Mometrix
TEST PREPARATION

ILTS

Learning Behavior Specialist I (290) Secrets Study Guide

I0892932

Dear Future Exam Success Story

First of all, **THANK YOU** for purchasing Mometrix study materials!

Second, congratulations! You are one of the few determined test-takers who are committed to doing whatever it takes to excel on your exam. **You have come to the right place.** We developed these study materials with one goal in mind: to deliver you the information you need in a format that's concise and easy to use.

In addition to optimizing your guide for the content of the test, we've outlined our recommended steps for breaking down the preparation process into small, attainable goals so you can make sure you stay on track.

We've also analyzed the entire test-taking process, identifying the most common pitfalls and showing how you can overcome them and be ready for any curveball the test throws you.

Standardized testing is one of the biggest obstacles on your road to success, which only increases the importance of doing well in the high-pressure, high-stakes environment of test day. Your results on this test could have a significant impact on your future, and this guide provides the information and practical advice to help you achieve your full potential on test day.

Your success is our success

We would love to hear from you! If you would like to share the story of your exam success or if you have any questions or comments in regard to our products, please contact us at **800-673-8175** or **support@mometrix.com**.

Thanks again for your business and we wish you continued success!

Sincerely,
The Mometrix Test Preparation Team

Need more help? Check out our flashcards at:
http://MometrixFlashcards.com/ILTS

TABLE OF CONTENTS

Introduction

Thank you for purchasing this resource! You have made the choice to prepare yourself for a test that could have a huge impact on your future, and this guide is designed to help you be fully ready for test day. Obviously, it's important to have a solid understanding of the test material, but you also need to be prepared for the unique environment and stressors of the test, so that you can perform to the best of your abilities.

For this purpose, the first section that appears in this guide is the **Secret Keys**. We've devoted countless hours to meticulously researching what works and what doesn't, and we've boiled down our findings to the five most impactful steps you can take to improve your performance on the test. We start at the beginning with study planning and move through the preparation process, all the way to the testing strategies that will help you get the most out of what you know when you're finally sitting in front of the test.

We recommend that you start preparing for your test as far in advance as possible. However, if you've bought this guide as a last-minute study resource and only have a few days before your test, we recommend that you skip over the first two Secret Keys since they address a long-term study plan.

If you struggle with **test anxiety**, we strongly encourage you to check out our recommendations for how you can overcome it. Test anxiety is a formidable foe, but it can be beaten, and we want to make sure you have the tools you need to defeat it.

Secret Key #1 – Plan Big, Study Small

There's a lot riding on your performance. If you want to ace this test, you're going to need to keep your skills sharp and the material fresh in your mind. You need a plan that lets you review everything you need to know while still fitting in your schedule. We'll break this strategy down into three categories.

Information Organization

Start with the information you already have: the official test outline. From this, you can make a complete list of all the concepts you need to cover before the test. Organize these concepts into groups that can be studied together, and create a list of any related vocabulary you need to learn so you can brush up on any difficult terms. You'll want to keep this vocabulary list handy once you actually start studying since you may need to add to it along the way.

Time Management

Once you have your set of study concepts, decide how to spread them out over the time you have left before the test. Break your study plan into small, clear goals so you have a manageable task for each day and know exactly what you're doing. Then just focus on one small step at a time. When you manage your time this way, you don't need to spend hours at a time studying. Studying a small block of content for a short period each day helps you retain information better and avoid stressing over how much you have left to do. You can relax knowing that you have a plan to cover everything in time. In order for this strategy to be effective though, you have to start studying early and stick to your schedule. Avoid the exhaustion and futility that comes from last-minute cramming!

Study Environment

The environment you study in has a big impact on your learning. Studying in a coffee shop, while probably more enjoyable, is not likely to be as fruitful as studying in a quiet room. It's important to keep distractions to a minimum. You're only planning to study for a short block of time, so make the most of it. Don't pause to check your phone or get up to find a snack. It's also important to **avoid multitasking**. Research has consistently shown that multitasking will make your studying dramatically less effective. Your study area should also be comfortable and well-lit so you don't have the distraction of straining your eyes or sitting on an uncomfortable chair.

The time of day you study is also important. You want to be rested and alert. Don't wait until just before bedtime. Study when you'll be most likely to comprehend and remember. Even better, if you know what time of day your test will be, set that time aside for study. That way your brain will be used to working on that subject at that specific time and you'll have a better chance of recalling information.

Finally, it can be helpful to team up with others who are studying for the same test. Your actual studying should be done in as isolated an environment as possible, but the work of organizing the information and setting up the study plan can be divided up. In between study sessions, you can discuss with your teammates the concepts that you're all studying and quiz each other on the details. Just be sure that your teammates are as serious about the test as you are. If you find that your study time is being replaced with social time, you might need to find a new team.

Secret Key #2 – Make Your Studying Count

You're devoting a lot of time and effort to preparing for this test, so you want to be absolutely certain it will pay off. This means doing more than just reading the content and hoping you can remember it on test day. It's important to make every minute of study count. There are two main areas you can focus on to make your studying count.

Retention

It doesn't matter how much time you study if you can't remember the material. You need to make sure you are retaining the concepts. To check your retention of the information you're learning, try recalling it at later times with minimal prompting. Try carrying around flashcards and glance at one or two from time to time or ask a friend who's also studying for the test to quiz you.

To enhance your retention, look for ways to put the information into practice so that you can apply it rather than simply recalling it. If you're using the information in practical ways, it will be much easier to remember. Similarly, it helps to solidify a concept in your mind if you're not only reading it to yourself but also explaining it to someone else. Ask a friend to let you teach them about a concept you're a little shaky on (or speak aloud to an imaginary audience if necessary). As you try to summarize, define, give examples, and answer your friend's questions, you'll understand the concepts better and they will stay with you longer. Finally, step back for a big picture view and ask yourself how each piece of information fits with the whole subject. When you link the different concepts together and see them working together as a whole, it's easier to remember the individual components.

Finally, practice showing your work on any multi-step problems, even if you're just studying. Writing out each step you take to solve a problem will help solidify the process in your mind, and you'll be more likely to remember it during the test.

Modality

Modality simply refers to the means or method by which you study. Choosing a study modality that fits your own individual learning style is crucial. No two people learn best in exactly the same way, so it's important to know your strengths and use them to your advantage.

For example, if you learn best by visualization, focus on visualizing a concept in your mind and draw an image or a diagram. Try color-coding your notes, illustrating them, or creating symbols that will trigger your mind to recall a learned concept. If you learn best by hearing or discussing information, find a study partner who learns the same way or read aloud to yourself. Think about how to put the information in your own words. Imagine that you are giving a lecture on the topic and record yourself so you can listen to it later.

For any learning style, flashcards can be helpful. Organize the information so you can take advantage of spare moments to review. Underline key words or phrases. Use different colors for different categories. Mnemonic devices (such as creating a short list in which every item starts with the same letter) can also help with retention. Find what works best for you and use it to store the information in your mind most effectively and easily.

Secret Key #3 – Practice the Right Way

Your success on test day depends not only on how many hours you put into preparing, but also on whether you prepared the right way. It's good to check along the way to see if your studying is paying off. One of the most effective ways to do this is by taking practice tests to evaluate your progress. Practice tests are useful because they show exactly where you need to improve. Every time you take a practice test, pay special attention to these three groups of questions:

- The questions you got wrong
- The questions you had to guess on, even if you guessed right
- The questions you found difficult or slow to work through

This will show you exactly what your weak areas are, and where you need to devote more study time. Ask yourself why each of these questions gave you trouble. Was it because you didn't understand the material? Was it because you didn't remember the vocabulary? Do you need more repetitions on this type of question to build speed and confidence? Dig into those questions and figure out how you can strengthen your weak areas as you go back to review the material.

Additionally, many practice tests have a section explaining the answer choices. It can be tempting to read the explanation and think that you now have a good understanding of the concept. However, an explanation likely only covers part of the question's broader context. Even if the explanation makes perfect sense, **go back and investigate** every concept related to the question until you're positive you have a thorough understanding.

As you go along, keep in mind that the practice test is just that: practice. Memorizing these questions and answers will not be very helpful on the actual test because it is unlikely to have any of the same exact questions. If you only know the right answers to the sample questions, you won't be prepared for the real thing. **Study the concepts** until you understand them fully, and then you'll be able to answer any question that shows up on the test.

It's important to wait on the practice tests until you're ready. If you take a test on your first day of study, you may be overwhelmed by the amount of material covered and how much you need to learn. Work up to it gradually.

On test day, you'll need to be prepared for answering questions, managing your time, and using the test-taking strategies you've learned. It's a lot to balance, like a mental marathon that will have a big impact on your future. Like training for a marathon, you'll need to start slowly and work your way up. When test day arrives, you'll be ready.

Start with the strategies you've read in the first two Secret Keys—plan your course and study in the way that works best for you. If you have time, consider using multiple study resources to get different approaches to the same concepts. It can be helpful to see difficult concepts from more than one angle. Then find a good source for practice tests. Many times, the test website will suggest potential study resources or provide sample tests.

Practice Test Strategy

If you're able to find at least three practice tests, we recommend this strategy:

Untimed and Open-Book Practice

Take the first test with no time constraints and with your notes and study guide handy. Take your time and focus on applying the strategies you've learned.

Timed and Open-Book Practice

Take the second practice test open-book as well, but set a timer and practice pacing yourself to finish in time.

Timed and Closed-Book Practice

Take any other practice tests as if it were test day. Set a timer and put away your study materials. Sit at a table or desk in a quiet room, imagine yourself at the testing center, and answer questions as quickly and accurately as possible.

Keep repeating timed and closed-book tests on a regular basis until you run out of practice tests or it's time for the actual test. Your mind will be ready for the schedule and stress of test day, and you'll be able to focus on recalling the material you've learned.

Secret Key #4 – Pace Yourself

Once you're fully prepared for the material on the test, your biggest challenge on test day will be managing your time. Just knowing that the clock is ticking can make you panic even if you have plenty of time left. Work on pacing yourself so you can build confidence against the time constraints of the exam. Pacing is a difficult skill to master, especially in a high-pressure environment, so **practice is vital**.

Set time expectations for your pace based on how much time is available. For example, if a section has 60 questions and the time limit is 30 minutes, you know you have to average 30 seconds or less per question in order to answer them all. Although 30 seconds is the hard limit, set 25 seconds per question as your goal, so you reserve extra time to spend on harder questions. When you budget extra time for the harder questions, you no longer have any reason to stress when those questions take longer to answer.

Don't let this time expectation distract you from working through the test at a calm, steady pace, but keep it in mind so you don't spend too much time on any one question. Recognize that taking extra time on one question you don't understand may keep you from answering two that you do understand later in the test. If your time limit for a question is up and you're still not sure of the answer, mark it and move on, and come back to it later if the time and the test format allow. If the testing format doesn't allow you to return to earlier questions, just make an educated guess; then put it out of your mind and move on.

On the easier questions, be careful not to rush. It may seem wise to hurry through them so you have more time for the challenging ones, but it's not worth missing one if you know the concept and just didn't take the time to read the question fully. Work efficiently but make sure you understand the question and have looked at all of the answer choices, since more than one may seem right at first.

Even if you're paying attention to the time, you may find yourself a little behind at some point. You should speed up to get back on track, but do so wisely. Don't panic; just take a few seconds less on each question until you're caught up. Don't guess without thinking, but do look through the answer choices and eliminate any you know are wrong. If you can get down to two choices, it is often worthwhile to guess from those. Once you've chosen an answer, move on and don't dwell on any that you skipped or had to hurry through. If a question was taking too long, chances are it was one of the harder ones, so you weren't as likely to get it right anyway.

On the other hand, if you find yourself getting ahead of schedule, it may be beneficial to slow down a little. The more quickly you work, the more likely you are to make a careless mistake that will affect your score. You've budgeted time for each question, so don't be afraid to spend that time. Practice an efficient but careful pace to get the most out of the time you have.

Secret Key #5 – Have a Plan for Guessing

When you're taking the test, you may find yourself stuck on a question. Some of the answer choices seem better than others, but you don't see the one answer choice that is obviously correct. What do you do?

The scenario described above is very common, yet most test takers have not effectively prepared for it. Developing and practicing a plan for guessing may be one of the single most effective uses of your time as you get ready for the exam.

In developing your plan for guessing, there are three questions to address:

- When should you start the guessing process?
- How should you narrow down the choices?
- Which answer should you choose?

When to Start the Guessing Process

Unless your plan for guessing is to select C every time (which, despite its merits, is not what we recommend), you need to leave yourself enough time to apply your answer elimination strategies. Since you have a limited amount of time for each question, that means that if you're going to give yourself the best shot at guessing correctly, you have to decide quickly whether or not you will guess.

Of course, the best-case scenario is that you don't have to guess at all, so first, see if you can answer the question based on your knowledge of the subject and basic reasoning skills. Focus on the key words in the question and try to jog your memory of related topics. Give yourself a chance to bring the knowledge to mind, but once you realize that you don't have (or you can't access) the knowledge you need to answer the question, it's time to start the guessing process.

It's almost always better to start the guessing process too early than too late. It only takes a few seconds to remember something and answer the question from knowledge. Carefully eliminating wrong answer choices takes longer. Plus, going through the process of eliminating answer choices can actually help jog your memory.

Summary: Start the guessing process as soon as you decide that you can't answer the question based on your knowledge.

How to Narrow Down the Choices

The next chapter in this book (**Test-Taking Strategies**) includes a wide range of strategies for how to approach questions and how to look for answer choices to eliminate. You will definitely want to read those carefully, practice them, and figure out which ones work best for you. Here though, we're going to address a mindset rather than a particular strategy.

Your odds of guessing an answer correctly depend on how many options you are choosing from.

Number of options left	5	4	3	2	1
Odds of guessing correctly	20%	25%	33%	50%	100%

You can see from this chart just how valuable it is to be able to eliminate incorrect answers and make an educated guess, but there are two things that many test takers do that cause them to miss out on the benefits of guessing:

- Accidentally eliminating the correct answer
- Selecting an answer based on an impression

We'll look at the first one here, and the second one in the next section.

To avoid accidentally eliminating the correct answer, we recommend a thought exercise called **the $5 challenge**. In this challenge, you only eliminate an answer choice from contention if you are willing to bet $5 on it being wrong. Why $5? Five dollars is a small but not insignificant amount of money. It's an amount you could afford to lose but wouldn't want to throw away. And while losing $5 once might not hurt too much, doing it twenty times will set you back $100. In the same way, each small decision you make—eliminating a choice here, guessing on a question there—won't by itself impact your score very much, but when you put them all together, they can make a big difference. By holding each answer choice elimination decision to a higher standard, you can reduce the risk of accidentally eliminating the correct answer.

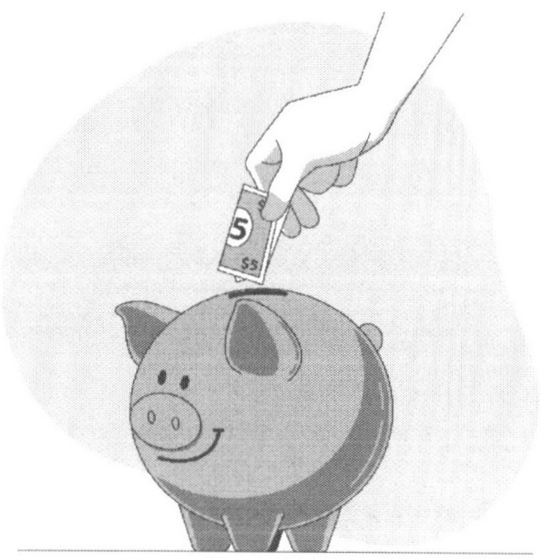

The $5 challenge can also be applied in a positive sense: If you are willing to bet $5 that an answer choice *is* correct, go ahead and mark it as correct.

Summary: Only eliminate an answer choice if you are willing to bet $5 that it is wrong.

Which Answer to Choose

You're taking the test. You've run into a hard question and decided you'll have to guess. You've eliminated all the answer choices you're willing to bet $5 on. Now you have to pick an answer. Why do we even need to talk about this? Why can't you just pick whichever one you feel like when the time comes?

The answer to these questions is that if you don't come into the test with a plan, you'll rely on your impression to select an answer choice, and if you do that, you risk falling into a trap. The test writers know that everyone who takes their test will be guessing on some of the questions, so they intentionally write wrong answer choices to seem plausible. You still have to pick an answer though, and if the wrong answer choices are designed to look right, how can you ever be sure that you're not falling for their trap? The best solution we've found to this dilemma is to take the decision out of your hands entirely. Here is the process we recommend:

Once you've eliminated any choices that you are confident (willing to bet $5) are wrong, select the first remaining choice as your answer.

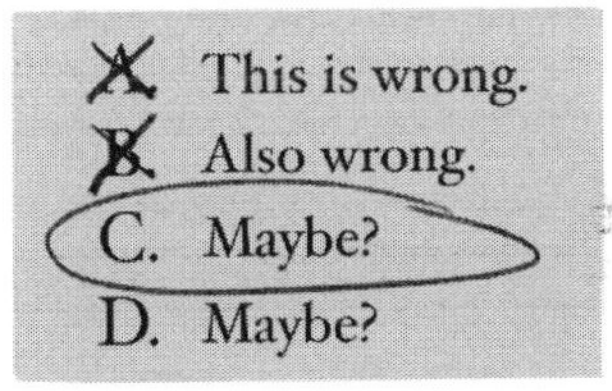

Whether you choose to select the first remaining choice, the second, or the last, the important thing is that you use some preselected standard. Using this approach guarantees that you will not be enticed into selecting an answer choice that looks right, because you are not basing your decision on how the answer choices look.

This is not meant to make you question your knowledge. Instead, it is to help you recognize the difference between your knowledge and your impressions. There's a huge difference between thinking an answer is right because of what you know, and thinking an answer is right because it looks or sounds like it should be right.

Summary: To ensure that your selection is appropriately random, make a predetermined selection from among all answer choices you have not eliminated.

Test-Taking Strategies

This section contains a list of test-taking strategies that you may find helpful as you work through the test. By taking what you know and applying logical thought, you can maximize your chances of answering any question correctly!

It is very important to realize that every question is different and every person is different: no single strategy will work on every question, and no single strategy will work for every person. That's why we've included all of them here, so you can try them out and determine which ones work best for different types of questions and which ones work best for you.

Question Strategies

☑ Read Carefully

Read the question and the answer choices carefully. Don't miss the question because you misread the terms. You have plenty of time to read each question thoroughly and make sure you understand what is being asked. Yet a happy medium must be attained, so don't waste too much time. You must read carefully and efficiently.

☑ Contextual Clues

Look for contextual clues. If the question includes a word you are not familiar with, look at the immediate context for some indication of what the word might mean. Contextual clues can often give you all the information you need to decipher the meaning of an unfamiliar word. Even if you can't determine the meaning, you may be able to narrow down the possibilities enough to make a solid guess at the answer to the question.

☑ Prefixes

If you're having trouble with a word in the question or answer choices, try dissecting it. Take advantage of every clue that the word might include. Prefixes can be a huge help. Usually, they allow you to determine a basic meaning. *Pre-* means before, *post-* means after, *pro-* is positive, *de-* is negative. From prefixes, you can get an idea of the general meaning of the word and try to put it into context.

☑ Hedge Words

Watch out for critical hedge words, such as *likely, may, can, often, almost, mostly, usually, generally, rarely*, and *sometimes*. Question writers insert these hedge phrases to cover every possibility. Often an answer choice will be wrong simply because it leaves no room for exception. Be on guard for answer choices that have definitive words such as *exactly* and *always*.

☑ Switchback Words

Stay alert for *switchbacks*. These are the words and phrases frequently used to alert you to shifts in thought. The most common switchback words are *but, although*, and *however*. Others include *nevertheless, on the other hand, even though, while, in spite of, despite*, and *regardless of*. Switchback words are important to catch because they can change the direction of the question or an answer choice.

✓ FACE VALUE

When in doubt, use common sense. Accept the situation in the problem at face value. Don't read too much into it. These problems will not require you to make wild assumptions. If you have to go beyond creativity and warp time or space in order to have an answer choice fit the question, then you should move on and consider the other answer choices. These are normal problems rooted in reality. The applicable relationship or explanation may not be readily apparent, but it is there for you to figure out. Use your common sense to interpret anything that isn't clear.

Answer Choice Strategies

✓ ANSWER SELECTION

The most thorough way to pick an answer choice is to identify and eliminate wrong answers until only one is left, then confirm it is the correct answer. Sometimes an answer choice may immediately seem right, but be careful. The test writers will usually put more than one reasonable answer choice on each question, so take a second to read all of them and make sure that the other choices are not equally obvious. As long as you have time left, it is better to read every answer choice than to pick the first one that looks right without checking the others.

✓ ANSWER CHOICE FAMILIES

An answer choice family consists of two (in rare cases, three) answer choices that are very similar in construction and cannot all be true at the same time. If you see two answer choices that are direct opposites or parallels, one of them is usually the correct answer. For instance, if one answer choice says that quantity *x* increases and another either says that quantity *x* decreases (opposite) or says that quantity *y* increases (parallel), then those answer choices would fall into the same family. An answer choice that doesn't match the construction of the answer choice family is more likely to be incorrect. Most questions will not have answer choice families, but when they do appear, you should be prepared to recognize them.

✓ ELIMINATE ANSWERS

Eliminate answer choices as soon as you realize they are wrong, but make sure you consider all possibilities. If you are eliminating answer choices and realize that the last one you are left with is also wrong, don't panic. Start over and consider each choice again. There may be something you missed the first time that you will realize on the second pass.

✓ AVOID FACT TRAPS

Don't be distracted by an answer choice that is factually true but doesn't answer the question. You are looking for the choice that answers the question. Stay focused on what the question is asking for so you don't accidentally pick an answer that is true but incorrect. Always go back to the question and make sure the answer choice you've selected actually answers the question and is not merely a true statement.

✓ EXTREME STATEMENTS

In general, you should avoid answers that put forth extreme actions as standard practice or proclaim controversial ideas as established fact. An answer choice that states the "process should be used in certain situations, if..." is much more likely to be correct than one that states the "process should be discontinued completely." The first is a calm rational statement and doesn't even make a definitive, uncompromising stance, using a hedge word *if* to provide wiggle room, whereas the second choice is far more extreme.

⊘ Benchmark

As you read through the answer choices and you come across one that seems to answer the question well, mentally select that answer choice. This is not your final answer, but it's the one that will help you evaluate the other answer choices. The one that you selected is your benchmark or standard for judging each of the other answer choices. Every other answer choice must be compared to your benchmark. That choice is correct until proven otherwise by another answer choice beating it. If you find a better answer, then that one becomes your new benchmark. Once you've decided that no other choice answers the question as well as your benchmark, you have your final answer.

⊘ Predict the Answer

Before you even start looking at the answer choices, it is often best to try to predict the answer. When you come up with the answer on your own, it is easier to avoid distractions and traps because you will know exactly what to look for. The right answer choice is unlikely to be word-for-word what you came up with, but it should be a close match. Even if you are confident that you have the right answer, you should still take the time to read each option before moving on.

General Strategies

⊘ Tough Questions

If you are stumped on a problem or it appears too hard or too difficult, don't waste time. Move on! Remember though, if you can quickly check for obviously incorrect answer choices, your chances of guessing correctly are greatly improved. Before you completely give up, at least try to knock out a couple of possible answers. Eliminate what you can and then guess at the remaining answer choices before moving on.

⊘ Check Your Work

Since you will probably not know every term listed and the answer to every question, it is important that you get credit for the ones that you do know. Don't miss any questions through careless mistakes. If at all possible, try to take a second to look back over your answer selection and make sure you've selected the correct answer choice and haven't made a costly careless mistake (such as marking an answer choice that you didn't mean to mark). This quick double check should more than pay for itself in caught mistakes for the time it costs.

⊘ Pace Yourself

It's easy to be overwhelmed when you're looking at a page full of questions; your mind is confused and full of random thoughts, and the clock is ticking down faster than you would like. Calm down and maintain the pace that you have set for yourself. Especially as you get down to the last few minutes of the test, don't let the small numbers on the clock make you panic. As long as you are on track by monitoring your pace, you are guaranteed to have time for each question.

⊘ Don't Rush

It is very easy to make errors when you are in a hurry. Maintaining a fast pace in answering questions is pointless if it makes you miss questions that you would have gotten right otherwise. Test writers like to include distracting information and wrong answers that seem right. Taking a little extra time to avoid careless mistakes can make all the difference in your test score. Find a pace that allows you to be confident in the answers that you select.

✓ KEEP MOVING

Panicking will not help you pass the test, so do your best to stay calm and keep moving. Taking deep breaths and going through the answer elimination steps you practiced can help to break through a stress barrier and keep your pace.

Final Notes

The combination of a solid foundation of content knowledge and the confidence that comes from practicing your plan for applying that knowledge is the key to maximizing your performance on test day. As your foundation of content knowledge is built up and strengthened, you'll find that the strategies included in this chapter become more and more effective in helping you quickly sift through the distractions and traps of the test to isolate the correct answer.

Now that you're preparing to move forward into the test content chapters of this book, be sure to keep your goal in mind. As you read, think about how you will be able to apply this information on the test. If you've already seen sample questions for the test and you have an idea of the question format and style, try to come up with questions of your own that you can answer based on what you're reading. This will give you valuable practice applying your knowledge in the same ways you can expect to on test day.

Good luck and good studying!

Understanding Students with Disabilities

Transform passive reading into active learning! After immersing yourself in this chapter, put your comprehension to the test by taking a quiz. The insights you gained will stay with you longer this way. Scan the QR code to go directly to the chapter quiz interface for this study guide. If you're using a computer, simply visit the online resources page at **mometrix.com/resources719/iltslbsi290** and click the Chapter Quizzes link.

Overview of Human Developmental Theories

Issues of Human Development

Historically, there have been a number of arguments that theories of human development seek to address. These ideas generally lie on a spectrum but are often essential concepts involved in developmental theories. For instance, the nature vs. nurture debate is a key concept involved in behaviorist camps of development, insisting that a substantial portion of a child's development may be attributed to his or her social environment.

- **Universality vs. context specificity**: Universality implies that all individuals will develop in the same way, no matter what culture they live in. Context specificity implies that development will be influenced by the culture in which the individual lives.
- **Assumptions about human nature** (three doctrines: original sin, innate purity, and tabula rasa):
    - Original sin says that children are inherently bad and must be taught to be good.
    - Innate purity says that children are inherently good.
    - Tabula rasa says that children are born as "blank slates" without good or bad tendencies and can be taught right and wrong.
- **Behavioral consistency**: Children either behave in the same manner no matter what the situation or setting or they change their behavior depending on the setting and who is interacting with them.
- **Nature vs. nurture**: Nature refers to the genetic influences on development. Nurture refers to the environmental and social influences on development.
- **Continuity vs. discontinuity**: Continuity states that development progresses at a steady rate and that the effects of change are cumulative. Discontinuity states that development progresses in a stair-step fashion and that the effects of early development have no bearing on later development.
- **Passivity vs. activity**: Passivity refers to development being influenced by outside forces. Activity refers to development influenced by the child him or herself and how he or she responds to external forces.
- **Critical vs. sensitive period**: The critical period is the window of time when the child will be able to acquire new skills and behaviors. The sensitive period refers to a flexible time period when a child will be receptive to learning new skills, even if it is later than the norm.

THEORETICAL SCHOOLS OF THOUGHT ON HUMAN DEVELOPMENT

- **Behaviorist Theory** – This philosophy discusses development in terms of conditioning. As children interact with their environments, they learn what behaviors result in rewards or punishments and develop patterns of behaviors as a result. This school of thought lies heavily within the nurture side of the nature/nurture debate, arguing that children's personalities and behaviors are a product of their environments.
- **Constructivist Theory** – This philosophy describes the process of learning as one in which individuals build or construct their understanding from their prior knowledge and experiences in an environment. In constructivist thought, individuals can synthesize their old information to generate new ideas. This school of thought is similar to behaviorism in that the social environment plays a large role in learning. Constructivism, however, places greater emphasis on the individual's active role in the learning process, such as the ability to generate ideas about something an individual has not experienced directly.
- **Ecological Systems Theory** – This philosophy focuses on the social environments in and throughout a person's life. Ecological systems theorists attempt to account for all of the complexities of various aspects of a person's life, starting with close relationships, such as family and friends, and zooming out into broader social contexts, including interactions with school, communities, and media. Alongside these various social levels, ecological systems discuss the roles of ethnicity, geography, and socioeconomic status in development across a person's lifespan.
- **Maturationist Theory** – This philosophy largely focuses on the natural disposition of a child to learn. Maturationists lean heavily into the nature side of the nature/nurture argument and say that humans are predisposed to learning and development. As a result, maturationists propose that early development should only be passively supported.
- **Psychoanalytic Theory** – Psychoanalytic theorists generally argue that beneath the conscious interaction with the world, individuals have underlying, subconscious thoughts that affect their active emotions and behaviors. These subconscious thoughts are built from previous experiences, including developmental milestones and past traumas. These subconscious thoughts interact with conscious thoughts to form a person's desires, personality, attitudes, and habits.

FREUD'S PSYCHOSEXUAL DEVELOPMENTAL THEORY

Sigmund Freud was a neurologist who founded the psychoanalytic school of thought. He described the distinction between the conscious and unconscious mind and the effects of the unconscious mind on personality and behavior. He also developed a concept of stages of development, in which an individual encounters various conflicts or crises, called psychosexual stages of development. The way in which an individual handles these crises were thought to shape the individual's personality over the course of life. This general formula heavily influenced other psychoanalytic theories.

ERIKSON'S PSYCHOSOCIAL DEVELOPMENTAL THEORY

Eric Erikson's psychosocial development theory was an expansion and revision of Freud's psychosexual stages. Erikson describes eight stages in which an individual is presented with a crisis, such as an infant learning to trust or mistrust his or her parents to provide. The choice to trust or mistrust is not binary, but is on a spectrum. According to the theory, the individual's resolution of the crisis largely carries through the rest of his or her life. Handling each of the eight conflicts well theoretically leads to a healthy development of personality. The conflicts are spaced out throughout life, beginning at infancy and ending at death.

Kohlberg's Stages of Moral Development

Kohlberg's stages of moral development are heavily influenced by Erikson's stages. He describes three larger levels of moral development with substages. In the first level, the **preconventional level**, morality is fully externally controlled by authorities and is motivated by the avoidance of punishment and pursuit of rewards. In the second level, the **conventional level**, the focus shifts to laws, social factors, and the pursuit of being seen by others as good or nice. In the third and final level, the **postconventional** or **principled level**, the individual looks beyond laws and social obligations to more complex situational considerations. A person in this stage might consider that a law may not always be the best for individuals or society and that a particular situation may warrant breaking the rule for the true good.

George Herbert Mead's Play and Game Stage Development Theory

George Herbert Mead was a sociologist and psychologist who described learning by stepping into **social roles**. According to his theory, children first interact with the world by imitating and playing by themselves. While engaged in this play, a child can experiment with concepts. Mead describes this development in terms of three stages characterized by increasing complexity of play. A child in the **preparatory stage** can **play** pretend and learn cooking concepts by pretending to cook. As a child develops socially, he or she learns to step in and out of increasingly abstract and complex **roles** and includes more interaction. This is known as the **play stage**, including early interactive roles. For instance, children may play "cops and robbers," which are more symbolically significant roles because they are not natural roles for children to play in society. As social understanding develops, children enter the **game stage**, in which the child can understand his or her own role and the roles of others in a game. In this stage, children can participate in more complex activities with highly structured rules. An example of a complex game is baseball, in which each individual playing has a unique and complex role to play. These stages are thought to contribute to an individual's ability to understand complex social roles in adulthood.

Ivan Pavlov

Ivan Pavlov was a predecessor to the behaviorist school and is credited with being the first to observe the process of classical conditioning, also known as Pavlovian conditioning. Pavlov observed that dogs would begin salivating at the sound of a bell because they were conditioned to expect food when they heard a bell ring. According to classical conditioning, by introducing a neutral stimulus (such as a bell) to a naturally significant stimulus (such as the sight of food), the neutral stimulus will begin to create a conditioned response on its own.

John B. Watson

Watson is credited as the founder of behaviorism and worked to expand the knowledge base of conditioning. He is famous for his experiments, including highly unethical experiments such as the "Little Albert" experiment in which he used classical conditioning to cause an infant to fear animals that he was unfamiliar with. Watson proposed that psychology should focus only on observable behaviors.

B.F. Skinner

Skinner expanded on Watson's work in behaviorism. His primary contributions to behaviorism included studying the effect of **reinforcement** and **punishment** on particular behaviors. He noted that stimuli can be both additive or subtractive and may be used to either increase or decrease behavior frequency and strengths.

Lev Vygotsky

Vygotsky's sociocultural theory describes development as a social process in which individuals mediate knowledge through social interactions and can learn by interacting with and watching others. Vygotsky's ideas have been widely adopted in the field of education, most notably his theory of the **zone of proximal development**. This theory describes three levels of an individual's ability to do tasks, including completely incapable of performing a task, capable with assistance, and independently capable. As an individual's experience grows, he or she should progress from less capable and independent to more capable and independent.

Review Video: Instructional Scaffolding
Visit mometrix.com/academy and enter code: 989759

Bandura's Social Learning Theory

Albert Bandura's social learning theory argues against some of the behaviorist thoughts that a person has to experience stimulus and response to learn behaviors and, instead, posits that an individual can learn from other peoples' social interactions. Bandura would say that most learning takes place from observing and predicting social behavior, not through direct experience. This becomes a more efficient system for learning because people are able to learn information more synthetically.

Bowlby's Attachment Theory

Bowlby's attachment theory describes the impact that early connections have on lifelong development. Working from an evolutionary framework, Bowlby described how infants are predisposed to be attached to their caregivers because this increases chance of survival. According to Bowlby's theory, infants are predisposed to stay close to known caregivers and use them as a frame of reference to help with learning what is socially acceptable and what is safe.

Piaget's Cognitive Development Theory

Piaget's theory of cognitive development describes how as individuals develop, their cognitive processes are able to become more complex and abstract. In the early stages, an infant may be able to recognize an item, such as a glass of water, on sight only. As that individual grows, he or she is able to think, compare, and eventually develop abstract thoughts about that concept. According to Piaget, this development takes place in all individuals in predictable stages.

Maslow's Hierarchy of Needs

Maslow defined human motivation in terms of needs and wants. His **hierarchy of needs** is classically portrayed as a pyramid sitting on its base divided into horizontal layers. He theorized that, as humans fulfill the needs of one layer, their motivation turns to the layer above. The layers consist of (from bottom to top):

- **Physiological**: The need for air, fluid, food, shelter, warmth, and sleep
- **Safety**: A safe place to live, a steady job, a society with rules and laws, protection from harm, and insurance or savings for the future
- **Love/belonging**: A network consisting of a significant other, family, friends, co-workers, religion, and community
- **Esteem or self-respect**: The knowledge that you are a person who is successful and worthy of esteem, attention, status, and admiration

- **Self-actualization**: The acceptance of your life, choices, and situation in life and the empathetic acceptance of others, as well as the feeling of independence and the joy of being able to express yourself freely and competently

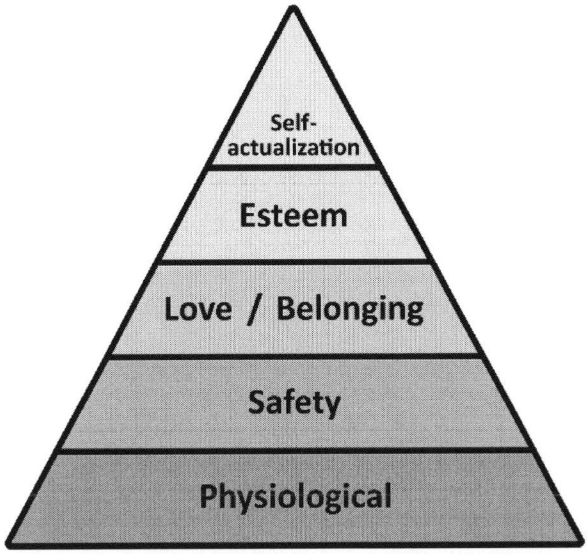

Review Video: Maslow's Hierarchy of Needs
Visit mometrix.com/academy and enter code: 461825

Cognitive Development

Piaget's Theory of Cognitive Development

Jean Piaget's theory of cognitive development consists of four stages that a child moves through throughout life. The four stages are the **sensorimotor stage** (birth-2 years), **preoperational stage** (2-7 years), **concrete operational stage** (7-11 years), and **formal operational stage** (12 years and beyond). Piaget believed that the way children think changes as they pass through these stages. In the **sensorimotor stage**, infants exist in the present moment and investigate their world for the first time through their senses, reflexes, and actions. Key skills infants acquire during this stage include object permanence and self-recognition. In the **preoperational stage**, children learn to express ideas symbolically, including through language and pretend play. Markers of this stage include engaging in animism, egocentrism, and the inability to understand conservation (the knowledge that the quantity of something does not change when its appearance does). In the **concrete operational stage**, children develop logical thought and begin understanding conservation. The **formal operational stage** brings the ability to think abstractly and hypothetically. Piaget believed that children learn through experimenting and building upon knowledge from experiences. He asserted that educators should be highly qualified and trained to create experiences that support development in each of these stages.

Review Video: Piaget's Cognitive Development Theory
Visit mometrix.com/academy and enter code: 100376

Skills Typically Acquired at Each Stage of Cognitive Development

- **Sensorimotor:** Children in the sensorimotor stage gain an increasing awareness of their bodies and the world around them and acquire a wide range of skills as they mature from infancy to toddlerhood. Early skills at this stage include sucking, tasting, smiling, basic vocalizations, and **gross motor skills** such as kicking and grasping. These skills increase in complexity over time and come to include abilities such as throwing and dropping objects, crawling, walking, and using simple words or phrases to communicate. As children near the end of this stage, they are typically able to exhibit skills such as stacking, basic problem solving, planning methods to achieve a task, and attempting to engage in daily routines, such as dressing themselves or brushing their hair.
- **Preoperational:** This stage is marked by significant leaps in **cognition** and **gross motor skills**. Children in the preoperational stage are able to use increasingly complex language to communicate, and they develop skills like jumping, running, and climbing as they gain increasing control over their bodies. Preoperational children begin learning the basic categorization of alike objects, such as animals, flowers, or foods. This stage is also characterized by the development of pretend play and includes skills such as creating imaginary friends, role playing, and using toys or objects to symbolize something else, such as using a box as a pretend house.
- **Concrete operational:** In this stage, children begin developing **logical reasoning** skills that allow them to perform increasingly complex tasks. Concrete operational children are able to distinguish subcategories, including types of animals, foods, or flowers, and can organize items in ascending or descending order based upon characteristics like height, weight, or size. Children at this stage develop the understanding that altering the appearance of an object or substance does not change the amount of it. A classic example of this is the understanding that liquid transferred from one container to another retains its volume. This concept is known as **conservation**.
- **Formal operational:** The formal operational stage is characterized by the development of **abstract** and **hypothetical** cognitive skills. Children at this stage are able to solve increasingly complex math equations, hypothesize and strategically devise a plan for engaging in science experiments, and develop creative solutions to problems. They are also able to theorize potential outcomes to hypothetical situations as well as consider the nuances of differing values, beliefs, morals, and ethics.

Substages of the Sensorimotor Stage

Piaget's sensorimotor stage is divided into six substages. In each, infants develop new skills for representing and interacting with their world. In the first substage, infants interact **reflexively** and involuntarily to stimuli in the form of muscle jerking when startled, sucking, and gripping. Subsequent stages are circular, or repetitive, in nature and are based on interactions with the self and, increasingly, the environment. **Primary circular reactions**, or intentionally repeated actions, comprise the second substage. Infants notice their actions and sounds and purposefully repeat them, but these actions do not extend past the infant's body. Interaction with the environment begins in the third substage as infants engage in **secondary circular reactions**. Here, infants learn that they can interact with and manipulate objects within their environment to create an effect, such as a sound from pressing a button. They then repeat the action and experience joy in this ability. In the fourth substage, secondary circular reactions become coordinated as infants begin planning movements and actions to create an effect. **Tertiary circular reactions** allow for exploration in the fifth substage, as infants start experimenting with cause and effect. In the sixth substage, infants begin engaging in **representational thought** and recall information from memory.

Examples of Primary, Secondary, and Tertiary Circular Reactions

The following are some common examples of primary, secondary, and tertiary circular reactions:

- **Primary:** Primary circular reactions are repeated **bodily** actions that the infant finds enjoyable. Such actions include thumb sucking, placing hands or feet in the mouth, kicking, and making basic vocalizations.
- **Secondary:** Secondary circular reactions refer to repeated enjoyable interactions between the infant and objects within their **environment** in order to elicit a specific response. Such actions include grasping objects, rattling toys, hitting buttons to hear specific sounds, banging two objects together, or reaching out to touch various items.
- **Tertiary:** Tertiary circular reactions are intentional and planned actions using objects within the environment to **achieve a particular outcome**. Examples include stacking blocks and knocking them down, taking toys out of a bin and putting them back, or engaging in a repeated behavior to gauge a caretaker's reaction each time.

Defining Characteristics of the Preoperational Stage of Development

The preoperational stage of development refers to the stage before a child can exercise operational thought and is associated with several defining characteristics including **pretend play**, **animism**, and **egocentrism**. As children learn to think and express themselves symbolically, they engage in pretend play as a means of organizing, understanding, and representing the world around them as they experience it. During this stage, children do not understand the difference between inanimate and animate objects and thus demonstrate animism, or the attribution of lifelike qualities to inanimate objects. Egocentrism refers to the child's inability to understand the distinction between him or herself and others and, consequentially, the inability to understand the thoughts, perspectives, and feelings of others. During the preoperational stage, the brain is not developed enough to understand **conservation**, which is the understanding that the quantity of something does not change just because its appearance changes. Thus, children in this stage exhibit **centration**, or the focusing on only one aspect of something at a time. Additionally, children struggle with **classification** during this stage, as they are not cognitively developed enough to understand that an object can be classified in multiple ways.

Milestones Achieved During the Concrete Operational Stage of Development

The concrete operational stage marks the beginning of a child's ability to think logically about the concrete world. In this stage, children develop many of the skills they lacked in the preoperational phase. For example, egocentrism fades as children in this stage begin to develop empathy and understand others' perspectives. Additionally, they develop an understanding of conservation, or the idea that the quantity of something does not change with its appearance. Children in this stage begin to learn to classify objects in more than one way and can categorize them based on a variety of characteristics. This allows them to practice **seriation**, or the arranging of objects based on quantitative measures.

Development of Cognitive Abilities in the Formal Operational Stage

In the formal operational stage, children can think beyond the concrete world and in terms of abstract thoughts and hypothetical situations. They develop the ability to consider various outcomes of events and can think more creatively about solutions to problems than in previous stages. This advanced cognitive ability contributes to the development of personal identity. In considering abstract and hypothetical ideas, children begin to formulate opinions and develop personal stances on intangible concepts, thus establishing individual character. The formal operational stage continues to develop through adulthood as individuals gain knowledge and experience.

LEV VYGOTSKY'S THEORY OF COGNITIVE DEVELOPMENT

Lev Vygotsky's theory on cognitive development is heavily rooted in a **sociocultural** perspective. He argued that the most important factors for a child's cognitive development reside in the cultural context in which the child grows up and social interactions that they have with adults, mentors, and more advanced peers. He believed that children learn best from the people around them, as their social interactions, even basic ones such as smiling, waving, or facial expressions, foster the beginning of more complex cognitive development. He is well-known for his concept of the **Zone of Proximal Development (ZPD)**, which is the gap between what a child can do independently and what the child can do with assistance from a more advanced individual or a collaborator. He believed that children could move through the ZPD and complete increasingly complicated tasks when receiving assistance from more cognitively advanced mentors. According to Vygotsky, children develop the most when passing through the ZPD. Vygotsky's contributions are heavily embedded in modern education and often take the form of teacher-led instruction and scaffolding to assist learners as they move through the ZPD.

Zone of Proximal Development

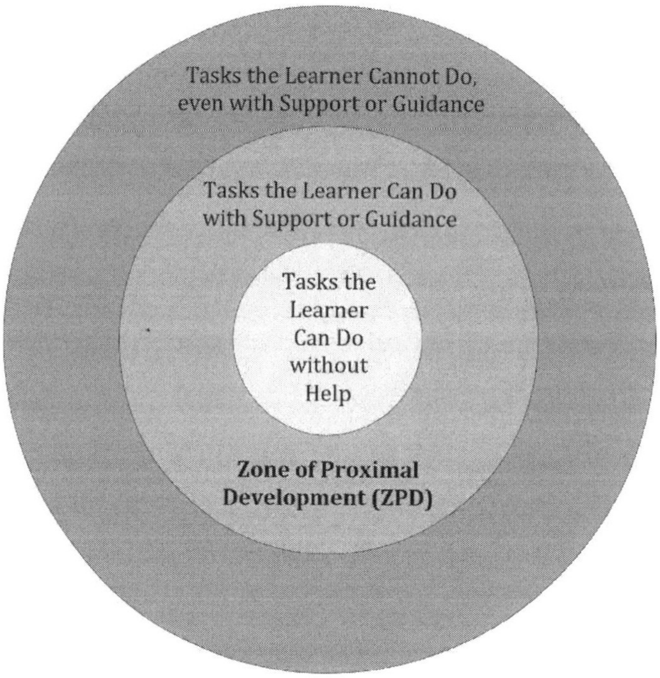

Review Video: Zone of Proximal Development (ZPD)
Visit mometrix.com/academy and enter code: 555594

Social and Emotional Development

ERIK ERIKSON'S EIGHT STAGES OF PSYCHOSOCIAL DEVELOPMENT

Erik Erikson defined eight predetermined stages of psychosocial development from birth to late adulthood in which an individual encounters a crisis that must be resolved to successfully transition to the next stage. The first is **trust vs. mistrust** (0-18 months), where the infant learns that the world is safe and that caregivers can be trusted to tend to his or her basic needs. The next stage is **autonomy vs. shame** (18 months-3 years), where children learn to control their actions and establish independence. In the **initiative vs. guilt stage** (3-5 years), children acquire a sense of purpose and initiative through social interactions. Next, children enter the **industry vs. inferiority stage** (6-11 years), where they develop mastery and pride in completing a task. The next stage is **identity vs. role confusion** (12-18 years), in which children explore and develop characteristics that will comprise their identities and determine their roles in society. The sixth stage is **intimacy vs. isolation** (19-40 years), where one forms relationships by sharing the identity developed in the previous stage with others. **Generativity vs. stagnation** (40-65 years) occurs in middle adulthood and focuses on contributing to society's next generation through finding one's life purpose. The last stage is **ego integrity vs. despair** (65 to death), in which one reflects on the productivity and success of his or her life.

Expected Behaviors at Each Stage of Psychosocial Development

Stage	Examples of expected behaviors
Trust vs. mistrust	In this stage, the infant's primary goal is ensuring the fulfillment of his or her **basic needs**. Infants will cry or make other vocalizations to indicate to caregivers when they want something, such as to be fed or picked up. Separation anxiety from parents is also typical during this stage.
Autonomy vs. shame	Children in this stage begin attempting to perform daily tasks **independently**, such as making food, dressing themselves, bathing, or combing their hair. As children in this stage begin to realize they have a separate identity, they often begin attempting to assert themselves to parents and caregivers.
Initiative vs. guilt	Children at this stage often begin actively engaging and playing with other children. In play settings, these children will often assume **leadership roles** among a group of peers, create new games or activities, and devise their own rules for them. The initiative vs. guilt stage is also characterized by the development of feelings of sadness or guilt when making a mistake or hurting another's feelings.
Industry vs. inferiority	In this stage, children begin attempting to master concepts or skills with the intention of seeking **approval** and **acceptance** from others, particularly those older than themselves, in order to secure a feeling of competency. Children in this stage often become more involved in striving to succeed academically, extracurricular activities, and competitive sports.
Identity vs. role confusion	This stage is characterized by experimentation and uncertainty as young adolescents strive to establish an **independent identity**. Typical behaviors include interacting with new peer groups, trying new styles of dress, engaging in new activities, and considering new beliefs, values, and morals. As young adolescents in this stage are impressionable, they may potentially engage in risky or rebellious behavior as a result of peer pressure.
Intimacy vs. isolation	Individuals in this stage have typically established their identities and are ready to seek **long-term relationships**. This stage marks the development of a social network composed of close friends and long-term romantic partners.

Stage	Examples of expected behaviors
Generativity vs. stagnation	During this stage, individuals begin engaging in **productive** activities to benefit others and elicit personal fulfillment. Such activities include advancing in a career, parenting, or participating in community service projects.
Integrity vs. despair	This stage occurs at the end of one's life and is characterized by **reflection** upon lifetime accomplishments and positive contributions to society. Doing so allows the individual to assess whether his or her purpose was fulfilled and begin accepting death.

Incorporating Life Skills into Curriculum

In addition to academic achievement, the ultimate goal of education is to develop the whole child and provide a successful transition to independence and adulthood. Incorporating valuable life skills, such as decision-making, goal setting, organization, self-direction, and workplace communication, in early childhood through grade 12 is vital in ensuring students become productive contributors to society. Furthermore, the implementation of these life skills in early childhood is integral in allowing children to successfully progress in independence and maturity. The acquisition of such skills instills in students the self-motivation and ability to set goals, make decisions on how to effectively organize and manage time to complete them, and overcome obstacles. Additionally, teaching students to apply these skills promotes effective communication when working with others toward a goal. Through incorporating life skills into curriculum, teachers instill a growth mindset and foster self-empowered, confident lifelong learners with the necessary tools to navigate real-life situations and achieve success as they transition to adulthood. In the classroom, activities that promote leadership skills, cooperative learning, goal setting, self-monitoring, and social interaction foster an increasing sense of independence as children develop.

External Environmental Factors on Social and Emotional Development

Social and emotional development is heavily influenced by a child's home environment. Children learn social and emotional skills such as self-regulation, self-awareness, coping, and relationship building through modeling from parents and caregivers. A positive and supportive home environment is integral for proper social and emotional development. External factors, including lack of affection and attention, parental divorce, and homelessness, pose profound negative impacts on this development. In terms of social development, such external factors could lead to attachment or abandonment issues as well as distrust. Furthermore, children exposed to negative environmental factors could struggle in forging relationships, cooperating, and following societal rules. Emotionally, negative impacts on development cause aggression, poor self-regulation, insecurity, anxiety, isolation, and depression. Since developmental domains are interconnected, the impacts that external factors have on social and emotional development ultimately damage cognitive and physical development. Underdeveloped social skills impair cognitive development because the inability to properly interact with peers impedes the ability to learn from them. Additionally, inadequate emotional skills can inhibit concentration and understanding in school, thus inhibiting cognitive development. Physically, struggling to interact with others leads to impaired development of gross and fine motor skills as well as large muscle development that would be achieved through play.

Physical Development

Physical Changes Occurring in Early Childhood Through Adolescence

Early Childhood

As children pass through stages of development from early childhood through middle childhood and adolescence, they experience significant physical changes. Children in early childhood experience rapid growth in height and weight as they transition away from physical characteristics of infancy. In this stage, children begin to gain independence as they develop and improve upon gross and fine motor skills. Throughout early childhood, children develop the ability to walk and run, and as they mature through this stage, they learn to throw, catch, climb, and hop. Of the locomotive skills listed, walking comes first, running and climbing can develop simultaneously, and hopping or jumping comes last. They improve in their fine motor skills and learn to hold and manipulate small objects such as zippers and buttons and can grasp writing utensils to create shapes, letters, and drawings with increasing accuracy.

Middle Childhood

Physical growth varies for individual children in middle childhood, as some children begin experiencing prepubescent bodily changes. Children in middle childhood experience further improvements and refinements of gross and fine motor skills and coordination. Significant physical and appearance changes occur in adolescence as children enter puberty. These changes often occur quickly, resulting in a period of awkwardness and lack of coordination as adolescents adjust to this rapid development.

Impact of External Factors on Physical Development

As children pass through physical development stages from early childhood to adolescence, it is important that environmental factors are supportive of proper growth and health. Physical development can be hindered by external factors, such as poor nutrition, lack of sleep, prenatal exposure to drugs, and abuse, as these can cause significant and long-lasting negative consequences. Exposure to such factors can lead to stunted physical growth, impaired brain development and function, poor bone and muscle development, and obesity. Furthermore, the negative impacts from such external factors ultimately impedes cognitive, social, and emotional development. Impaired brain development and function negatively affect cognitive development by impacting the ability to concentrate and grasp new concepts. In terms of emotional development, physical impairments due to external factors can cause a child to become depressed, withdrawn, aggressive, prone to low self-esteem, and unable to self-regulate. Improper physical growth and health impacts social development in that physical limitations could hinder a child's ability to properly interact with and play with others. Impacted brain development and function can limit a child's ability to understand social cues and norms.

Language Development

Stages of Language Development

The first stage of language development and acquisition, the **pre-linguistic stage**, occurs during an infant's first year of life. It is characterized by the development of gestures, making eye contact, and sounds like cooing and crying. The **holophrase** or **one-word sentence stage** develops in infants between 10 and 13 months of age. In this stage, young children use one-word sentences to communicate meaning in language. The **two-word sentence stage** typically develops by the time a child is 18 months old. Each two-word sentence usually contains a noun or a verb and a modifier, such as "big balloon" or "green grass." Children in this stage use their two-word sentences to communicate wants and needs. **Multiple-word sentences** form by the time a child is two to two and a half years old. In this stage, children begin forming sentences with subjects and predicates, such as "tree is tall" or "rope is long." Grammatical errors are present, but children in this stage begin demonstrating how to use words in appropriate context. Children ages two and a half to three years typically begin using more **complex grammatical structures**. They begin to include grammatical structures that were not present before, such as conjunctions and prepositions. By the age of five or six, children reach a stage of **adult-like language development**. They begin to use words in appropriate context and can move words around in sentences while maintaining appropriate sentence structure. Language development and acquisition has a wide range of what is considered normal development. Some children do not attempt to speak for up to two years and then may experience an explosion of language development at a later time. In these cases, children often emerge from their silent stage with equivalent language development to babies who were more expressive early on. A child who does not speak after two years, however, may be exhibiting signs of a developmental delay.

Oral Language Development

Oral language development begins well before students enter educational environments. It is learned first without formal instruction, with **environmental factors** being a heavy influence. Children tend to develop their own linguistic rules as a result of genetic disposition, their environments, and how their individual thinking processes develop. Oral language refers to both speaking and listening. Components of oral language development include phonology, syntax, semantics, morphology, and pragmatics. **Phonology** refers to the production and recognition of sounds. **Morphology** refers to how words are formed from smaller pieces, called morphemes. **Semantics** refers to the meaning of words and phrases and has overlap with morphology and syntax, as morphemes and word order can both change the meaning of words. Semantic studies generally focus on learning and understanding vocabulary. **Syntax** refers to how words and morphemes are combined to make up meaningful phrases. In English, word order is the primary way that many components of grammar are communicated. Finally, **pragmatics** refers to the practical application of language based on various social situations. For instance, a college student is likely to use different vocabulary, complexity, and formality of language when speaking with a professor than when speaking with his or her peer group. Each of these five components of language are applied in oral language. Awareness and application of these components develops over time as students gain experience and education in language use. **Oral language development** can be nurtured by caregivers and teachers well before children enter educational environments. Caregivers and teachers can promote oral language development by providing environments full of language development opportunities. Additionally, teaching children how conversation works, encouraging interaction among children, and demonstrating good listening and speaking skills are good strategies for nurturing oral language development.

> **Review Video: Components of Oral Language Development**
> Visit mometrix.com/academy and enter code: 480589

Helping Students Develop Oral Language Abilities

Children pick up oral language skills in their home environments and build upon these skills as they grow. Early language development is influenced by a combination of genetic disposition, environment, and individual thinking processes. Children with **oral language acquisition difficulties** often experience difficulties in their **literacy skills**, so activities that promote good oral language skills also improve literacy skills. **Strategies** that help students develop oral language abilities include developing appropriate speaking and listening skills; providing instruction that emphasizes vocabulary development; providing students with opportunities to communicate wants, needs, ideas, and information; creating language learning environments; and promoting auditory memory. Developing appropriate speaking and listening skills includes teaching turn-taking, awareness of social norms, and basic rules for speaking and listening. Emphasizing **vocabulary development** is a strategy that familiarizes early learners with word meanings. Providing students with opportunities to **communicate** is beneficial for developing early social skills. Teachers can create **language learning environments** by promoting literacy in their classrooms with word walls, reading circles, or other strategies that introduce language skills to students. Promoting **auditory memory** means teaching students to listen to, process, and recall information.

> **Review Video: Types of Vocabulary Learning (Broad and Specific)**
> Visit mometrix.com/academy and enter code: 258753

Helping Students Monitor Errors in Oral Language

Oral language is the primary way people communicate and express their knowledge, ideas, and feelings. As oral language generally develops, their **speaking and listening skills** become more refined. This refinement of a person's language is called fluency, which can be broken down into the subdisciplines of language, reading, writing, speaking, and listening. **Speaking fluency** usually describes the components of rate, accuracy, and prosody. **Rate** describes how fast a person can speak, and **prosody** describes the inflection and expressions that a person puts into speech. **Accuracy** describes how often a person makes an error in language production. In early stages of language development, individuals generally do not have enough language knowledge to be able to monitor their own speech production for errors and require input from others to notice and correct their mistakes. As an individual becomes more proficient, he or she will be able to monitor his or her own language usage and make corrections to help improve fluency. In the classroom, the teacher needs to be an active component of language monitoring to help facilitate growth. Teachers can monitor **oral language errors** with progress-monitoring strategies. Teachers can also help students monitor their own **oral language development** as they progress through the reading curriculum. Students can monitor their oral language by listening to spoken words in their school and home environments, learning and practicing self-correction skills, and participating in reading comprehension and writing activities. Students can also monitor oral language errors by learning oral language rules for phonics, semantics, syntax, and pragmatics. These rules typically generalize to developing appropriate oral language skills.

Expressive and Receptive Language

Expressive language refers to the aspects of language that an individual produces, generally referring to writing and speaking. **Receptive language** refers to the aspects of language that an individual encounters or receives and generally refers to reading and listening. Both expressive and receptive language are needed for communication from one person to another.

	Expressive	**Receptive**
Written	Writing	Reading
Oral	Speaking	Listening

Expressive Language Skills

Expressive language skills include the ability to use vocabulary, sentences, gestures, and writing. People with good **expressive language skills** can label objects in their environments, put words in sentences, use appropriate grammar, demonstrate comprehension verbally by retelling stories, and more. This type of language is important because it allows people to express feelings, wants, needs, thoughts, ideas, and individual points of view. Strong expressive language skills include pragmatic knowledge, such as using gestures and facial expressions or using appropriate vocabulary for the listener or reader and soft skills, such as checks for comprehension, use of analogies, and grouping of ideas to help with clarity. Well-expressed language should be relatively easy for someone else to comprehend.

Receptive Language Skills

Receptive language refers to a person's ability to perceive and understand language. Good receptive language skills involve gathering information from the environment and processing it into meaning. People with good **receptive language skills** perceive gestures, sounds, words, and written information well. Receptive language is important for developing appropriate communication skills. Instruction that targets receptive language skills can include tasks that require sustained attention and focus, recognizing emotions and gestures, and listening and reading comprehension. Games that challenge the players to communicate carefully, such as charades or catchphrase, can be a great way to target receptive language skills. As one student tries to accurately express an idea with words or gestures, the rest of the class must exercise their receptive language skills. Lastly, focusing on **social skills and play skills instruction** encourages opportunities for children to interact with their peers or adults. This fosters receptive language skills and targets deficits in these skills.

Stages of Literacy Development

The development of literacy in young children is separated into five stages. Names and ranges of these stages sometimes vary slightly, but the stage milestones are similar. Stage 1 is the **Emergent Reader stage**. In this stage, children ages 6 months to 6 years demonstrate skills like pretend reading, recognizing letters of the alphabet, retelling stories, and printing their names. Stage 2 is the **Novice/Early Reader stage** (ages 6–7 years). Children begin to understand the relationships between letters and sounds and written and spoken words, and they read texts containing high-frequency words. Children in this stage should develop orthographic conventions and semantic knowledge. In Stage 3, the **Decoding Reader stage**, children ages 7–9 develop decoding skills in order to read simple stories. They also demonstrate increased fluency. Stage 4 (ages 8–15 years) is called the **Fluent, Comprehending/Transitional Reader stage**. In this stage, fourth to eighth graders read to learn new ideas and information. In Stage 5, the **Expert/Fluent Reader stage**, children ages 16 years and older read more complex information. They also read expository and narrative texts with multiple viewpoints.

Review Video: Stages of Reading Development
Visit mometrix.com/academy and enter code: 121184

Relationship between Language Development and Early Literacy Skills

Language development and early literacy skills are interconnected. **Language concepts** begin and develop shortly after birth with infant/parent interactions, cooing, and then babbling. These are the earliest attempts at language acquisition for infants. Young children begin interacting with written and spoken words before they enter their grade school years. Before they enter formal classrooms, children begin to make **connections** between speaking and listening and reading and writing. Children with strong speaking and listening skills demonstrate strong literacy skills in early grade school. The development of **phonological awareness** is connected to early literacy skills. Children with good phonological awareness recognize that words are made up of different speech sounds. For example, children with appropriate phonological awareness can break words (e.g., "bat" into separate speech sounds, "b-a-t"). Examples of phonological awareness include rhyming (when the ending parts of words have the same or similar sounds) and alliteration (when words all have the same beginning sound). Success with phonological awareness (oral language) activities depends on adequate development of speech and language skills.

Promoting Literacy During the Early Stages of Literacy Development

Teachers and parents can implement strategies at different stages of literacy development in order to build **good reading skills** in children with and without disabilities. During the **Emergent Reader stage**, teachers and parents can introduce children to the conventions of reading with picture books. They can model turning the pages, reading from left to right, and other reading conventions. Book reading at this stage helps children begin to identify letters, letter sounds, and simple words. Repetitive reading of familiar texts also helps children begin to make predictions about what they are reading. During the **Novice/Early Reader** and **Decoding Reader stages**, parents and teachers can help children form the building blocks of decoding and fluency skills by reading for meaning and emphasizing letter-sound relationships, visual cues, and language patterns. In these stages, increasing familiarity with sight words is essential. In the **Fluent, Comprehending/Transitional Reader stage**, children should be encouraged to read book series, as the shared characters, settings, and plots help develop their comprehension skills. At this stage, a good reading rate (fluency) is an indicator of comprehension skills. **Expert/Fluent readers** can independently read multiple texts and comprehend their meanings. Teachers and parents can begin exposing children to a variety of fiction and non-fiction texts before this stage in order to promote good fluency skills.

Review Video: Phonics (Encoding and Decoding)
Visit mometrix.com/academy and enter code: 821361

Review Video: Fluency
Visit mometrix.com/academy and enter code: 531179

Types of Disabilities

Medical disabilities include problems related to diseases, illnesses, trauma, and genetic conditions. **Physical disabilities** include problems related to fine and gross motor skills and can include sensory input or sensory perception disorders. Medical and physical disabilities often manifest with other disabilities, such as **learning disabilities**. Medical disabilities that affect educational performance usually fall under the "other health impairment" or "traumatic brain injury" categories of the Individuals with Disabilities Education Act (IDEA). Students with physical disabilities, such as cerebral palsy, can be eligible for special education under IDEA's "orthopedic impairment" category. However, for either medical or physical disabilities to qualify, they must **adversely affect educational performance**. For example, a student with cerebral palsy would not be eligible for special education or an **Individualized Education Program (IEP)** if the disability does not affect educational performance. The student would receive accommodations and modifications under a 504 Plan.

Review Video: Medical Conditions in Education
Visit mometrix.com/academy and enter code: 531058

Low-Incidence Disabilities and High-Incidence Disabilities

Low-incidence disabilities account for up to 20 percent of all students' disabilities. Students with low-incidence disabilities have sometimes received assistance for their disabilities starting from an early age. **Low-incidence disabilities** include intellectual disabilities, multiple disabilities, hearing impairments, orthopedic impairments, other health impairments, visual impairments, certain autism spectrum conditions, deaf-blindness, traumatic brain injury, and significant developmental delays. **High-incidence disabilities** account for up to 80 percent of all students' disabilities. While students with high-incidence disabilities present with academic, social, communication, or behavioral problems, they can often be held to the same standards as their regular education peers. Children with high-incidence disabilities may perform at the same capacities as their similar-aged peers but have deficits in reading, math, writing, handwriting, or maintaining attention. High-incidence disabilities include speech and language impairments, learning disabilities, attention-deficit/hyperactivity disorder, emotional disorders, mild intellectual disabilities, certain autism spectrum conditions, and cognitive delays.

Interventions for Students with Physical Disabilities

A physical disability refers to any disability that limits **gross mobility** and prevents **normal body movement**. For example, muscular dystrophy is a physical disability that weakens muscles over time. Students with physical disabilities require early interventions and should begin to receive them before grade school. When students with physical disabilities enter grade school, they may receive interventions and related services if they qualify for special education and receive IEPs or **504 Plans**. When physical disabilities do not affect the students' academic success, they may be put on 504 Plans to receive appropriate related services, accommodations, or modifications. When physical disabilities are present with other disabilities or the physical disabilities affect academic performance, students may be put on IEPs and receive appropriate related services, accommodations, and modifications. Teachers, intervention specialists, physiotherapists, occupational therapists, and speech language pathologists work as a team in implementing appropriate accommodations, modifications, and related services to assist students with physical disabilities.

Working with Students with Physical Disabilities

Students with physical disabilities should be included in **general education classrooms** with accommodations if their disabilities do not coexist with other disabilities, such as learning disabilities. The Individuals with Disabilities Education Act states that students must be assigned to a classroom that conforms with the student's least restrictive environment, which generally means the general education classroom, unless appropriate accommodations cannot be made. If sufficient accommodations or modifications are not able to be made within the general education classroom, a student may be placed in a more specialized environment that provides for his or her particular needs. In any of these settings, it is essential for educators to practice **instructional strategies** that facilitate the learning processes and accommodate the needs of students with physical disabilities. Classrooms should be arranged so they can be **navigated** easily by everyone. This includes giving students using wheelchairs adequate aisle space and workspace. **Partner work** is helpful for students with physical disabilities, who may struggle with handwriting or using keyboards. Partners can assist these students with skills like note-taking, which may be difficult for students with physical disabilities. Additionally, assignments can include **accommodations** or **modifications** to meet the specific needs of students with physical disabilities. For example, text-to-speech software can be provided for students who struggle with using regular keyboards.

Accommodations and Modifications

Students with **speech, language, visual,** or **hearing impairments** (including **deafness**) that adversely affect their educational performance receive **accommodations**, modifications, and related services specific to their disabilities. Students with these impairments may be educated alongside peers and provided with related services outside of the general education classroom. Accommodations, modifications, and related services are provided based on the severity of the disability.

An **orthopedic impairment (OI)** severely hinders mobility or motor activity. Accommodations, modifications, and related services in the classroom environment may be appropriate for students with OI. Students with **intellectual disabilities**, such as Down syndrome, often need supports in place for communication, self-care, and social skills. The educational implications of a **traumatic brain injury** are unique to the individual and are therefore treated on a case-by-case basis. Students with **multiple disabilities** have needs that cannot be met in any one program. Sometimes their needs are so great that they must be educated in partial inclusion or self-contained settings.

Disability Categories in IDEA

- **Specific Learning Disabilities (SLD)** is the umbrella term for children who struggle with issues in their abilities to read, write, speak, listen, reason, or do math.
- **Other Health Impairment (OHI)** is the umbrella term for a disability that limits a child's strength, energy, or alertness.
- **Autism Spectrum Disorder (ASD)** is a disability that mostly affects a child's social and communication skills, and sometimes behavior.
- **Emotional Disturbance (ED)** is a disability category for a number of mental disorders.
- **Speech or Language Impairment** covers children with language impairments.
- **Visual Impairment or Blindness** is a disability category for children with visual impairments that significantly impact their abilities to learn.
- **Deafness** is the category for students who cannot hear even with a hearing aid.
- **Hearing Impairment** describes hearing loss that is not as pervasive as deafness. This is distinguished from deafness categorically, as the types of interventions needed are very different.

- **Deaf-Blindness** covers children diagnosed with both deafness and blindness.
- Those with **Orthopedic Impairments** have impairments to their bodies that interfere with the performance of daily living skills.
- An **Intellectual Disability** is the diagnosis for children with below-average intellectual abilities or intelligence quotients (IQs).
- **Traumatic Brain Injury (TBI)** covers children who have suffered from TBIs.
- **Multiple Disabilities** as a category means a child has more than one disability defined by the Individuals with Disabilities Education Act and requires educational interventions that go beyond standard interventions for one category.

> **Review Video: Understanding Learning Disability Needs of Students**
> Visit mometrix.com/academy and enter code: 662775

Specific Learning Disability

Early Indications of a Specific Learning Disability

Early indications of specific learning disabilities (SLDs) can include medical history, problems with speech acquisition, problems with socialization, academic delays, and behavioral delays. Delays in certain milestones may indicate learning disabilities, but these delays may also be due to other causes. Premature birth, serious childhood illnesses, frequent ear infections, and sleep disorders are **medical factors** that can influence the development of learning disabilities. Children that develop SLDs may demonstrate early delays in **speech**. Late speech development, pronunciation problems, and stuttering may indicate SLDs, but they may also be issues that are unrelated to SLDs and can be addressed by individualized speech instruction. Students with SLDs may also have problems adjusting **socially** and may demonstrate social skills that are not age appropriate. Depending on when the children enter academic settings, they may demonstrate academic delays compared to similar-aged peers. These delays are usually determined using formal and informal assessments in educational settings. **Behaviors** such as hyperactivity or difficulty following directions may also indicate a child has an SLD. However, these indicators do not definitely mean that a child has a learning disability, and some of the indicators overlap with characteristics of other disabilities.

Instructional Strategies for Teaching Students with Specific Learning Disabilities

While there is no one strategy that works effectively with all students with specific learning disabilities, there are some strategies that tend to produce **positive outcomes** for these students. Direct instruction, learning strategy instruction, and a multi-sensory approach are three large-scale interventions that can be used to promote student learning. **Direct instruction** is teacher-driven instruction that targets specific skills; this is sometimes delivered in resource rooms. **Learning strategy instruction** is a method for teaching students with disabilities different tools and techniques useful for learning new content or skills. This includes techniques like chunking the content, sequencing tasks, and small group instruction. A **multi-sensory approach** ensures that students are receiving and interacting with new information and skills using more than one sense at a time. This approach is helpful for students with learning disabilities because it targets many different ways of learning.

Dyslexia and Dysgraphia Disorders

Students with dyslexia are eligible for special education under the specific learning disability category in the Individuals with Disabilities Education Act if their educational performance is significantly impacted by their disabilities. **Dyslexia** is a permanent condition that makes it difficult for people to read. This affects reading accuracy, fluency, and comprehension. Dyslexia also generalizes to difficulties in the content areas of writing, mathematics, and spelling. Children who have dyslexia often have difficulties with **phonemic awareness skills** and **decoding**. It is not a disability that affects vision or the way people see letters. Dyslexia may coexist with other conditions such as **dysgraphia**, which is a disorder that causes issues with written expression. With dysgraphia, children often struggle with holding pencils and writing letters accurately. It is difficult for students with dysgraphia to distinguish shapes, use correct letter spacing, read maps, copy text, understand spelling rules, and more.

Review Video: Disorders That Impair Reading Comprehension
Visit mometrix.com/academy and enter code: 306758

Sensory Processing Disorders

A person with a deficit in the brain's ability to interpret sensory information has a sensory processing disorder (**SPD**). In people without SPD, brain receptors can interpret sensory input, and then the person demonstrates appropriate reactions. In people with SPD, sensory input is blocked from brain receptors, resulting in abnormal reactions. Previously known as a sensory integration disorder, SPD is not a disability specifically defined or eligible under IDEA. However, many students with disabilities defined by IDEA, like autism, also experience some sort of sensory processing disorder. Students with SPD may display **oversensitive or under-sensitive responses** to their environments, stimuli, and senses. They may not understand physical boundaries, such as where their bodies are in space, and may bump into things and demonstrate clumsiness. These students may get upset easily, throw tantrums, demonstrate high anxiety, and struggle with changes.

Importance of Enforcing Word Recognition

Many students with specific learning disabilities demonstrate **deficits in their reading abilities**. This includes **word recognition abilities**. Teaching **word identification** is important for these students because developing age-appropriate word recognition skills is one of the essential building blocks for creating efficient readers. Children who do not develop adequate reading skills in elementary school are generally below-average readers as they age in school. Most districts and teachers use **basal reading programs** that teach word recognition and phonics. Teachers often supplement basal reading programs with **instructional programs** that can be used at home and at school. These are especially useful for students with disabilities or students who are at risk and struggle with word recognition abilities. Elements of basal and supplementary reading programs include instruction for helping students make connections between letters and sounds, opportunities to become comfortable with reading, alphabetic knowledge, phonemic awareness, letter-sound correlations, word identification strategies, spelling, writing, and reading fluency.

Other Health Impairments

Qualifications to Be Eligible for Special Education Under the Category of OHI

The category of other health impairment (**OHI**) under IDEA indicates that a child has **limited strength, vitality, or alertness**. This includes hyper-alertness or hypo-alertness to environmental stimuli. In order to be eligible for special education under this category according to IDEA, the disability must **adversely affect educational performance**. It must also be due to **chronic or acute health problems**, such as attention-deficit/hyperactivity disorder, diabetes, epilepsy, heart conditions, hemophilia, lead poisoning, leukemia, nephritis, rheumatic fever, sickle cell anemia, or Tourette's syndrome. Since the OHI category encompasses a number of different disabilities, teachers and parents must rely on a student's Individualized Education Program to ensure that individual academic needs are met and appropriate accommodations and modifications are provided.

Educational Implications for Students with ADHD

IDEA does **not** recognize attention-deficit/hyperactivity disorder (ADHD) in any of its 13 major disability categories. Students may be diagnosed with ADHD by a physician, but this diagnosis is not enough to qualify them for **special education services**. When ADHD is present alongside an IDEA-recognized disability, the student qualifies for special education services under that disability. A student whose ability to learn is affected by ADHD can receive services with a 504 Plan in place. **Section 504 of the Rehabilitation Act of 1973** requires that any child whose disability affects a major life activity receive appropriate **accommodations** and **modifications** in the learning environment. Parents who think a child's ADHD adversely affects educational functioning may request a formal evaluation to be performed by the school. If the child is found to qualify for special education services, they then receive services under IDEA's **other health impairment** category.

ADHD

Children with **attention-deficit/hyperactivity disorder (ADHD)** may demonstrate inattention and/or hyperactivity and impulsivity. Students with ADHD may have difficulties with attention span, following instructions, and concentrating to the point that their educational performance is affected. Since ADHD symptoms are common among children, their presence does not necessarily indicate that a child has ADHD. ADHD is not caused by certain environmental factors, such as diet or watching too much television. Symptoms may be exacerbated by these factors, but the causes can be heredity, chemical imbalances, issues with brain functions, environmental toxins, or prenatal trauma, such as the mother smoking or drinking during pregnancy.

Autism Spectrum Disorder

Autism is a **spectrum disorder**, which means the characteristics associated with the disability vary depending on the student. However, there are common repetitive and patterned behaviors associated with communication and social interactions for this population of students. Students with autism may demonstrate delayed or different speech patterns, the inability to understand body language or facial expressions, and the inability to exhibit appropriate speech patterns, body language, or facial expressions. In a classroom environment, students with autism may demonstrate **repetitive behaviors** that are distracting, such as hand flapping or making vocalizations. Some students with autism demonstrate **preoccupation** with doing activities, tasks, or routines in certain ways. This preoccupation can lead to difficulties when the students are asked to make changes to activities, tasks, or routines. Furthermore, some students with autism prefer to **participate** in a limited range of activities and may get upset when asked to participate in activities outside of their self-perceived ranges. This preference for a limited range of activities may even translate into repetitive behaviors or obsessive and fanatic focus on particular topics. Extreme interest in one topic can lead to disruptions when students with autism are asked to speak or write about different topics.

Review Video: Autism Spectrum Disorder
Visit mometrix.com/academy and enter code: 395410

Concurrent Autism Spectrum Disorder and Other Learning Disabilities

Misinformation about autism spectrum disorder (ASD) and its relation to other learning disabilities runs rampant within school communication and needs clarification to prevent harmful stereotyping of students. As a spectrum disorder, the way ASD presents varies widely and does not always affect students in the same ways. Autism spectrum disorder is frequently confused with intellectual disabilities, which is when an individual has a low IQ; however, students with ASD can have IQs ranging from significantly delayed to above average or gifted. ASD is also distinctive in that it largely involves difficulties with social understanding and communication, as well as fixations on repetitive routines and behaviors. It is important for an educational professional to understand the difference between ASD and other types of disabilities that commonly co-occur or which have overlapping symptoms. For instance, students with learning disabilities and students with ASD may both have challenges with reading nonverbal cues, staying organized, and expressing themselves, but that does not mean that they have the same underlying conditions or needs. The professional educational community must be aware and cautious when describing various disabilities to prevent the spread of misinformation and harmful stereotyping.

Early Signs of a Child Having ASD

Early signs of **autism spectrum disorder (ASD)** include impairments or delays in social interactions and communication, repetitive behaviors, limited interests, and abnormal eating habits. Students with ASD typically do not interact in conversations in the same ways as similar-aged peers without ASD. They may demonstrate inability to engage in pretend play and may pretend they don't hear when being spoken to. Hand flapping, vocal sounds, or compulsive interactions with objects are repetitive behaviors sometimes demonstrated by students with ASD. They may only demonstrate interest in talking about one topic or interacting with one object. They may also demonstrate self-injurious behavior or sleep problems, in addition to having a limited diet of preferred foods. **Early intervention** is key for these students in order to address and improve functioning. These students may also benefit from **applied behavior analysis** to target specific behaviors, and they may require speech and language therapy, occupational therapy, social skills instruction, or other services geared toward improving intellectual functioning.

Characteristics of Social Skill Delays in Students with ASD

Autism spectrum disorder (ASD) is a disability that can affect a student's social, communication, and behavioral abilities. **Social skill delays and deficits** are common for students with ASD. Social skill delays go hand in hand with **communication limitations** for students with ASD. This includes conversational focus on one or two narrow topics or ideas, which makes it difficult for students with ASD to hold two-way conversations about things that do not interest them. Some students with ASD engage in repetitive language or echolalia or rely on standard phrases to communicate with others. Their **speech and language skills** may be delayed compared to their similar-aged peers. This may also impact their abilities to engage in effective conversations. The **nonverbal skills** of students with ASD may also be misinterpreted, such as when they avoid eye contact while speaking or being spoken to.

Early Communication and Social Skill Delays in Students with ASD

Students with delays in communication development often need and receive some type of assistance or instruction with communication and social skills. Early intervention for these students is key, as communication difficulties may be a symptom of **autism spectrum disorder (ASD)**. For students with ASD, the need for communication and social skills instruction varies depending on the individual student. Key characteristics of **early communication difficulties** for a student with ASD include not responding to his or her name, not pointing at objects of interest, avoiding eye contact, not engaging in pretend play, delayed speech or language skills, or repeating words or phrases. Children with ASD may also exhibit overreaction or underreaction to environmental stimuli. Key characteristics of **early social skill difficulties** for a student with ASD may include preferring to play alone, trouble understanding personal feelings or the feelings of others, not sharing interests with others, and difficulty with personal space boundaries. Infants with ASD may not respond to their names and demonstrate reduced babbling and reduced interest in people. Toddlers with ASD may demonstrate decreased interest in social interactions, difficulty with pretend play, and a preference for playing alone.

Socratic Method for Students with ASD

With the Socratic method of teaching, students are **guided** by their teachers in their own educational discovery learning processes. This involves students intrinsically seeking knowledge or answers to problems. This method can be helpful for facilitating and enhancing the **social and emotional abilities** of students with disabilities, particularly autism spectrum disorder (ASD). The Socratic method requires **dialogue** in order to successfully facilitate the teacher/student guided learning process. This is beneficial for students with ASD, who generally struggle with appropriate communication and social skills. This method emphasizes **information seeking and communication skills** by engaging students in class discussions, assignment sharing, and group work. Communication for information-seeking purposes is often a deficit of students with ASD. Sharing of ideas is a concept that develops naturally in guided learning and often requires flexibility in the thought process, another skill that students with ASD struggle with. These skills can be taught to and reinforced in students with and without disabilities in order to develop skills essential to lifelong learning processes.

Fostering the Communication Development of Students with ASD

Students with **autism spectrum disorder (ASD)** vary in their need for communication and social skill assistance and instruction. Some students with ASD may demonstrate slight to extreme delays in language; difficulty sustaining conversations; and the inability to understand body language, tone of voice, and facial expressions. Since ASD is a **spectrum disorder**, there typically is no single instructional strategy or technique that works for all students with the disorder. Some **evidence-based strategies** are effective for teaching appropriate communication skills to students with ASD. **Applied behavior analysis (ABA)** is an evidence-based strategy that involves providing an intervention and analyzing its effectiveness for a student with ASD. **Discrete trial training (DTT)** is a teaching strategy that is more structured than ABA. It focuses on teaching and reinforcing skills in smaller increments. **Pivotal response treatment (PRT)** is an ABA-derived approach that focuses more on meaningful reinforcement when generally positive behaviors occur. Where ABA targets very specific tasks, PRT targets behaviors categorically or more generally. Furthermore, instead of using an unrelated, supplemented reward system, such as giving candy for completing a task, the rewards used should be related to the desired behavior. For instance, suppose a targeted goal is to have the individual work on politely asking for things generally. The PRT-based reward might be giving the individual the toy or desired object as a reward for asking for it.

Emotional Disturbances

A diagnosis of an emotional disturbance (**ED**) can also be referred to as a **behavioral disorder** or **mental illness**. Causes of emotional disturbances are generally unclear. However, heredity, brain disorders, and diet are some factors that influence the development of emotional disturbances. The emotional disturbance category includes psychological disorders, such as anxiety disorders, bipolar disorder, eating disorders, and obsessive-compulsive disorder. Children who have emotional disturbances that affect their educational performance are eligible for **special education** under the Individuals with Disabilities Education Act. Indicators of emotional disturbances include hyperactivity, aggression, withdrawal, immaturity, and academic difficulties. While many children demonstrate these indicators throughout their development, an emotional disturbance is associated with **prolonged demonstration** of these behaviors.

Issues Students with Emotional Disturbances Experience in the Instructional Setting

Students with the diagnosis of emotional disturbance (ED) as defined by the Individuals with Disabilities Education Act require **emotional and behavioral support** in the classroom. Students with ED may also require **specialized academic instruction** in addition to behavioral and emotional support. The amount of support given varies according to the needs of individual students. These students also need **scaffolded instruction** in social skills, self-awareness, self-esteem, and self-control. Students with ED often exhibit behaviors that impede their learning or the learning of others. **Positive behavioral interventions and supports (PBIS)** is a preventative instructional strategy that focuses on promoting positive behaviors in students. With PBIS, teachers or other professionals make changes to students' environments in order to decrease problem behaviors. PBIS involves collecting information on a problem behavior, identifying positive interventions to support the student before behaviors escalate, and implementing supports to decrease targeted negative behaviors. Supports can be implemented schoolwide or in the classroom. However, for students with ED, **classroom supports** are more effective because they can be individualized.

SPEECH AND LANGUAGE IMPAIRMENTS

Speech and language impairments, sometimes referred to as **communication disorders**, are disabilities recognized by the Individuals with Disabilities Education Act. Students diagnosed with communication disorders are eligible for special education if they qualify for services. Early indicators of communication disorders include but are not limited to:

- Not smiling or interacting with others
- Lack of babbling or cooing in infants
- Lack of age-appropriate comprehension skills
- Speech that is not easily understood
- Issues with age-appropriate syntax development
- Issues with age-appropriate social skills
- Deficits in reading and writing skills
- Beginning or ending words with incorrect sounds
- Hearing loss
- Stuttering

These indicators may also be linked to other disabilities, such as hearing impairments or autism spectrum disorder. Although prolonged demonstration of these indicators may suggest communication disorders, some children demonstrate delays and then self-correct over time.

FACILITATING LEARNING FOR STUDENTS WITH SPEECH OR LANGUAGE IMPAIRMENTS

In order to teach students with speech or language impairments, also referred to as **communication disorders**, teachers and other professionals can use the **strategies** listed below:

- Use visuals and concrete examples to help students with communication disorders take in new information. Link the visuals with spoken words or phrases.
- Use visuals or photographs to introduce or reinforce vocabulary.
- Use repetition of spoken words to introduce or reinforce vocabulary.
- Model conversational and social skills, which helps students with communication disorders become familiar with word pronunciation.
- Speak at a slower rate when necessary, especially when presenting new information.
- Consistently check for understanding.
- Be aware that communication issues may sometimes result in other issues, such as behavioral or social skill issues.
- Pair actions and motions with words to emphasize meaning, especially for students with receptive language disorders.

Receptive Language Disorders

Children with receptive language disorders often demonstrate appropriate expressive language skills and hear and read at age-appropriate levels. However, they may seem like they are not paying attention or engaging in activities, or they may appear to have difficulties following or understanding directions. They may refrain from asking questions or interrupt frequently during activities, especially during read-aloud activities. It may appear as if they are not listening, but children with receptive language disorders have difficulty perceiving **meaning** from what they hear. Children with this disorder may consistently leave tasks incomplete unless the tasks are broken down into smaller steps. This is due to issues with processing directions, especially **verbal directions**. Children with receptive language disorders may not respond appropriately or at all to questions from peers or adults. Answers to comprehension questions, especially when texts are read aloud, may be off topic or incorrect. Children with receptive language disorders have trouble gathering and connecting meaning to what they hear. A receptive language disorder is not exclusively a learning disability. However, children who have receptive disorders may have learning disabilities.

Expressive Language Disabilities

Expressive language is the ability to express wants and needs. Children with disabilities related to **expressive language disabilities** may have trouble conversing with peers and adults and have trouble with self-expression. Answers to questions may be vague or repetitive. They may not demonstrate age-appropriate social skills with peers and adults. Children with expressive language disabilities have a limited vocabulary range and rely on familiar vocabulary words in their expressive language. They can be very quiet and seclude themselves from classroom activities because of difficulties expressing their thoughts and feelings. They may not be able to accurately express what they understand because children with expressive language difficulties have trouble speaking in sentences. Expressive language disabilities indicate issues with **language processing centers** in the brain. Children with these disabilities can sometimes understand language but have trouble **expressing** it. Children with traumatic brain injuries, dyslexia, autism, or learning disabilities demonstrate issues with expressive language.

Implications of Literacy Development for Children with Disabilities

Children may not always meet the **literacy stage milestones** at specified ages. However, this does not always indicate a disability. Children who fall significantly behind in their literacy development, continually struggle with skill acquisition, or do not consistently retain skill instruction are more likely to be identified as having **disabilities**. Furthermore, children with **speech and language disorders** are more likely to experience problems learning to read and write. These issues are typically apparent before children enter grade school but can also become evident during their early grade school years. **Early warning signs** include disinterest in shared book reading, inability to recognize or remember names of letters, difficulty understanding directions, and persistent baby talk.

Effects of Deficits in Language Development on the Learning Processes

Without interventions, children with deficits in language development will likely have issues with overall academic success. **Academic success** is inextricably linked with good language development. Good **language development skills** include the ability to understand spoken and written words, as well as literacy skills. When a core knowledge of language is developed in young children, it can be built upon as the children grow and develop during their grade school years. Reading and writing are language-based skills. **Phonological awareness** is an essential skill and key building block for language development. Phonological awareness is a term that refers to students' awareness of sounds, syllables, and words. Students that develop strong phonological skills typically develop good literacy skills. Students with deficits in reading, writing, or math may have difficulties with phonological awareness and miss some building blocks essential for academic success. These deficits generalize to core subject areas as students are required to demonstrate grade-level appropriate skills.

Visual Impairment or Blindness

Visual impairments range from low vision to blindness. The Individuals with Disabilities Education Act defines a **visual impairment** as an impairment in vision that is great enough to affect a child's educational performance. **Blindness** is defined as a visual acuity of 20/200 or less in the dominant eye. Some people diagnosed with blindness still have minimal sight. Early indicators of a visual impairment or blindness in children include:

- Holding things close to the eyes or face
- Experiencing fatigue after looking at things closely
- Having misaligned eyes
- Squinting
- Tilting the head or covering one eye to see things up close or far away
- Demonstrating clumsiness
- Appearing to see better during the day

Students with visual impairments benefit the most from early interventions, especially when the impairments are present with other disabilities. Appropriate interventions vary based on students' needs and whether or not they have other disabilities. Modifications, such as magnified text, Braille, auditory support, and text-tracking software, can help level the learning plane for these students.

Deafness, Hearing Impairment, and Deaf-Blindness

Deafness, hearing impairment, and deaf-blindness are each considered their own categories under the Individuals with Disabilities Education Act, as the types and levels of intervention vary widely between them. **Deafness** is defined as a complete or near-complete loss of hearing, to the degree that a hearing aid cannot help. Deaf students often need specialized interventions to help with safety and communication, such as communication aids, assistive devices, and sign language. **Hearing impairments** consist of all qualifying degrees of hearing loss that are not severe enough to qualify as deafness. Interventions may include communication aids and training, as well as hearing aids. **Deaf-blindness** is restricted to students who are both deaf and blind concurrently. Deaf-blind students usually require considerable help with communication and daily living skills.

Effect of Hearing Loss on Language Development

Hearing language is part of learning language. Children with **hearing loss** miss out on sounds associated with language, and this can affect their listening, speaking, reading, social skills, and overall school success. Hearing loss can sometimes lead to delayed speech and language, learning disabilities in school, insecurities, and issues with socialization and making friends. Children with hearing loss may:

- Have trouble learning abstract vocabulary like *since* and *before*
- Omit article words in sentences like *a* and *an*
- Fall behind in core components of learning and development without early interventions
- Have difficulty speaking in and understanding sentences
- Speak in shorter sentences
- Have difficulty including word endings like *-ing* and *-s*
- Have issues speaking clearly because they cannot accurately hear sounds

- Omit quiet sounds like *p, sh,* or *f*
- Be unable to hear what their own voices sound like

Children with hearing loss are more likely to fall behind in school due to their hearing deficits. They can easily fall behind without support from interventions, teachers, and their families. Early **hearing testing** is essential to ensure that interventions, such as sign language, can be introduced to promote school and life success for children with hearing loss.

ORTHOPEDIC IMPAIRMENT

QUALIFICATIONS TO RECEIVE SPECIAL EDUCATION FOR ORTHOPEDIC IMPAIRMENT

Students who qualify to receive special education under the Individuals with Disabilities Education Act orthopedic impairment category have an orthopedic impairment that adversely affects educational performance. This includes children with congenital anomalies, impairments caused by disease, or impairments from other causes, such as cerebral palsy or amputations. An orthopedic impairment alone does not qualify a student for special education and an IEP. Once a student's educational performance is proven to be affected by the orthopedic impairment, the student becomes eligible for special education and placed on an IEP. The **IEP** determines the student's least restrictive environment, individualized goals for academic skills or adaptive behavior, and any appropriate accommodations or modifications. Students with orthopedic impairments whose educational performance is not affected may receive accommodations and modifications on **504 Plans**, if appropriate. Strategies for instruction should be determined and implemented on a case-by-case basis, as the orthopedic impairment category covers a broad range of disabilities.

INTELLECTUAL DISABILITIES

DETERMINING IF A CHILD MAY HAVE AN INTELLECTUAL DISABILITY

Intellectual disability (**ID**) is primarily diagnosed when a child displays impairments in adaptive functioning. Often, these children will score lower than 70 on an IQ test, but IQ scores are not diagnostic and are particularly inaccurate on the low end of the scale. Students diagnosed with intellectual disabilities demonstrate deficits in academic skills, abstract thinking, problem solving, language development, new skill acquisition, and retaining information. Students with ID often do not adequately meet developmental or social milestones. They demonstrate **deficits in functioning** with one or more basic living skills. Students with ID struggle conceptually and may have difficulties with time and money concepts, short-term memory, time management, pre-academic skills, planning, and strategizing. Students with ID demonstrate poor social judgment and decision-making skills because they have trouble understanding social cues and rules. They may grasp concrete social concepts before abstract ones and significantly later than their similar-aged, regular education peers. These students also tend to struggle with self-care skills, household tasks, and completing tasks that may be easy for similar-aged peers.

DETERMINING SEVERITY OF INTELLECTUAL DISABILITIES

There are four levels of intellectual disabilities: mild, moderate, severe, and profound. Specific factors are used to determine whether a disability is mild, moderate, severe, or profound. Intellectual levels are measured using cognitive- and research-based assessments. An **intellectual disability (ID)** is defined as significant cognitive deficits to intellectual functioning, such as reasoning, problem solving, abstract thinking, and comprehension. A **mild intellectual disability** is the most common type of intellectual disability. People with mild to moderate ID can generally participate in independent living activities and learn practical life skills and adaptive behaviors. People diagnosed with **severe intellectual disabilities** demonstrate major developmental delays. They struggle with simple routines and self-care skills. Additionally, they often understand speech but have trouble with expressive communication. People with **profound ID** cannot live independently, and they depend heavily on care from other people and resources. They are likely to have concurrent congenital disorders that affect their intellectual functioning.

Educational Implications for Students with Intellectual Disabilities

According to IDEA, students who are eligible for special education under the category of **intellectual disability** have significantly lower intellectual abilities, along with adaptive behavior deficits. Previously, intellectual disability was referred to as "mental retardation" in IDEA. In 2010, President Obama signed **Rosa's Law**, which changed the term to "intellectual disability." The definition of the disability category remained unchanged. Educational implications of a diagnosis of an intellectual disability differ depending on students' needs as determined by their IEPs. Students with intellectual disabilities often display **limitations to mental functioning** in areas like communication, self-care, and social skills (adaptive behavior). In many cases, these skills must be addressed in the educational environments in addition to any academic skill deficits. Learning adaptive behaviors and academic skills takes longer for students with intellectual disabilities. Their special education placements depend on what environments are least restrictive. This depends on the individual student and is determined in the IEP.

Promoting a Positive Performance for Students with Intellectual Disabilities

Students with intellectual disabilities often present with skill levels that are far below those of similar-aged peers. Because of deficits in academic, behavioral, and social skills, these students require **specialized instruction**, which varies depending on the needs of each individual student. An effective strategy for promoting a positive educational performance is to collect observations and data on the academic, behavioral, and social skill levels of the individual student. Teachers usually work with professionals in related services, like speech language pathologists, to address needs and implement educational interventions that work for this population of students. These students can benefit from **communication interventions** focused on interactions they may have with adults and peers. Students may benefit from augmentative and alternative communication devices, visual activity schedules and other visual supports, and computer-based instruction when learning communication and social skills. Students with intellectual disabilities may also require **behavioral interventions** to teach appropriate behaviors or decrease negative behaviors. They may also benefit from increased **peer interactions** through structured social groups in order to promote appropriate communication skills.

Multiple Disabilities

Components of the Multiple Disability Eligibility Category According to IDEA

The multiple disabilities category according to IDEA applies to students who have two or more disabilities occurring simultaneously. The multiple disability category does not include deaf-blindness, which has its own category under IDEA. Students with **multiple disabilities** present with such **severe educational needs** that they cannot be accommodated in special education settings that address only one disability. Placement in special education programs is determined by students' **least restrictive environments** as defined in their **Individualized Education Programs**. Students with multiple disabilities often present with communication deficits, mobility challenges, and deficits in adaptive behavior and need one-on-one instruction or assistance when performing daily activities.

Intervention Strategies for the Instruction of Students with Multiple Disabilities

Working with students with multiple disabilities can be challenging. However, strategies used in other special education settings can be implemented to promote the success of students with multiple disabilities. Effective strategies include the following:

- Setting **long-term goals**, which may last for a few years depending on how long students are in the same classrooms
- Working **collaboratively** with team members, like paraprofessionals and related service professionals, to ensure that they carry out students' educational objectives consistently
- Developing and maintaining **group goals** that the adults and students in the classrooms can strive to achieve together
- Working with students and paraprofessionals and consulting paraprofessionals frequently for **feedback**
- Demonstrating **patience** when waiting for students to respond or complete tasks
- Learning about how students **communicate**, which may involve gestures, a Picture Exchange Communication System, or other methods
- Driving instruction and education goals based on how students **learn best**
- Considering how students will **respond** when designing lessons, including accounting for response time during instruction

Culture and Language Differences in Special Education

Role of Cultural Competence in Schools and Special Education

Cultural competence, the awareness and appreciation of cultural differences, helps avoid **cultural and linguistic bias**. Schools that demonstrate **cultural competence** have an appreciation of families and their unique backgrounds. Cultural competence is important because it assists with incorporating knowledge and appreciation of other cultures into daily practices and teaching. This helps increase the quality and effectiveness of services for students with unique cultural and linguistic backgrounds. It also helps produce better outcomes for these students. In special education, being culturally competent means being aware of cultural and linguistic differences, especially when considering children for the identification process. Adapting to the **diversity** and **cultural contexts** of the surrounding communities allows teachers to better understand flags for referrals. Teachers that continually assess their awareness of the cultures and diversity of the communities where they teach demonstrate cultural competence. In order for schools and teachers to be described as culturally competent, they should have a process for recognizing diversity.

Cultural and Linguistic Differences vs. Learning Difficulties

Many schools are enriched with cultural diversity. It is important for special educators to identify if a suspected learning disability may instead be a **cultural or linguistic difference**. Teachers and schools must increase awareness of cultural and linguistic differences in order to avoid overidentification of certain populations as having learning difficulties. Some ways a child's behavior may represent cultural or linguistic differences are demonstrated in the **interactions** between teachers and students. In some cultures, children are asked to make eye contact to ensure they are listening, whereas in other cultures, children are taught to look down or away when being spoken to by an adult. Certain facial expressions and behaviors may be interpreted differently by students because of their cultural backgrounds. Additionally, teaching methods that are comfortable and effective for some students may be ineffective for others due to differing cultural backgrounds. Cultural values and characteristics may vary between teachers and students and contribute to the students' school performance. It is important for teachers to be **self-aware** and constantly **assess** whether ineffective teaching methods are due to learning difficulties or cultural and linguistic diversity.

Strategies for Teaching ELLs and Students with Disabilities

English language learners (ELLs) are often at risk of being unnecessarily referred for special education services. This is frequently a result of **inadequate planning** for the needs of English language learners rather than skill deficits. To ensure that the needs of ELLs are met and discrimination is avoided, educators can implement strategies for **targeting their learning processes**. Strategies similar to those utilized in inclusive special education settings, such as using visuals to supplement instruction, are helpful. This type of nonlinguistic representation helps convey meaning to ELLs. Working in groups with peers helps students with disabilities and ELLs demonstrate communication and social skills while working toward common goals. Allowing students to write and speak in their first languages until they feel comfortable speaking in English is a scaffolding strategy that can also be implemented. Sentence frames that demonstrate familiar sentence formats help all students to practice speaking and writing in structured, formal ways.

Review Video: ESL/ESOL/Second Language Learning
Visit mometrix.com/academy and enter code: 795047

Teaching Appropriate Communication Skills to ELLs with Disabilities

Students with disabilities who are also ELLs have the additional challenge of **language barriers** affecting their access to learning. These barriers, combined with the disabilities, can make instruction for these students challenging. For ELL students with disabilities, it is important for teachers to rely on **appropriate instructional strategies** in order to determine what is affecting the students' access to information. Strategies for teaching ELLs are similar to those for teaching nonverbal students. Pairing **visuals** with words helps students make concrete connections between the written words and the pictures. Consistently seeing the words paired with the visuals helps the students interpret word meanings. Using sign language or other gestures is another way teachers can facilitate understanding of word meanings. When used consistently, students make connections between the visual word meanings and the written words. Teachers can also provide opportunities for ELLs to access language by having all students in the classroom communicate in a **consistent manner**. The goal of this instructional strategy is for peers to model appropriate verbal communication as it applies to different classroom situations.

Chapter Quiz

Ready to see how well you retained what you just read? Scan the QR code to go directly to the chapter quiz interface for this study guide. If you're using a computer, simply visit the online resources page at **mometrix.com/resources719/iltslbsi290** and click the Chapter Quizzes link.

Assessing Students and Developing Individualized Programs

Transform passive reading into active learning! After immersing yourself in this chapter, put your comprehension to the test by taking a quiz. The insights you gained will stay with you longer this way. Scan the QR code to go directly to the chapter quiz interface for this study guide. If you're using a computer, simply visit the online resources page at **mometrix.com/resources719/iltslbsi290** and click the Chapter Quizzes link.

Assessment Methodology

Assessment Methods

Effective teaching requires multiple methods of assessment to evaluate student comprehension and instructional effectiveness. Assessments are typically categorized as diagnostic, formative, summative, and benchmark and are applicable at varying stages of instruction. **Diagnostic** assessments are administered before instruction and indicate students' prior knowledge and areas of misunderstanding to determine the path of instruction. **Formative** assessments occur continuously to measure student engagement, comprehension, and instructional effectiveness. These assessments indicate instructional strategies that require adjustment to meet students' needs in facilitating successful learning and include strategies like checking for understanding, observations, total participation activities, and exit tickets. **Summative** assessments are given at the end of a lesson or unit to evaluate student progress in reaching learning targets and identify areas of misconception for reteaching. Such assessments can be given in the form of exams and quizzes or be project-based activities in which students demonstrate their learning through hands-on, personalized methods. Additionally, portfolios serve as valuable summative assessments in allowing students to demonstrate their progress over time and provide insight regarding individual achievement. **Benchmark** assessments occur less frequently and encompass large portions of curriculum. These assessments are intended to evaluate the progress of groups of students in achieving state and district academic standards.

Assessment Types

- **Diagnostic:** These assessments can either be formal or informal and are intended to provide teachers with information regarding students' level of understanding prior to beginning a unit of instruction. Examples include pretests, KWL charts, anticipation guides, and brainstorming activities. Digital resources, such as online polls, surveys, and quizzes are also valuable resources for gathering diagnostic feedback.
- **Formative:** These assessments occur throughout instruction to provide the teacher with feedback regarding student understanding. Examples include warm-up and closure activities, checking frequently for understanding, student reflection activities, and providing students with color-coded cards to indicate their level of understanding. Short quizzes and total participation activities, such as four corners, are also valuable formative assessments. Numerous digital resources, including polls, surveys, and review games, are also beneficial in providing teachers with formative feedback to indicate instructional effectiveness.

- **Summative:** Summative assessments are intended to indicate students' levels of mastery and progress toward reaching academic learning standards. These assessments may take the form of written or digital exams and include multiple choice, short answer, or long answer questions. Examples also include projects, final essays, presentations, or portfolios to demonstrate student progress over time.
- **Benchmark:** Benchmark assessments measure students' progress in achieving academic standards. These assessments are typically standardized to ensure uniformity, objectivity, and accuracy. Benchmark assessments are typically given as a written multiple choice or short answer exam, or as a digital exam in which students answer questions on the computer.

Review Video: Formative and Summative Assessments
Visit mometrix.com/academy and enter code: 804991

Determining Appropriate Assessment Strategies

As varying assessment methods provide different information regarding student performance and achievement, the teacher must consider the most applicable and effective assessment strategy in each stage of instruction. This includes determining the **desired outcomes** of assessment as well as the information the teacher intends to ascertain and how they will apply the results to further instruction. **Age-** and **grade-level**-appropriateness must be considered when selecting which assessment strategies will enable students to successfully demonstrate their learning. Additionally, the teacher must be cognizant of students' individual differences and learning needs to determine which assessment model is most **accommodating** and reflective of their progress. It is also important that teachers consider the practicality of assessment strategies and methods they will use to implement the assessment for maximized feedback regarding individual and whole-class progress in achieving learning goals.

Assessments That Reflect Real-World Applications

Assessments that reflect **real-world applications** enhance relevancy and students' ability to establish personal connections to learning that deepen understanding. Implementing such assessments provides authenticity and enhances engagement by defining a clear and practical purpose for learning. These assessments often allow for hands-on opportunities for demonstrating learning and can be adjusted to accommodate students' varying learning styles and needs while measuring individual progress; however, assessments that focus on real-world applications can be subjective, thus making it difficult to extract concrete data and quantify student progress to guide future instructional decisions. In addition, teachers may have difficulty analyzing assessment results on a large scale and comparing student performance with other schools and districts, as individual assessments may vary.

Diagnostic Tests

Diagnostic tests are integral to planning and delivering effective instruction. These tests are typically administered prior to beginning a unit or lesson and provide valuable feedback for guiding and planning instruction. Diagnostic tests provide **preliminary information** regarding students' levels of understanding and prior knowledge. This serves as a baseline for instructional planning that connects and builds upon students' background knowledge and experiences to enhance success in learning. Diagnostic tests allow the teacher to identify and clarify areas of student misconception prior to engaging in instruction to ensure continued comprehension and avoid the need for remediation. They indicate areas of student strength and need as well as individual instructional aids that may need to be incorporated into lessons to support student achievement. In addition, these tests enable the teacher to determine which instructional strategies, activities, groupings, and materials will be most valuable in maximizing engagement and learning. Diagnostic tests can be **formal** or **informal** and include pre-tests, pre-reading activities, surveys, vocabulary inventories, and graphic organizers (such as KWL charts). These tests are used to assess student understanding prior to engaging in learning. Diagnostic tests are generally not graded, as there is little expectation that all students in a class possess the same baseline of proficiency at the start of a unit.

Formative Assessments

Formative assessments are any assessments that take place in the **middle of a unit of instruction**. The goals of formative assessments are to help teachers understand where a student is in his or her progress toward **mastering** the current unit's content and to provide the students with **ongoing feedback** throughout the unit. The advantage of relying heavily on formative assessments in instruction is that it allows the teacher to continuously **check for comprehension** and adjust instruction as needed to ensure that the whole class is adequately prepared to proceed at the end of the unit. To understand formative assessments well, teachers need to understand that any interaction that can provide information about the student's comprehension is a type of formative assessment which can be used to inform future instruction.

Formative assessments are often a mixture of formal and informal assessments. **Formal formative assessments** often include classwork, homework, and quizzes. Examples of **informal formative assessments** include simple comprehension checks during instruction, class-wide discussions of the current topic, and exit slips, which are written questions posed by teachers at the end of class, which helps the teacher quickly review which students are struggling with the concepts.

Summative Assessments

Summative assessment refers to an evaluation at the end of a discrete unit of instruction, such as the end of a course, unit, or semester. Classic examples of summative assessments include end-of-course assessments, final exams, or even qualifying standardized tests such as the SAT or ACT. Most summative assessments are created to measure student mastery of particular **academic standards**. Whereas formative assessment generally informs current instruction, summative assessments are used to objectively demonstrate that each individual has achieved adequate mastery of the standards in question. If a student has not met the benchmark, he or she may need extra instruction or may need to repeat the course.

These assessments usually take the form of **tests** or formal portfolios with rubrics and clearly defined goals. Summative assessments are usually high-stakes, heavily-weighted, and they should always be formally graded. These types of assessments often feature a narrower range of question types, such as multiple choice, short answer, and essay questions to help with systematic grading.

Project-based assessments are beneficial in evaluating achievement, as they incorporate several elements of instruction and highlight real-world applications of learning. This allows students to demonstrate understanding through a hands-on, individualized approach that reinforces connections to learning and increases retainment. **Portfolios** of student work over time serve as a valuable method for assessing individual progress toward reaching learning targets. Summative assessments provide insight regarding overall instructional effectiveness and are necessary for guiding future instruction in subsequent years but are not usually used to modify current instruction.

Review Video: Assessment Reliability and Validity
Visit mometrix.com/academy and enter code: 424680

Benchmark Assessments

Benchmark assessments are intended to quantify, evaluate, and compare individual and groups of students' achievement of school-wide, district, and state **academic standards.** They are typically administered in specific intervals throughout the school year and encompass entire or large units of curriculum to determine student mastery and readiness for academic advancement. Benchmark assessments provide data that enable the teacher to determine students' progress toward reaching academic goals to guide current and continued instruction. This data can be utilized by the school and individual teachers to create learning goals and objectives aligned with academic standards. It can also be used to plan instructional strategies, activities, and assessments to support students in achieving these academic standards. In addition, benchmark assessments provide feedback regarding understanding and the potential need for remediation to allow the teacher to instill necessary supports in future instruction that prepare students for success in achieving learning targets.

Alignment of Assessments with Instructional Goals and Objectives

To effectively monitor student progress, assessments must align with **instructional goals** and **objectives**. This allows the teacher to determine whether students are advancing at an appropriate pace to achieve state and district academic standards. When assessments are aligned with specific learning targets, the teacher ensures that students are learning relevant material to establish a foundation of knowledge necessary for growth and academic achievement. To achieve this, teachers must determine which instructional goals and objectives their students must achieve and derive instruction, content, and activities from these specifications. Instruction must reflect and reinforce learning targets, and the teacher must select the most effective strategies for addressing students' needs as they work to achieve them. Assessments must be reflective of content instruction to ensure they are aligned with learning goals and objectives, as well as to enable the teacher to evaluate student progress in mastering them. The teacher must clearly communicate learning goals and objectives throughout all stages of instruction to provide students with clarity on expectations. This establishes a clear purpose and focus for learning that enhances relevancy and strengthens connections to support student achievement.

Clearly Communicating Assessment Criteria and Standards

Students must be clear on the purpose of learning throughout all stages of instruction to enhance understanding and facilitate success. When assessment **criteria** and **standards** are clearly communicated, the purpose of learning is established, and students are able to effectively connect instructional activities to learning goals and criteria for assessment. Communicating assessment criteria and standards provides students with clarity on tasks and learning goals they are expected to accomplish as they prepare themselves for assessment. This allows for more **focused instruction** and engagement in learning, as it enhances relevancy and student motivation. Utilizing appropriate forms of **rubrics** is an effective strategy in specifying assessment criteria and standards, as it informs students about learning goals they are working toward, the quality of work they are expected to achieve, and skills they must master to succeed on the assessment. Rubrics indicate to students exactly how they will be evaluated, thus supporting their understanding and focus as they engage in learning to promote academic success.

Rubrics for Communicating Standards

The following are varying styles of rubrics that can be used to communicate criteria and standards:

- **Analytic:** Analytic rubrics break down criteria for an assignment into several categories and provide an explanation of the varying levels of performance in each one. This style of rubric is beneficial for detailing the characteristics of quality work as well as providing students with feedback regarding specific components of their performance. Analytic rubrics are most effective when used for summative assessments, such as long-term projects or essays.
- **Holistic:** Holistic rubrics evaluate the quality of the student's assignment as a whole rather than scoring individual components. Students' scores are determined based upon their performance across multiple performance indicators. This style of rubric is beneficial for providing a comprehensive evaluation but limits the amount of feedback that students receive regarding their performance in specific areas.
- **Single-point:** Single-point rubrics outline criteria for assignments into several categories. Rather than providing a numeric score to each category, however, the teacher provides written feedback regarding the students' strengths and ways in which they can improve their performance. This style of rubric is beneficial in providing student-centered feedback that focuses on their overall progress.
- **Checklist:** Checklists typically outline a set of criteria that is scored using a binary approach based upon completion of each component. This style increases the efficiency of grading assignments and is often easy for students to comprehend but does not provide detailed feedback. This method of grading should generally be reserved for shorter assignments.

Communicating High Academic Expectations in Assessments

The attitudes and behaviors exhibited by the teacher are highly influential on students' attitudes toward learning. Teachers demonstrate belief in students' abilities to be successful in learning when they communicate **high academic expectations**. This promotes students' **self-concept** and establishes a **growth mindset** to create confident, empowered learners that are motivated to achieve. High expectations for assessments and reaching academic standards communicates to students the quality of work that is expected of them and encourages them to overcome obstacles as they engage in learning. When communicating expectations for student achievement, it is important that the teacher is aware of students' individual learning needs to provide the necessary support that establishes equitable opportunities for success in meeting assessment criteria and standards. Setting high expectations through assessment criteria and standards while supporting students in their learning enhances overall achievement and establishes a foundation for continuous academic success.

Effective Communication and Impact on Student Learning

Communicating high academic expectations enhances students' self-concept and increases personal motivation for success in learning. To maximize student achievement, it is important that the teacher set high academic expectations that are **clearly** communicated through **age-appropriate** terms and consistently reinforced. Expectations must be reflected through learning goals and objectives and must be **visible** at all times to ensure student awareness. Teachers must be **specific** in communicating what they want students to accomplish and clearly detail necessary steps for achievement while assuming the role of facilitator to guide learning and provide support. Providing constructive **feedback** throughout instruction is integral in reminding students of academic expectations and ensuring they are making adequate progress toward reaching learning goals. When high academic expectations are communicated and reinforced, students are empowered with a sense of confidence and self-responsibility for their own learning that promotes their desire to learn. This ultimately enhances achievement and equips them with the tools necessary for future academic success.

Analyzing and Interpreting Assessment Data

Teachers can utilize multiple techniques to effectively analyze and interpret assessment data. This typically involves creating charts and graphs outlining different data subsets. They can list each learning standard that was assessed, determine how many students overall demonstrated proficiency on the standard, and identify individual students who did not demonstrate proficiency on each standard. This information can be used to differentiate instruction. Additionally, they can track individual student performance and progress on each standard over time.

Teachers can take note of overall patterns and trends in assessment data. For example, they can determine if any subgroups of students did not meet expectations. They can consider whether the data confirms or challenges any existing beliefs, implications this may have on instructional planning and what, if any, conclusions can be drawn from this data.

Analyzing and interpreting assessment data may raise new questions for educators, so they can also determine if additional data collection is needed.

Using Assessment Data to Differentiate Instruction for Individual Learners

By analyzing and interpreting assessment data, teachers can determine if there are any specific learning standards that need to be retaught to their entire classes. This may be necessary if the data shows that all students struggled in these specific areas. Teachers may consider reteaching these standards using different methods if the initial methods were unsuccessful.

Teachers can also form groups of students who did not demonstrate proficiency on the same learning standards. Targeted instruction can be planned for these groups to help them make progress in these areas. Interventions can also be planned for individual students who did not show proficiency in certain areas. If interventions have already been in place and have not led to increased learning outcomes, the interventions may be redesigned. If interventions have been in place and assessment data now shows proficiency, the interventions may be discontinued.

If assessment data shows that certain students have met or exceeded expectations in certain areas, enrichment activities can be planned to challenge these students and meet their learning needs.

Aligning Assessments with Instructional Goals and Objectives

Assessments that are congruent to instructional goals and objectives provide a **clear purpose** for learning that enhances student understanding and motivation. When learning targets are reflected in assessments, instructional activities and materials become more **relevant**, as they are derived from these specifications. Such clarity in purpose allows for more focus and productivity as students engage in instruction and fosters connections that strengthen overall understanding for maximized success in learning. Aligning assessments with instructional goals and objectives ensures that students are learning material that is relevant to the curriculum and academic standards to ensure **preparedness** as they advance in their academic careers. In addition, it enables the teacher to evaluate and monitor student progress to determine whether they are progressing at an ideal pace for achieving academic standards. With this information, the teacher can effectively modify instruction as necessary to support students' needs in reaching desired learning outcomes.

NORM-REFERENCED TESTS

On **norm-referenced tests**, students' performances are compared to the performances of sample groups of similar students. Norm-referenced tests identify students who score above and below the average. To ensure reliability, the tests must be given in a standardized manner to all students.

Norm-referenced tests usually cover a broad range of skills, such as the entire grade-level curriculum for a subject. They typically contain a few questions per skill. Whereas scores in component areas of the tests may be calculated, usually overall test scores are reported. Scores are often reported using percentile ranks, which indicate what percentage of test takers scored lower than the student being assessed. For example, a student's score in the 75th percentile means the student scored better than 75% of other test takers. Other times, scores may be reported using grade-level equivalency.

One advantage of norm-referenced tests is their objectivity. They also allow educators to compare large groups of students at once. This may be helpful for making decisions regarding class placements and groupings. A disadvantage of norm-referenced tests is that they only indicate how well students perform in comparison to one another. They do not indicate whether or not students have mastered certain skills.

CRITERION-REFERENCED TESTS

Criterion-referenced tests measure how well students perform on certain skills or standards. The goal of these tests is to indicate whether or not students have mastered certain skills and which skills require additional instruction. Scores are typically reported using the percentage of questions answered correctly or students' performance levels. Performance levels are outlined using terms such as *below expectations*, *met expectations*, and *exceeded expectations*.

One advantage of criterion-referenced tests is that they provide teachers with useful information to guide instruction. They can identify which specific skills students have mastered and which skills need additional practice. Teachers can use this information to plan whole-class, small-group, and individualized instruction. Analyzing results of criterion-referenced tests over time can also help teachers track student progress on certain skills. A disadvantage of criterion-referenced tests is that they do not allow educators to compare students' performances to samples of their peers.

WAYS THAT STANDARDIZED TEST RESULTS ARE REPORTED

- **Raw scores** are sometimes reported and indicate how many questions students answered correctly on a test. By themselves, they do not provide much useful information. They do not indicate how students performed in comparison to other students or to grade-level expectations.
- **Grade-level equivalents** are also sometimes reported. A grade-level equivalent score of 3.4 indicates that a student performed as well as an average third grader in the fourth month of school. It can indicate whether a student is performing above or below grade-level expectations, but it does not indicate that the student should be moved to a different grade level.
- **Standard scores** are used to compare students' performances on tests to standardized samples of their peers. Standard deviation refers to the amount that a set of scores differs from the mean score on a test.
- **Percentile ranks** are used on criterion-referenced tests to indicate what percentage of test takers scored lower than the student whose score is being reported.

- **Cutoff scores** refer to predetermined scores students must obtain in order to be considered proficient in certain areas. Scores below the cutoff level indicate improvement is needed and may result in interventions or instructional changes.

Formal and Informal Assessments

Assessments are any method a teacher uses to gather information about student comprehension of curriculum, including improvised questions for the class and highly-structured tests. **Formal assessments** are assessments that have **clearly defined standards and methodology** and which are applied consistently to all students. Formal tests should be objective and scrutinized for validity and reliability since they tend to carry higher weight for the student. Summative assessments, such as end-of-unit tests, lend themselves to being formal tests because it is necessary that a teacher test the comprehension of all students in a consistent and thorough way.

Although formal assessments can provide useful data about student performance and progress, they can be costly and time-consuming to implement. Administering formal assessments often interrupts classroom instruction and may cause testing anxiety.

Informal assessments are assessments that do not adhere to formal objectives, and they do not have to be administered consistently to all students. As a result, they do not have to be scored or recorded as a grade and generally act as a **subjective measure** of class comprehension. Informal assessments can be as simple as asking the students to raise their hands if they are ready to proceed to the next step or asking a particular question of an individual student.

Informal assessments do not provide objective data for analysis, but they can be implemented quickly and inexpensively. Informal assessments can also be incorporated into regular classroom instruction and activities, making them more authentic and less stressful for students.

Using Various Assessments

The goal of **assessment** in education is to gather data that, when evaluated, can be used to further student learning and achievement. **Standardized tests** are helpful for placement purposes and to reflect student progress toward goals set by a school district or state. If a textbook is chosen to align with district learning standards, the textbook assessments can provide teachers with convenient, small-scale, regular checks of student knowledge against the target standard.

In order be effective, teachers must know where their students are in the learning process. Teachers use a multitude of **formal and informal assessment methods** to do this. Posing differentiated discussion questions is an example of an informal assessment method that allows teachers to gauge individual student progress rather than their standing in relation to a universal benchmark.

Effective teachers employ a variety of assessments, as different formats assess different skills, promote different learning experiences, and appeal to different learners. A portfolio is an example of an assessment that gauges student progress in multiple skills and through multiple media. Teachers can use authentic or performance-based assessments to stimulate student interest and provide visible connections between language-learning and the real world.

Assessment Reliability

Assessment reliability refers to how well an assessment is constructed and is made up of a variety of measures. An assessment is generally considered **reliable** if it yields similar results across multiple administrations of the assessment. A test should perform similarly with different test administrators, graders, test-takers, and over multiple iterations. Factors that affect reliability include the day-to-day wellbeing of the student (students can sometimes underperform), the physical environment of the test, the way it is administered, and the subjectivity of the scorer (with written-response assessments).

Perhaps the most important threat to assessment reliability is the nature of the **exam questions** themselves. An assessment question is designed to test knowledge of a certain construct. A question is reliable in this sense if students who understand the content answer the question correctly. Statisticians look for patterns in student marks, both within the single test and over multiple tests, as a way of measuring reliability. Teachers should watch out for circumstances in which a student or students answer correctly a series of questions about a given concept (demonstrating their understanding) but then answer a related question incorrectly. The latter question may be an unreliable indicator of concept knowledge.

Measures of Assessment Reliability

- **Test-retest reliability** refers to an assessment's consistency of results with the same test-taker over multiple retests. If one student shows inconsistent results over time, the test is not considered to have test-retest reliability.
- **Intertester reliability** refers to an assessment's consistency of results between multiple test-takers at the same level. Students at similar levels of proficiency should show similar results.
- **Inter-rater reliability** refers to an assessment's consistency of results between different administrators of the test. This plays an especially critical role in tests with interactive or subjective responses, such as Likert-scales, cloze tests, and short answer tests. Different raters of the same test need to have a consistent means of evaluating the test-takers' performance. Clear rubrics can help keep two or more raters consistent in scoring.
- **Intra-rater reliability** refers to an assessment's consistency of results with one rater over time. One test rater should be able to score different students objectively to rate subjective test formats fairly.
- **Parallel-forms reliability** refers to an assessment's consistency between multiple different forms. For instance, end-of-course assessments may have many distinctive test forms, with different questions or question orders. If the different forms of a test do not provide the same results, the test is said to be lacking in parallel-forms reliability.
- **Internal consistency reliability** refers to the consistency of results of similar questions on a particular assessment. If there are two or more questions targeted at the same standard and at the same level, they should show the same results across each question.

Assessment Validity

Assessment validity is a measure of the relevancy that an assessment has to the skill or ability being evaluated and the degree to which students' performance is representative of their mastery of the topic of assessment. In other words, a teacher should ask how well an assessment's results correlate to what it is looking to assess. Assessments should be evaluated for validity on both the **individual question** level and as a **test overall**. This can be especially helpful in refining tests for future classes. The overall validity of an assessment is determined by several types of validity measures.

An assessment is considered **valid** if it measures what it is intended to measure. One common error that can reduce the validity of a test (or a question on a test) occurs if the instructions are written at a reading level the students can't understand. In this case, it is not valid to take the student's failed answer as a true indication of his or her knowledge of the subject. Factors internal to the student might also affect exam validity: anxiety and a lack of self-esteem often lower assessments results, reducing their validity as a measure of student knowledge.

An assessment has content validity if it includes all the **relevant aspects** of the subject being tested—if it is comprehensive, in other words. An assessment has **predictive validity** if a score on the test is an accurate predictor of future success in the same domain. For example, SAT exams purport to have validity in predicting student success in a college. An assessment has construct validity if it accurately measures student knowledge of the subject being tested.

MEASURES OF ASSESSMENT VALIDITY

- **Face validity** refers to the initial impression of whether an assessment seems to be fit for the task. As this method is subjective to interpretation and unquantifiable, it should not be used singularly as a measurement of validity.
- **Construct validity** asks if an assessment actually assesses what it is intended to assess. Some topics are more straightforward, such as assessing if a student can perform two-digit multiplication. This can be directly tested, which gives the assessment a strong content validity. Other measures, such as a person's overall happiness, must be measured indirectly. If an assessment asserted that a person is generally happy if he or she smiles frequently, it would be fair to question the construct validity of that assessment because smiling is unlikely to be a consistent measure of all peoples' general happiness.
- **Content validity** indicates whether the assessment is comprehensive of all aspects of the content being assessed. If a test leaves out an important topic, then the teacher will not have a full picture as a result of the assessment.
- **Criterion validity** refers to whether the results of an assessment can be used to **predict** a related value, known as **criterion**. An example of this is the hypothesis that IQ tests would predict a person's success later in life, but many critics believe that IQ tests are not valid predictors of success because intelligence is not the only predictor of success in life. IQ tests have shown validity toward predicting academic success, however. The measure of an assessment's criterion validity depends on how closely related the criterion is.
- **Discriminant validity** refers to how well an assessment tests only that which it is intended to test and successfully discriminates one piece of information from another. For instance, a student who is exceptional in mathematics should not be able to put that information into use on a science test and gain an unfair advantage. If the student is able to score well due to his or her mathematics knowledge, the science test did not adequately discriminate science knowledge from mathematics knowledge.
- **Convergent validity** is related to discriminant validity, but takes into account that two measures may be distinct but correlated. For instance, a personality test should distinguish self-esteem from extraversion so that they can be measured independently, but if an assessment has convergent validity, it should show a correlation between related measures.

PRACTICALITY

An assessment is **practical** if it uses an appropriate amount of human and budgetary resources. A practical exam doesn't take very long to design or score, nor does it take students very long to complete in relation to other learning objectives and priorities. Teachers often need to balance a desire to construct comprehensive or content-valid tests with a need for practicality: lengthy exams consume large amounts of instruction time and may return unreliable results if students become tired and lose focus.

Assessment Bias

An assessment is considered biased if it disadvantages a certain group of students, such as students of a certain gender, race, cultural background, or socioeconomic class. A **content bias** exists when the subject matter of a question or assessment is familiar to one group and not another. For example, a reading comprehension passage that discusses an event in American history would be biased against students new to the country. An **attitudinal bias** exists when a teacher has a preconceived idea about the likely success of an assessment of a particular individual or group. A **method bias** arises when the format of an assessment is unfamiliar to a given group of students. **Language bias** occurs when an assessment utilizes idioms, collocations, or cultural references unfamiliar to a group of students. Finally, **translation bias** may arise when educators attempt to translate content-area assessments into a student's native language—rough or hurried translations often result in a loss of nuance important for accurate assessment.

Authentic Assessments

An authentic assessment is an assessment designed to closely resemble something that a student does, or will do, in the real world. For example, students will never encounter a multiple-choice test requiring them to choose the right tense of a verb, but they will encounter contexts in which they have to write a narration of an event that has antecedents and consequents spread out in time—like narrating their version of what caused a traffic accident. The latter is an example of a potential **authentic assessment**.

Well-designed authentic assessments require a student to exercise **advanced cognitive skills** (e.g., solving problems, integrating information, performing deductions), integrate **background knowledge**, and confront **ambiguity**. Research has demonstrated that mere language proficiency is not predictive of future language success—learning how to utilize knowledge in a complex context is an essential additional skill.

The terms "authentic" and "performance-based" are often used interchangeably when describing assessments; however, a performance-based assessment doesn't necessarily have to be grounded in a possible authentic experience.

Performance-Based Assessments

A performance-based assessment is one in which students demonstrate their learning by performing a **task** rather than by answering questions in a traditional test format. Proponents of **performance-based assessments** argue that they lead students to use **high-level cognitive skills** since they focus on how to put their knowledge to use and plan a sequence of stages in an activity or presentation. They also allow students more opportunities to individualize their presentations or responses based on preferred learning styles. Research suggests that students welcome the chance to put their knowledge to use in real-world scenarios.

Advocates of performance-based assessments suggest that they avoid many of the problems of language or cultural bias present in traditional assessments, allowing more accurate assessment of how well students learned the underlying concepts. In discussions regarding English as a second language, they argue that performance assessments come closer to replicating what should be the true goal of language learning—the effective use of language in real contexts—than do more traditional exams. Critics point out that performance assessments are difficult and time-consuming for teachers to construct and for students to perform. Finally, performative assessments are difficult to grade in the absence of a well-constructed and detailed rubric.

TECHNOLOGY-BASED ASSESSMENTS

Technology-based assessments provide teachers with multiple resources for evaluating student progress to guide instruction. They are applicable in most formal and informal instructional settings and can be utilized as formative and summative assessments. Technology-based assessments simplify and enhance the efficiency of determining comprehension and instructional effectiveness, as they quickly present the teacher with information regarding student progress. This data enables the teacher to make necessary adjustments to facilitate student learning and growth. Implementing this assessment format simplifies the process of aligning them to school and district academic standards. This establishes objectivity and uniformity for comparing results and progress among students. It also helps ensure that all students are held to the same academic expectations. While technology-based assessments are beneficial, there are some shortcomings to consider. This format may not be entirely effective for all learning styles in demonstrating understanding, as individualization in technology-based assessment can be limited. These assessments may not illustrate individual students' growth over time but rather their mastery of an academic standard, thus hindering the ability to evaluate overall achievement. As technology-based evaluation limits hands-on opportunities, the real-world application and relevancy of the assessment may be unapparent to students.

ADVANTAGES AND DISADVANTAGES OF TECHNOLOGY-BASED ASSESSMENTS

Technology-based assessments can have many advantages. They can be given to large numbers of students at once, limited only by the amounts of technological equipment schools possess. Many types of technology-based assessments are instantly scored, and feedback is provided quickly. Students are sometimes able to view their results and feedback at the conclusion of their testing sessions. Data can be quickly compiled and reported in easy-to-understand formats. Technology-based assessments can also often track student progress over time.

Technology-based assessments can have some disadvantages as well. Glitches and system errors can interfere with the assessment process or score reporting. Students must also have the necessary prerequisite technological skills to take the assessments, or the results may not measure the content they are designed to measure. For example, if students take timed, computer-based writing tests, they should have proficient typing skills. Otherwise, they may perform poorly on the tests despite strong writing abilities. Other prerequisite skills include knowing how to use a keyboard and mouse and understanding how to locate necessary information on the screen.

PORTFOLIO ASSESSMENTS

A **portfolio** is a collection of student work in multiple forms and media gathered over time. Teachers may assess the portfolio both for evidence of progress over time or in its end state as a demonstration of the achievement of certain proficiency levels.

One advantage of **portfolio assessments** is their breadth. Unlike traditional assessments, which focus on one or two language skills, portfolios may contain work in multiple forms, such as writing samples, pictures, and graphs designed for content courses, video and audio clips, student reflections, teacher observations, and student exams. A second advantage is that they allow a student to develop work in authentic contexts, including in other classrooms and at home.

In order for portfolios to function as an objective assessment tool, teachers should negotiate with students in advance of what genres of work will be included and outline a grading rubric that makes clear what will be assessed, such as linguistic proficiency, use of English in academic contexts, and demonstrated use of target cognitive skills.

Curriculum-Based Assessments

Curriculum-based assessments, also known as **curriculum-based measurements (CBM)**, are short, frequent assessments designed to measure student progress toward meeting curriculum **benchmarks**.

Teachers implement CBMs by designing **probes**, or short assessments that target specific skills. For example, a teacher might design a spelling probe, administered weekly, that requires students to spell 10 unfamiliar but level-appropriate words. The data from these assessments can be tracked over time to measure student progress toward defined grade-level goals.

CBM has several clear advantages. If structured well, the probes have high reliability and validity. Furthermore, they provide clear and objective evidence of student progress—a welcome outcome for students and parents who often grapple with less-clear and subjective evidence. Used correctly, CBMs also motivate students and provide them with evidence of their own progress; however, while CBMs are helpful in identifying areas of student weaknesses, they do not identify the causes of those weaknesses or provide teachers with strategies for improving instruction.

Textbook Assessments

Textbook assessments are the assessments provided at the end of a chapter or unit in an approved textbook. **Textbook assessments** present several advantages for a teacher: they are already made; they are likely to be accurate representations of the chapter or unit materials; and, if the textbook has been prescribed or recommended by the state, it is likely to correspond closely to Common Core or other tested standards.

Textbook assessments can be limiting for students who lag in the comprehension of academic English or whose preferred learning style is not verbal. While textbooks may come with DVDs or recommended audio links, ESOL teachers will likely need to supplement these assessment materials with some of their own findings. Finally, textbook assessments are unlikely to represent the range of assessment types used in the modern classroom, such as a portfolio or performance-based assessments.

Peer Assessment

A peer assessment is when students grade one another's work based on a teacher-provided framework. **Peer assessments** are promoted as a means of saving teacher time and building student metacognitive skills. They are typically used as **formative** rather than summative assessments, given concerns about the reliability of student scoring and the tensions that can result if student scores contribute to overall grades. Peer assessments are used most often to grade essay-type written work or presentations. Proponents point out that peer assessments require students to apply metacognition, build cooperative work and interpersonal skills, and broaden the sense that the student is accountable to peers and not just the teacher. Even advocates of the practice agree that students need detailed rubrics in order to succeed. Critics often argue that low-performing students have little to offer high-performing students in terms of valuable feedback—and this disparity may be more pronounced in ESOL classrooms or special education environments than in mainstream ones. One way to overcome this weakness is for the teacher to lead the evaluation exercise, guiding the students through a point-by-point framework of evaluation.

Developmental Screening

Types of Developmental Assessments

Developmental assessments measure the development of infants, toddlers, and preschoolers. These **norm-referenced tests** measure fine and gross motor skills; communication and language; and social, cognitive, and self-help milestones that young children should achieve at certain ages. When a child is suspected of having a **developmental delay**, a developmental assessment is useful in identifying the child's strengths and weaknesses. These assessments map out the **progress** of a child compared to the progress of similar-aged children. Developmental assessments are also useful in identifying if the delay is significant or can be overcome with time. These assessments can be used to determine what **educational placement** is most appropriate for a child with a developmental delay. Developmental assessments are administered via observations and questionnaires. Parents, legal guardians, caregivers, and instructors who are most familiar with the child provide the most insight on developmental strengths and weaknesses.

> **Review Video: Identifying Appropriate Evaluation Strategies**
> Visit mometrix.com/academy and enter code: 100353

Screening Tests for Identifying Students Who Need Special Education

When determining if a child needs special education, **screening tests** are the first step. The Individuals with Disabilities Education Act offers guidance for schools to implement screening tests. Districts and schools often have school-wide processes in place for screening students for **special education**. Screening tests can also be used to identify students who are falling behind in class. The advantage of screening tests is that they are easily administered. They require few materials and little time and planning in order to administer. Additionally, they can be used to quickly assess students' strengths and weaknesses, they do not have to be administered one-on-one, and they can be used for everyone in the class. Screening tests can be as simple as paper-and-pencil quizzes assessing what students know. They are used for measuring visual acuity, auditory skills, physical health, development, basic academic skills, behavioral problems, risk of behavioral problems, language skills, and verbal and nonverbal intelligence.

Individual Intelligence Tests vs. Individual Academic Achievement Tests

Intelligence tests measure a student's capacity for abstract thinking, mental reasoning, judgment, and decision-making. These **norm-referenced tests** help determine a student's **overall intelligence**, which correlates with **potential academic performance**. Intelligence tests can be used to determine if a student's deficits are due to intellectual disabilities or related to specific learning disabilities or emotional disorders. They can also measure verbal skills, motor performance, and visual reasoning. Intelligence tests are also known as **intelligence quotient tests (IQ tests)**. IQ tests should be administered by trained professionals to ensure the tests are administered accurately. Unlike intelligence tests, individual academic achievement tests measure a student's strengths and weaknesses in individual skills. They are also norm referenced and used to determine if a student needs **special education services**. Results from individual academic tests help determine areas of concern or possible deficits for an individual student. Unlike intelligence tests, individual academic tests can be administered by teachers.

Adaptive Behavior Scale Assessments

Adaptive behavior scales are useful for diagnosing a student with an **intellectual disability** that affects the development or progression of adaptive behavior. They are used in preschools and for determining eligibility for **special education** in grade schools. They are also used in planning the

curriculum for students with intellectual disabilities. Adaptive behavior scales are standardized but not always norm referenced because of difficulties comparing expectations for some adaptive and maladaptive skills exhibited by similar-aged peers. In terms of curriculum planning, these assessments can determine the type and quantity of assistance a student may need. Adaptive behavior scale assessments identify a student's level of **independence**. Adaptive behavior scales can be used to determine **skill abilities** associated with daily living, community functioning, social skills, communication, motor functions, and basic academic skills. Teachers and other professionals can administer adaptive behavior scales to students with intellectual disabilities to determine starting points for improving their adaptive behavior deficits.

Curriculum-Based Measurement of Student Academic Progress

Curriculum-based measurement (**CBM**) is a way for teachers to track how students are **progressing** in mathematics, language arts, social studies, science, and other skills. It is also useful for communicating progress to parents or legal guardians. CBM results can determine whether or not current **instructional strategies** are effective for particular students. In the same respect, CBM can determine if students are meeting the **standards** laid out in their Individualized Education Program goals. If CBM results show that instructional strategies are not effective or goals are not being met, teachers should change instructional strategies. CBM can be revisited to determine whether or not the newly implemented strategies are effective. Progress can sometimes be charted to present a visual for how a student is progressing in a particular content area or with a specific skill.

Woodcock-Johnson Tests

High-Incidence Disabilities

Woodcock-Johnson tests can be used as diagnostic tools for identifying children with **high-incidence disabilities**. The Woodcock-Johnson Tests of Achievement, the Woodcock-Johnson Tests of Cognitive Abilities, and the Woodcock-Johnson Tests of Oral Language are comprehensively useful for assessing children's:

- Intellectual abilities
- Cognitive abilities
- Aptitude
- Oral language
- Academic achievements

These norm-referenced tests are valuable in understanding children's strengths and weaknesses and how they compare to cohorts of normally progressing, similar-aged peers. For example, **Woodcock-Johnson tests (WJ tests)** are useful in identifying children with language disorders because children with language disorders typically score lower on the listening comprehension and fluid reasoning test sections. The WJ tests are useful diagnostic tools for identifying children with attention-deficit/hyperactivity disorder (ADHD) as well. While children with ADHD may perform similarly to children with learning disabilities, their key deficits are in the cognitive efficiency, processing speed, academic fluency, short-term memory, and long-term retrieval test sections.

Prenatal, Perinatal, and Neonatal Disabilities

Prenatal, perinatal, and neonatal risk factors can be genetic or environmental. These factors put infants at risk for developing **intellectual disabilities** that affect their day-to-day lives. An intellectual disability is a disability that significantly limits a child's overall cognitive abilities. **Prenatal** risk factors include genetic syndromes (e.g., Down syndrome), brain malformation, maternal diseases, and environmental influences. Drugs, alcohol, or poison exposure can all affect an unborn child. **Perinatal** (during delivery) risk factors include labor and delivery trauma or anoxia at birth. **Neonatal** (post-birth) risk factors include hypoxic ischemic brain injury, traumatic brain injury, infections, seizure disorders, and toxic metabolic syndromes. Early screening and applicable assessments are tools used to identify young children with intellectual disabilities and can assist with providing special education services under the Individuals with Disabilities Education Act. These tools can also help assess the severity of deficits and the need for special services, such as occupational therapy.

Learning Disabilities in Reading and Mathematics

The Woodcock-Johnson tests (WJ tests) include tests of achievement, cognitive abilities, and oral language. Together, these assessments are useful in the diagnostic process of identifying a student with a **disability**. Additionally, they are helpful for identifying specific **deficits** in a student's reading or math skills. WJ tests are norm-referenced and compare the results of a child's performance to that of a cohort of children of similar age and average intellectual abilities. These assessments provide information about **reading disorders**, such as dyslexia, because they measure phonological awareness, rapid automatized naming, processing speed, and working memory. WJ tests report on a child's cognitive functioning in these test areas. These assessments also provide useful information for students with learning deficits in **mathematics**. Performance on the math calculation skills and math reasoning test sections provides information on specific deficits in general comprehension, fluid reasoning, and processing speed. Deficits in these areas are correlated with learning disabilities in mathematics.

The Wechsler Intelligence Scales

The Wechsler Intelligence Scales are assessments that measure the cognitive abilities of children and adults. The **Wechsler Intelligence Scale for Children (WISC)**, now in its fifth edition (WISC-V), is used for children ages 6–16 and measures the child's intellectual ability through 10 primary subtests and 6 secondary subtests. The result is an overall composite score, the Full-Scale Intelligence Quotient (FSIQ), as well as index scores in subcategories such as verbal comprehension, fluid reasoning, and quantitative reasoning. WISC-V results are useful tools for evaluating a student with a disability. Test results can be used to measure and report on a student's general intelligence and provide insight into the student's cognitive abilities in order to determine an appropriate educational pathway. Results can be reported in a student's Evaluation Team Report (ETR) and Individualized Education Program (IEP) in order to justify special education services or have a starting point for IEP goals. WISC-V results are especially important in an ETR, and they are generally completed at least once every three years, because they contribute to describing the **overall performance profile** of a student with a disability.

Kaufman Assessment Battery for Children

The Kaufman Assessment Battery for Children (KABC), updated to a second edition in 2008 with a normative update in 2014 (**KABC-II NU**) is a unique standardized test because it is used to evaluate preschoolers, minority groups, and children with learning disabilities. The KABC-II NU can be used to assess children ages 3–18 and is meant to be used with children who are nonverbal, bilingual, or English-speaking. However, it is especially useful in assessing the abilities of students who are **nonverbal**. The KABC-II NU can be used to help determine students' educational placements and assist with their educational planning. This assessment consists of subtests that may be combined and interpreted according to one of two different models depending on the child's language background. The subtests lead to both individual scaled scores and a global score. The scales are:

- Simultaneous
- Sequential

- Planning
- Learning
- Knowledge

The KABC-II NU is also unique because it includes a **nonverbal scale** that can be administered to children with hearing or speech impairments and children who do not speak English.

Vineland Adaptive Behavior Scales

The Vineland Adaptive Behavior Scales, Third Edition (**Vineland-3**), assesses the personal and social skills of children and adults. **Adaptive behavior** refers to the skills needed for day-to-day activities and independent living. Children with disabilities sometimes have deficits in adaptive behavior, and the Vineland-3 is useful for planning their **educational pathways**. It is an especially useful tool for developing **transition plans and goals** for students of appropriate ages on Individualized Education Programs. The Vineland-3 is a process that involves people who know the students best, like parents and teachers. The teacher version and parent version of this assessment can be delivered via interview or survey. The parent version focuses on a student's adaptive behavior at home, while the teacher version focuses on adaptive behavior in the school setting. Vineland-3 assesses four **domains**: communication, activities of daily living, social relationships, and motor skills. A student's parents or caregivers fill out a form pertaining to home life, and a teacher fills out a form pertaining to school settings. The comprehensive score from both the teacher and parent version are used to report abilities in the four domains.

Types of Cognitive Assessments

Cognitive tests assess the **cognitive functioning abilities** of children and adults. They are useful tools for diagnosing or identifying children with disabilities who are eligible for **special education services** under the Individuals with Disabilities Education Act. Examples of cognitive tests used in diagnosing or identifying children with disabilities include aptitude tests and intelligence quotient (IQ) tests. There are also cognitive assessments that measure verbal reasoning, numerical reasoning, abstract reasoning, spatial ability, verbal ability, and more. Children's cognitive abilities are related to how quickly they **process** information. Assessment results can be good measurements of how quickly children may learn new information or tasks. Cognitive assessments provide specific information about children's cognitive functioning by providing measurements of their intelligence, attention, concentration, processing speed, language and communication, visual-spatial abilities, and short- and long-term memory capabilities. Results can also be used on a child's Evaluation Team Report or to develop goals for an Individualized Education Program.

Advantages and Disadvantages of Curriculum-Based Assessments

Curriculum-based assessments (**CBAs**) determine if students are making adequate progress through the curriculum. They can be administered by a teacher, special educator, or school psychologist. CBAs have advantages over norm-referenced assessments, like developmental assessments, because they are not used to compare performance between students. Other types of assessments measure a student's cumulative abilities across multiple skills instead of assessing individual skills. CBAs measure student progress in more **individualized** ways. They are especially useful for measuring IEP goal progress. Since CBAs are **teacher-created assessments**, they provide opportunities to assess students informally and formally on IEP goals. For example, a teacher may verbally quiz a student on ten addition problems to determine if the student is making progress on math IEP goals. CBAs are also used in the "response to intervention" process to identify students with special needs by measuring the effectiveness of interventions provided to them.

Assessment for Students with Disabilities

Alternate Assessments

Students with and without disabilities are typically expected to take the same standardized tests, sometimes with accommodations and modifications. Some students with disabilities take **alternate assessments**, which are forms of the standardized tests that other students take. Students that participate in alternate assessments are unable to participate in state standardized tests even with accommodations. Less than one percent of students in public school districts participate in alternate assessments. They are mostly intended for students with **intellectual disabilities** or **severe cognitive delays**. Alternate assessments are based on **alternate achievement standards**, which are modified versions of state achievement standards. Alternate assessments are a way for students' progress to be assessed with standards that are more appropriate for their skills. For example, a state standard for math may not be appropriate for a student with an intellectual disability. Instead, the student may have the alternate standard of demonstrating the ability to count money to make a purchase. Teachers, parents, and students work collaboratively to demonstrate that the achievement standards are met.

Role of Formal Assessments in the Education of a Student with Disabilities

Formal assessments measure how well a student has mastered learning material and are useful in detecting if a student is **falling behind** in general or at the end of a unit. Formal test results can be used to compare the performance of a student with disabilities against other students of similar demographics. **Developmental assessments** are norm-referenced tests that are designed to assess the development of young children. Developmental assessments are used to identify the strengths and weaknesses of a child suspected of having a disability. **Intelligence tests** are another type of norm-referenced test that can determine a student's potential to learn academic skills. Intelligence tests, sometimes called IQ tests, also indicate a student's specific level of intelligence. This is helpful in knowing if a student's learning problems are associated with sub-average intellectual abilities or other factors, such as an emotional disturbance. A student with an emotional disturbance or specific learning disability would have an average or above-average intelligence score, whereas a student with intellectual disabilities would have a sub-average score. **Curriculum-based assessments** are also helpful in determining where, specifically, a student needs the most help within a content area.

Interest Inventories

Interest inventories are tools for measuring people's interests or preferences in activities. They are useful for gathering information about a student's likes and dislikes. In special education, interest inventories are sometimes used to help develop the **transition portion** of an Individualized Education Program (IEP). A student's interests as determined by an interest inventory can be used to drive the entire IEP. For an older student with a driving interest in mind, interest inventories can also be reflected in the annual IEP goals. Interest inventories can come in the form of observations, ability tests, or self-reported inventories. They can also work as age-appropriate **transition assessments** used in the transition statement section of the IEP. An advantage of interest inventories is that they help students get to know their own strengths and interests. They are also useful in guiding students with disabilities into thinking about postsecondary careers, education, or independent living.

Role of Informal Assessments in the Education of a Student with Disabilities

Informal assessments are a little more flexible for teachers, particularly in the ways they can be administered in the classroom. In special education, informal assessments play an important role in **adjusting instruction** to meet the specific needs of a student. Using informal assessment outcomes to drive instruction helps ensure that academic or behavioral student needs are met. Informal assessments are also helpful in adjusting instruction to meet **specific goals or objectives** on a student's IEP. Checklists, running records, observations, and work samples are all informal assessments from which data for IEP goals can be collected. **Checklists** can include behaviors or academic skills the student is meant to achieve. **Running records** help provide insight into student behavior over time by focusing on a sequence of events. **Work samples** are helpful in providing a concrete snapshot of a student's academic capabilities.

Individualized Education Programs

Developing and Writing Measurable IEP Goals

According to the Individuals with Disabilities Education Act, students eligible for special education receive Individualized Education Program (IEP) goals, which must contain specific **components**. Components of a **measurable IEP goal** include condition, performance, criteria, assessment, and standard. Measurable goals also include how skill mastery will be **assessed**, such as through observations or work samples. In the provided example below, the criterion is clearly measurable, as Jacob will either succeed or fail at multiple trials, and the ratio of successes to numbers of attempts should be recorded and dated throughout the IEP year to show his progress. Goals should also be **standards-based** whenever possible and may be required.

For example, an IEP goal may state, "By the end of this IEP, Jacob will use appropriate skills to communicate his needs in four out of five trials."

- **Condition** refers to when, where, and how the disability will be addressed. "By the end of this IEP" is the condition of the goal.
- **Performance** is what the student is expected to accomplish during the condition of the goal. In this case, that is "Jacob will use appropriate skills to communicate his needs."
- The last part of the goal stating "in four out of five trials" is the **criterion** that outlines how well the goal will be performed.

Review Video: IEPs
Visit mometrix.com/academy and enter code: 153484

Role of Local Education Agency Representatives in IEP Meetings

A local education agency (**LEA**) representative is a member of the IEP team who is trained in special education curriculum, general education curriculum, and community resources. In many cases, a school building leader or principal may fulfill the role of LEA representative. An LEA rep must be a licensed professional who knows the student and is familiar with the IEP process. The role of LEA representatives in IEP meetings is to make sure the information presented is compliant with the Individuals with Disabilities Education Act (IDEA) standards. LEA representatives are also responsible for ensuring that the school district is **compliant** with procedural components of IDEA and that eligible students are receiving free and appropriate public educations. This role is necessary on the IEP team because whereas the whole IEP team should have the students' best interests in mind, they may not understand the doctrines of IDEA and be able to consider compliance. As a result, the LEA representative must act as the primary advocate for effective implementation of the IEP.

Involvement of Students with IEPs in the Transition Process in High School

Most states require **transition statements** to be made when students reach age 14 during the IEP year. Federal law requires students 16 years of age or older to have transition statements; postsecondary goals for independent living, employment, and education; and summaries of performance that include the results of the most recent transition assessments. Per federal law, students of transition age must be invited to their **IEP meetings**. It is important for students on IEPs to **participate** in the transition process because it helps them figure out what they want to do after they graduate from high school. Participation in the process gets them thinking about living independently, postsecondary education options, and employment options. Students usually have opportunities to participate in formal and informal assessments like interest inventories that help them define their interests. Transition goals for independent living, employment, and education should be based on the results of these assessments and any other interests the students have expressed. The students participate in the **implementation** of the transition goals by completing activities associated with their indicated interests.

Student Support Teams

A **student support team (SST)** is a team made up of parents and educational professionals who work to support students in the general education classroom who are struggling with academics, discipline, health problems, or any other anticipated or actual problem that does not qualify the student for special education or supports from an Individualized Education Program. In this support team model, a group of educators works to identify and provide early intervention services for any student exhibiting academic or behavioral problems. The purpose of this kind of SST is to offer different supports, such as monitoring student progress, developing intervention plans, and referring students for intervention services. While the primary goal of this kind of SST is to provide support for students **struggling with school**, it can also shift focus to supporting students at risk of **dropping out of school**. Another primary objective of an SST is to identify students who are likely to have disabilities or who may need 504 Plans to succeed in school and to recommend them for referrals so they are not left without necessary supports.

Amendments to an Individualized Education Program

A student's IEP is in effect for one year. Academic goals, objectives, benchmarks, transition goals, and any accommodations and modifications are to be in place for the student for the duration of the IEP. An **amendment** to the IEP can be made when a change is needed before the year is over. An amendment is an agreement between the student, parents or legal guardians, and the IEP team. IEP meetings for amendments can be requested at any time. IEP amendments can be requested if a student is not making adequate progress toward the goals, if the goals become inappropriate in some way for the student, or when the student has met all IEP goals and requires new ones. If new information about the student becomes available, the IEP can be amended. Students, parents, and other team members may also request amendment meetings if they think that other accommodations and modifications are needed or should be removed.

How the Needs of Students with IEPs Are Met in the School Environment

IEPs communicate what **services** are to be provided for children with disabilities in the school setting, the children's **present levels of performance**, and how their disabilities affect **academic performance**. IEPs also specify **annual goals** appropriate to the students' specific needs and any accommodations or modifications that need to be provided. Schools and teachers have the responsibility to implement these IEP components when working with students with disabilities. Additionally, schools and teachers working with students with disabilities must ensure that students' individualized annual goals are met within a year of the students' IEP effective dates. It is up to the IEP teams to determine what classroom settings would most benefit the students while also appropriately meeting their IEP goals with the fewest barriers. Special educators must determine how data is collected and then obtain and record data on how the students are meeting their IEP goals. Special educators are responsible for providing intervention services based on the data results. They must also ensure that any accommodations or modifications listed on the IEPs are implemented in both general education and self-contained classrooms.

ACCOMMODATION VS. MODIFICATION IN IEPS

Formal accommodations, adaptations, and modifications for a student with a disability are listed on the Individualized Education Program. **Accommodations** change *how* a student learns the material, while an **adaptation** or **modification** changes *what* a student is taught or expected to learn.

- **Accommodations** are changes to the instruction or assessment that do *not* alter the curricular requirements. For instance, a student with accommodations may be allowed to answer a test orally instead of writing the answers or might be given pre-structured notes to help organize thoughts during instruction. These types of changes do not fundamentally change the information taught or the requirements for passing.
- **Adaptations** or **modifications** are changes to the instruction or assessment that fundamentally change the curricular requirements, but which enable a student with a disability to participate. Examples of adaptations include substitution of activities for related materials, exemption from answering particular types of questions on assessments, and removing or reducing time limits when taking tests.

For state standardized tests, accommodations like extra time and frequent breaks can be provided. Students that need modifications to state tests may complete alternate assessments that may not cover the same material as the standard exams.

Review Video: Adapting and Modifying Lessons or Activities
Visit mometrix.com/academy and enter code: 834946

DETERMINING THE PLACEMENT OF A STUDENT WITH A DISABILITY

With every student, the ideal goal is placement in the **general education classroom** as much as possible while still meeting the student's educational needs and ensuring a successful educational experience. The Individuals with Disabilities Education Act does not require that students be placed in the regular education classroom, but it does require that students be placed in their **least restrictive environment** as defined by the student's IEP team. Ultimately, the IEP team determines what **environment** best suits the student based on the student's specific needs. The IEP team is responsible for determining what educational environment would provide the student with the maximum appropriate educational benefit. While justification for removing a student from the regular education classroom is common and appropriate, as occurs when a student is placed in a resource room, the IEP team must explain the reasoning in the student's IEP. **Justification** must specifically state why the student cannot be educated with accommodations and services in the regular education classroom during any part of the school day. Justification for removal cannot be the perceived instructional limitations of the regular education teacher or concerns over extra instructional time needed to educate a student with a disability.

CREATING A SMART ANNUAL GOAL IN AN IEP

A good IEP goal describes how far the student is expected to **progress** toward the goal by the next IEP. Since IEPs should be revised once a year, a good annual IEP goal should describe what the student is capable of doing in a one-year time frame. Creating **SMART** IEP goals can help the student determine realistic expectations of what can be achieved in a year. SMART IEP goals are specific, measurable, attainable, relevant, and time-bound. Goals are **specific** when they list the targeted result in the skill or subject area. Goals should also be specific to the student's needs. Goals that are **measurable** state the way a student's progress will be measured. Measurable goals list how accurately a student should meet the goal. **Attainable** goals are realistic for the student to achieve in one year. **Relevant** goals outline what a student needs to do to accomplish the goal. For example, a SMART goal may state, "During the school week, Robert will use his device to communicate greetings 80 percent of the time in four out of five trials." **Time-bound** goals include a time frame for the student to achieve the goal. They also list when and how often progress will be measured.

Review Video: SMART Goals
Visit mometrix.com/academy and enter code: 100378

Role of an Initial Evaluation Assessment in Qualifying for Special Education

When a student is determined to need special education, it means the student has a disability or disabilities adversely affecting educational performance. It may also mean the student's needs cannot be addressed in the general education classroom with or without accommodations and that **specially designed instruction** is required. An **initial evaluation** of the student is required for special education eligibility. The evaluation is comprehensive and includes existing data collected on the student and additional assessments needed to determine eligibility. Individual school districts decide what assessments should be completed for the student's initial evaluation. Each district is responsible for and should provide assessments that measure functional, developmental, and academic information. The student's parents or legal guardians are responsible for providing outside information relevant to the student's education, such as medical needs assessed outside of the school district by qualified providers.

Purpose of an IEP

The purpose of an IEP is to guide the learning of a student with a **disability** in the educational environment. An IEP is a written statement for a student eligible for **special education**. An initial IEP is **implemented** once the child has been evaluated and determined to be in need of special education. After the initial IEP, **IEP meetings** are conducted annually (or more often) in order to update the plan to meet the needs of the student. IEPs are created, reviewed, and revised according to individual state and federal laws. These plans include the amount of time the student will spend in the special education classroom based on the level of need. They also include any related services the student might need (such as speech-language therapy) as well as academic and behavioral goals for the year. As the student learns and changes, performance levels and goals change as well. A student's present levels of performance are included and updated yearly, as are the academic and behavioral goals.

Members of an Individualized Education Program Team

IEPs are updated **annually** following the initial IEP. IEP team members meet at least once a year to discuss a student's progress and make changes to the IEP. The required members of a student's IEP team include the student's parents or legal guardians, one of the student's general education teachers, the special education teacher, a school representative, an individual who can interpret the instructional implications of evaluation results, and if appropriate, the student. Anyone else who has knowledge or expertise about the student may also attend. **Parents and legal guardians** contribute unique expertise about the student, typically having the benefit of knowing the child well. **General education teachers** can speak to how the student is performing in the general education classroom. The **special education teacher** can report on progress made toward academic and behavioral goals and present levels of performance. A **school representative** must be qualified to provide or supervise specially designed instruction, be knowledgeable of the general education curriculum, and be knowledgeable about school resources. The **individual who can interpret evaluation results** can be an existing team member or someone else who is qualified to report on evaluation results. **Advocates**, such as counselors or therapists who see the student outside the school day, can also attend the meeting to speak on the student's behalf.

Legal Rights of Parents or Legal Guardians

IEP meetings occur annually for each student. However, it is a **parent or legal guardian's right** to request a meeting at any point during the school year. The student's school is responsible for identifying and evaluating the child; developing, reviewing, or revising the IEP; and determining what placement setting best suits the needs of the student. It is within the parent or legal guardian's rights to have **input** in all processes related to the student. Under the Individuals with Disabilities Education Act, parents have the right to participate in IEP meetings, have an independent evaluation in addition to the one the school provides, give or deny consent for the IEP, contest a school's decision, and obtain private education paid for by the public school. In specific circumstances, if the student is determined to need services that the public school cannot provide, the public school district may need to pay for the student's tuition at a private school where the student's needs can be met.

Collaborative Consultation between Educational Professionals

Collaborative consultation refers to the special educator or other professional providing advice to the general education teacher about a student on an IEP. Special educators and other IEP team members, such as school psychologists and related service professionals, serve as the **experts** and have knowledge about how individual students learn and behave. This is especially important when students with IEPs are included in the general education classroom. Special educators and general education teachers must work collaboratively to ensure that students are reaching their potential in the general education setting. Examples of **collaborative consultation** include the special educator serving as a consultant to the general education teacher by providing advice on a student's IEP, accommodations, modifications, and IEP goal tracking. Another way the special educator or other professional can assist the general educator is by providing skill and strategy instruction to students on IEPs outside the general education classroom. The idea behind this method is for students to generalize these skills and strategies to the general education classroom.

Review Video: Collaborating with Other Professionals
Visit mometrix.com/academy and enter code: 100351

Public School Responsibilities to Parents of Students on IEPs

The school must invite the parents or legal guardians to any **IEP meetings** and provide advance notice of the meetings. Each meeting notice is required to include the purpose of the meeting, its time and location, and who will attend. The location of the meeting is likely the student's school, but legally it must be held at a mutually agreed-upon place and time. If the parent or legal guardian cannot attend the IEP meeting, the school must ensure participation in another way, such as video or telephone conference. The meeting can be conducted without the parent or legal guardian if the school district cannot get the parent or legal guardian to attend. A parent or legal guardian can request a meeting, and the school can refuse or deny the request. If denied, the school must provide a **prior written notice** explaining their refusal. A prior written notice is a document outlining important school district decisions about a student on an IEP.

Chapter Quiz

Ready to see how well you retained what you just read? Scan the QR code to go directly to the chapter quiz interface for this study guide. If you're using a computer, simply visit the online resources page at **mometrix.com/resources719/iltslbsi290** and click the Chapter Quizzes link.

Supporting Development and Learning

Transform passive reading into active learning! After immersing yourself in this chapter, put your comprehension to the test by taking a quiz. The insights you gained will stay with you longer this way. Scan the QR code to go directly to the chapter quiz interface for this study guide. If you're using a computer, simply visit the online resources page at **mometrix.com/resources719/iltslbsi290** and click the Chapter Quizzes link.

Instructional Planning

Designing Lesson Plans and Units to Align with Instructional Goals

The effective sequencing of units and lesson plans is key to developing coherent, comprehensible instruction that aligns with instructional goals and fosters success in learning. Teachers must first determine the instructional goals that students will be expected to achieve based on state academic standards as a framework and students' individual needs, knowledge, and abilities. Teachers must then logically arrange specific units of instruction aimed toward achieving the determined instructional goals. Each unit should build upon knowledge from the prior unit. Within each unit, teachers must determine what students must achieve as they work toward instructional goals and determine objectives that facilitate success based on individual need and ability. Once objectives are defined, teachers must design lesson plans in a logical sequence that will facilitate students in reaching these objectives and increasingly build upon knowledge as students work toward achieving the learning goal. When planning lessons, teachers must decide which activities, procedures, and materials are necessary for successfully completing lesson objectives while ensuring that individual learning needs are met. The teacher must also decide what will be assessed at the end of each lesson and unit to determine student success in achieving instructional goals.

Review Video: Creating Effective Lesson Plans
Visit mometrix.com/academy and enter code: 100377

Creating Developmentally Appropriate Learning Experiences and Assessments

Multiple factors must be considered when designing developmentally appropriate learning experiences and assessments that effectively facilitate student growth and achievement. Teachers must consider the general cognitive, physical, social, and emotional developmental levels of students as well as individual differences in background, skill, knowledge, and learning needs. With this understanding, teachers must then evaluate whether learning experiences are simultaneously appropriate to students' developmental levels and individual needs. This includes ensuring that learning activities and teaching strategies are varied in approach, are tailored to students' interests, and that they incorporate student choice in learning. Learning experiences must build upon students' background knowledge and experiences and provide challenging yet attainable learning opportunities based on individual skills and abilities. Additionally, teachers must consider whether learning experiences promote student participation and engagement as well as cooperative learning to ensure development across domains. Just as with learning experiences, the developmental appropriateness of assessments must also be evaluated. The teacher must consider whether assessments allow for choice in how students demonstrate their learning so as to address individual learning needs. Furthermore, it is important that teachers consider the purpose of each assessment regarding the feedback they are seeking and how it can help determine further instruction.

Role of Learning Theory in Instructional Process and Student Learning

Multiple learning theories exist to explain how people acquire knowledge, abilities, and skills. Each theory proposes its own approach for best practices in teaching and learning, and their effectiveness varies depending on the context of learning and individual student needs. These theories serve as frameworks for the instructional process and facilitating student learning. Teachers must understand the principles of various learning philosophies as well as their students' unique learning needs to effectively design and implement instruction from the perspective of the most applicable theory. Upon identifying desired learning outcomes, teachers can draw on applicable learning theories to make informed decisions about designing instruction, activities, and assessments that are most effective based on their students' learning styles, skills, and abilities.

The following are examples of some common learning theories that can be used as a framework in the instructional process:

- **Constructivism (Jean Piaget):** This theory proposes that students learn by interacting with the learning environment and connecting new information to their background knowledge to build understanding. This active process allows students to personalize their learning and construct their own perceptions of the world through the lens of their previous experiences.
- **Humanism (Abraham Maslow, Carl Rogers):** This theory proposes that learning should take a person-centered approach, with a focus on the individual's innate capacity for personal growth and self-actualization. It operates axiomatically from the principle that all humans have a natural desire to learn; therefore, a failure to learn is due to the learning situation or environment rather than a person's inability to learn. Teachers should act as facilitators and strive to create a safe, accepting learning environment, celebrate students' differences, and praise academic and personal achievement.
- **Connectivism (George Siemens, Stephen Downes):** This theory proposes that learning occurs by making a series of connections across pieces of information, ideas, concepts, and perspectives. Connectivism is rooted in the notion that learning occurs externally, and technology facilitates connections by giving learners access to several outlets for acquiring and processing new information.
- **Experiential Learning (David Kolb):** This theory proposes that students learn and retain information best through physical exploration and interaction with the learning environment. In the classroom, teachers can facilitate this student-led approach by providing students with varying relevant experiences and opportunities for hands-on learning, such as projects or learning centers.
- **Multiple Intelligences (Howard Gardner):** Gardner's theory proposes there are several versions of intelligence, and as such, the process of learning differs among individuals. Some learners may have a stronger intelligence in one domain but have difficulty in another and, therefore, learn best when instruction is presented through the lens of their dominant intelligence. Intelligences are categorized as logical-mathematical, verbal-linguistic, visual-spatial, bodily-kinesthetic, interpersonal, intrapersonal, musical, and naturalistic.

Connecting New Information and Ideas to Prior Knowledge

When students connect new information to prior knowledge, learning becomes relevant and engaging. Effective instruction encourages students to connect learning to background knowledge and experiences, which increases retainment, deepens understanding, and enhances the effectiveness of the overall learning experience. Fostering personal connections to learning is achieved through incorporating an array of strategies and technologies into instruction. Activities including KWL charts, anticipatory guides, graphic organizers, and brainstorming encourage students to consider what they know before learning new concepts, thus allowing them to build upon their prior knowledge and ability to make connections that strengthen learning. Cooperative learning strategies promote sharing and building prior knowledge with other students, thus increasing students' connections to new information. Numerous technologies exist to enhance the learning experience by fostering connections between prior knowledge and new information. Teachers can incorporate a wide range of apps and games across subject areas that build upon prior knowledge by providing activities with increasing levels of difficulty. Online polls, surveys, and word association websites allow students to demonstrate prior understanding of a topic to begin making connections. Self-reflection and closure opportunities at the end of instruction further strengthen learning by encouraging students to connect new material to prior knowledge and experiences.

Making Learning Meaningful and Relevant

Effective instruction occurs when learning is meaningful and relevant. When the purpose of learning is clear, students are engaged, motivated, and retain new information. Instruction must be student-centered, foster personal connections, and be applicable to real-life situations to create meaningful and relevant instruction. Teachers achieve this through an array of methods and technologies that are tailored to students' learning needs. Through forging positive relationships with students, teachers learn their unique interests, preferences, and experiences. Activities such as interest inventories, surveys, and community building develop a positive rapport between teachers and students. This allows teachers to make learning meaningful by creating learner-centered instruction that facilitates personal connections and builds upon prior knowledge. Field trips and community outreach programs are effective in enhancing relevancy through demonstrating the real-world applications of instruction. Additionally, technologies including virtual field trips and tours, videos, and documentaries assist in increasing students' understanding the purpose of learning by illustrating the real-world applications of instruction. Self-assessments make learning meaningful and relevant through encouraging student ownership and responsibility over learning as students seek areas for improvement. Moreover, closure activities serve to demonstrate overall purpose for learning through encouraging students to connect learning to the lesson's objective and their prior knowledge.

Intradisciplinary and Interdisciplinary Instruction

Intradisciplinary and interdisciplinary instruction are both valuable strategies for teaching and learning. In **intradisciplinary** instruction, several elements of a single broad subject area are incorporated into the lesson. For example, in a science lesson, the teacher could incorporate elements of chemistry, biology, and physics into instruction. This method of instruction is beneficial in deepening students' understanding of the nuances of a particular subject area through demonstrating the various components that comprise the overarching discipline. **Interdisciplinary** instruction refers to the simultaneous integration of ideas, knowledge, and skills from several subject areas when approaching an idea, problem, or theme and applying principles of one subject area to another. For example, in an interdisciplinary unit on food, the teacher could incorporate elements of math by teaching students to measure ingredients, language arts by teaching them to read or write a recipe, science through examining chemical reactions of the cooking process, and social studies through having students explore the impact of food agriculture on economy and society. Interdisciplinary instruction is beneficial in deepening students' understanding across subject areas and developing real-world critical thinking skills by encouraging them to make connections between disciplines and teaching them to consider an idea or problem from multiple perspectives.

Examples of Intradisciplinary Instruction

- **Language arts:** A single language arts lesson can incorporate components of reading, writing, grammar, and listening skills. For example, a lesson on a particular poem can include a close reading of the poet's use of grammar, symbolism, imagery, and other literary techniques as well as an audio recording of the poet reading aloud. At the end of the unit, students can be assigned to use what they learned to compose their own original poems.
- **Social studies:** Social studies units can incorporate elements of history, anthropology, archaeology, sociology, psychology, or any other field that involves the study of humans, civilizations, cultures, and historical events. For example, a unit on the Aztec people may include an examination of their religious beliefs, customs, architecture, and agricultural practices.
- **Science:** Intradisciplinary units in science can include several branches within the field, such as chemistry, biology, physics, earth science, botany, or geology. For example, a unit on volcanoes may incorporate lessons on plate tectonics, the Earth's layers, chemicals released during a volcanic eruption, islands formed from cooled volcanic rock, as well as plants that grow best near volcanoes.
- **Mathematics:** An intradisciplinary math lesson may simultaneously include several branches within the field, such as arithmetic, algebra, or geometry. For example, in a geometry lesson on the Pythagorean theorem, students must utilize algebraic equations and arithmetic to determine the length of the sides of a right triangle.

Examples of Interdisciplinary Instruction

- **Language arts:** A unit based in language arts may also incorporate several other disciplines, such as social studies, art, or music. For example, a unit on William Shakespeare's *Romeo and Juliet* may include a reading of the play, an analysis of the use of literary techniques within it, and study of William Shakespeare's life and the society in which he lived, thereby incorporating social studies into the language arts lesson. Students can also act out the play to incorporate the arts and participate in a rhythmic study on iambic pentameter to incorporate music.
- **Social studies:** Units based in social studies can include lessons focused on multiple disciplines, including language arts, music, science, and math. For example, an interdisciplinary unit on Ancient Egypt may include a historical study of the culture, religion, architecture, and practices of the Ancient Egyptians while integrating other subject areas, such as a study of hieroglyphics to incorporate language arts and creating Egyptian masks to incorporate art. Students can also study the scientific advancements of the Ancient Egyptians and incorporate math to study how the ancient pyramids were constructed.
- **Science:** Scientific units can also incorporate elements of art, math, social studies, and language arts in order to become interdisciplinary. For example, a unit on Punnett squares focuses on biology and genetics but can also include several other subject areas. Math can be incorporated by integrating lessons on probability or students can be assigned to research their genetics, create a family tree, and write a report on their findings to incorporate language arts and social studies. Art can also be incorporated by having students create portraits of the potential outcomes from Punnett squares.

- **Mathematics:** Interdisciplinary units in mathematics can also include lessons focused on art, social studies, science, and music. For example, a geometry unit on measuring triangles may also incorporate songs to memorize equations, lessons on the pyramids of Ancient Egypt to incorporate social studies, as well as an art project in which students use only triangles to create an original piece.

Incorporating Cooperative Learning and Consideration from Multiple Viewpoints

In any classroom, teachers will encounter a wide range of diversities among students' backgrounds, cultures, interests, skills, and abilities. Thus, providing students with several opportunities for cooperative learning gives them access to others' perspectives and is highly valuable in teaching students to consider ideas from multiple viewpoints. As each student has different experiences and background knowledge, collaborative learning allows them to share their views on ideas with others. Additionally, in working together, students have the opportunity to work with others from different backgrounds that they may have otherwise never encountered and gain exposure to approaching ideas from multiple viewpoints. Cooperative learning opportunities allow students to understand and appreciate others' perspectives and teach them that there are multiple approaches to problem solving and ideas.

Learning Experiences That Develop Real-World Life Skills

The ultimate goal of education is to develop the whole child into a productive, contributing member of society; therefore, it is imperative to provide learning experiences that will develop life skills that are applicable and beneficial in the real world. In an increasingly fast-paced global society, students must be prepared to enter the professional and societal world as confident, independent, responsible, and adaptive individuals. They must have the leadership skills necessary to compete in the professional arena. Students must be able to work cooperatively with others, respect and value multiple perspectives, and be effective problem solvers and critical thinkers in order to be successful outside of the classroom. Teachers must also aim to help students develop the skills necessary to become lifelong learners to ensure continuous growth and development as they enter society; therefore, learning experiences that promote the development of real-world life skills in addition to academic skills are necessary in adequately preparing students for success.

Cross-Curricular Instruction for Exploring Content from Varied Perspectives

Cross-curricular instruction allows teachers to demonstrate that elements from one subject area can be applied to ideas or problems in another. Thus, this instructional strategy is highly valuable in developing students' abilities to explore content from varied perspectives. As this method incorporates several disciplines in approaching a topic, it deepens students' understanding that there are several perspectives that one can take when solving a problem and that elements of one subject area are relevant in another. In addition, cross-curricular instruction prepares students for the real world through developing critical thinking skills and allowing them to make connections between disciplines, thus allowing them to understand how to successfully approach ideas from varied perspectives.

Benefits of Multicultural Learning Experiences

Multicultural learning experiences demonstrate to students the array of diversities that exist both inside and outside of the classroom. Just as each culture has its own values, norms, and traditions, each has its own perspectives and approaches to ideas and problem solving. Incorporating multicultural experiences in the classroom exposes students to cultures and groups that they may have otherwise never encountered and teaches them to respect and value perspectives outside of their own. As students learn other cultures' beliefs, customs, and attitudes, they develop the understanding that each culture solves problems and considers ideas from multiple viewpoints and that each approach is valuable. As students learn other perspectives, they can apply this knowledge and build problem solving and critical thinking skills that will be beneficial in developing successful lifelong learning habits.

Incorporating Multiple Disciplines into a Thematic Unit

In **cross-curricular** (or **interdisciplinary**) instruction, multiple disciplines are incorporated into a thematic unit in order to deepen students' understanding through fostering connections and demonstrating multiple perspectives and methods of problem solving. Effective interdisciplinary instruction requires careful planning to ensure that all activities are relevant to the overall lesson theme and effectively support students in achieving desired learning outcomes. Teachers must first select a thematic unit based on state academic standards and then determine desired learning outcomes. Then, teachers must design lessons and activities for students to reach learning goals and objectives. When integrating multiple disciplines into a thematic unit, teachers must seek out materials, resources, and activities from various subject areas that are applicable to the main topic and reinforce lesson objectives. Teachers can then integrate these elements into lesson planning to create multifaceted instruction. Additionally, teachers can create activities that approach the overarching lesson theme from the perspective of different subject areas. The activities and materials should be coordinated and relate to one another in order to deepen students' understanding of the overall concept.

Effectively Allocating Time When Creating Lessons and Units

Effective time management is vital for successful teaching and learning. To ensure that all academic standards are covered within a school year, teachers must consider how to best allocate specific amounts of time for units and lessons that allow for review, enrichment, and reteaching. A unit plan for the school year is an effective strategy in allowing the teacher to visualize and plan the amount of content that must be covered. A unit plan can also be utilized on a smaller scale, as a framework for designing and allotting time for instructional goals, objectives, and lessons within each unit. By setting learning goals and daily objectives within individual units, teachers can determine the amount of time available for completing each unit. This ensures more effective lesson planning by allowing teachers to develop daily schedules with dedicated time for teaching and learning. When planning lessons, teachers must consider how much instructional time is necessary to cover each topic and the time students will need to complete lesson activities. Additionally, teachers must ensure that they allow time at the end of each lesson for reteaching if students have misconceptions, as extra time can be utilized for enrichment if reteaching is unnecessary.

Opportunities for Reflection

Opportunities for reflection within lesson plans enhance learning experiences through strengthening student understanding and influencing further instruction. When students are given the opportunity to reflect, they are able to connect their learning back to the original objective and better understand the overall purpose for learning, thus fostering engagement. Reflection deepens students' understanding by allowing them to connect new concepts to their own personal experiences, which ultimately helps in comprehension and retainment by making learning relevant. Reflecting on performance empowers students to become self-motivated lifelong learners by allowing them to analyze what they understood and did well. Reflection also encourages students to identify areas for improvement. Teachers can utilize students' reflections to influence and drive further instruction. Students' reflections allow teachers to identify areas in which students excelled and areas in which they need improvement. They can also aid teachers in tailoring future lesson plans to adapt to students' needs and interests.

Opportunities for Self-Assessment

Including self-assessments within lessons is a valuable formative assessment strategy that enriches student learning and provides insight to the teacher. Providing students with the opportunity to monitor their progress and assess their learning supports them in developing a wide range of skills that are beneficial both inside and outside of the classroom. Self-assessments create a sense of ownership and responsibility over learning, which foster self-motivation and engagement. They also serve to create a sense of independence and objectivity within students to effectively review their own work and identify areas of improvement, which is a vital skill needed to become a lifelong learner. When students evaluate their own performance, teachers are able to effectively assess student understanding, thus allowing them to identify areas of weakness or misconception for reteaching.

Opportunities for Closure Activities

Closure activities at the end of each lesson or topic are short activities that allow teachers to formatively assess student understanding of content covered within a lesson and identify areas of misconception for reteaching. Additionally, closure activities are valuable in measuring whether the intended lesson objective was achieved before moving to the next topic. For students, closures at the end of a lesson provide structure and organization to learning as well as emphasize the purpose for instruction by allowing them to connect what they learned back to the original objective. Moreover, in having students restate what they have learned in a closure activity, learning is strengthened by giving students the opportunity to internalize new information. In demonstrating their understanding, they can better make personal connections between their own learning, background knowledge, and experiences.

Instructional Techniques

Implementing Multiple Instructional Techniques to Maximize Student Learning

Incorporating multiple instructional techniques into the classroom maximizes student learning by enhancing intellectual involvement and overall engagement. When instructional material is presented through a variety of means, it facilitates an **active learning** environment in which students' interest is captured and they are motivated to participate in learning. Varying teaching strategies stimulates engagement and fosters achievement by encouraging students to actively participate in their own learning and implement critical thinking skills to consider information more deeply. Students' understanding is strengthened when content is presented in different ways through various instructional techniques by providing them with multiple frames of reference for making connections and internalizing new concepts. In addition, utilizing multiple instructional techniques allows the teacher to effectively **differentiate instruction** to access multiple learning styles and address individual student needs to ensure understanding and enhance the overall learning process.

Instructional Strategies to Differentiate Instruction

Implementing a variety of strategies for differentiation helps to ensure that instruction appeals to students' varying learning styles and needs. By incorporating **multiple modalities** into direct instruction, such as visual representations, written directions, video or audio clips, songs, graphs, or mnemonic devices, teachers can differentiate the presentation of new concepts and information. Using strategies to differentiate instructional activities is also beneficial in diversifying the learning experience. By providing opportunities for **independent, collaborative**, and **hands-on** learning, teachers can ensure that learning is accessible and engaging to all students. In addition, learning activities should allow for a degree of flexibility in order to appeal to students' varying needs and preferences. Activities such as task cards, educational technology resources, and learning stations provide this **flexibility** and allow for a student-directed experience in which students can choose to learn in the way that best suits their needs. Similarly, assigning open-ended projects as summative assessments allows for a degree of **student-choice**, thus differentiating the method in which students demonstrate their understanding.

Varying the Teacher and Student Roles in the Instructional Process

Varying the roles of the teacher and students as an instructional technique is beneficial in creating an engaging, dynamic classroom environment that maximizes learning. When different roles are implemented, instruction is diversified, thus stimulating student interest and engagement. In addition, certain teacher and student roles are most applicable and effective in specific learning situations. When teachers acknowledge this and understand when to adopt and assign particular roles, they can effectively deliver instruction in a way that deepens student understanding and fosters success in learning. In presenting new content, directions, or modeling new skills, for example, the roles of **lecturer** and student **observer** are effective. In hands-on learning situations, students can take on the role of **active participant** while the teacher acts as a **facilitator** to create a student-centered and engaging learning environment in which students are given ownership over their own learning. Such variation enhances intellectual involvement by promoting critical thinking and problem-solving skills through self-directed learning. Skillfully assigning different roles throughout the learning process also allows the teacher to effectively address students' individual learning needs and preferences to promote engagement and enhance the learning experience.

Fostering Intellectual Involvement and Engagement

Effective instruction includes a variety of strategies for fostering intellectual involvement and engagement to promote academic success. Presenting instruction using various approaches provides multiple avenues for learning new content, thus ensuring and strengthening student understanding to facilitate achievement. In addition, diversifying instructional strategies creates variety in the classroom that effectively stimulates students' interest and motivation to engage in learning. Strategies such as **cooperative learning**, **discussion**, and **self-directed opportunities** encourage active student participation that enhances intellectual involvement by allowing students to build on background knowledge, deepen understanding by exploring others' perspectives, and take ownership over their own learning. This ultimately increases student engagement and motivation for success in learning. Similarly, incorporating **inquiry**, **problem-solving**, and **project-based** strategies promotes curiosity in learning, creativity, and the development of critical thinking skills that stimulate intellectual participation and engagement to create a productive learning environment. Implementing **digital resources** and media throughout instruction is integral in enhancing academic success by making learning relevant, interesting, and differentiated to accommodate various learning needs. At the end of a lesson or activity, allowing students the opportunity to reflect is a valuable strategy in increasing intellectual involvement, retainment, and academic success by facilitating personal connections with learning to build understanding.

Actively Engaging Students by Incorporating Discussion into Instruction

Classroom discussion is a valuable instructional technique in engaging students throughout the learning process. When teachers skillfully pose higher-level questions in discussions, they establish an active learning environment in which students are encouraged and motivated to participate, thus enhancing overall engagement. Effective discussions prompt students to become **intellectually invested** in instruction by promoting the use of **critical** and **higher-order thinking** skills to consider information more deeply and devise creative solutions to problems. In addition, discussions stimulate engagement by providing students the opportunity to express their own thoughts and reasoning regarding a given topic to establish a sense of ownership over their learning. Furthermore, discussions foster a collaborative learning environment that actively engages students by prompting them to understand others' perspectives, consider alternative approaches, and build on one another's experiences to make deeper connections to learning.

Promoting Student Inquiry

The promotion of inquiry is a valuable instructional technique in enhancing student engagement and intellectual involvement. In an **inquiry-based** learning environment, students are encouraged to explore instructional material and devise their own conclusions or solutions to problems. This increases the effectiveness of the learning process by providing students with a sense of agency over their own learning. In addition, implementing this strategy fosters curiosity, self-motivation, and active participation, as it allows for hands-on, **student-led** learning that increases overall engagement. Incorporating inquiry into the classroom stimulates critical and higher-order thinking skills as students construct their own understanding by interacting with learning materials, analyzing their findings, and synthesizing their learning to create new conclusions, results, and responses. To effectively incorporate inquiry into the learning process, the teacher must provide several opportunities for self-directed learning, project-based learning, and student choice to stimulate curiosity. Questions must be open-ended, and students must be encouraged to hypothesize, predict, and experiment in their learning. The teacher must be flexible in instruction to allow space and opportunity for exploration and allow time for reflection and extended learning opportunities to facilitate further inquiry.

Incorporating Problem-Solving into Instruction

Providing opportunities for creative problem solving within instruction effectively creates an engaging and successful learning experience. Students become more **intellectually involved** when encouraged to actively participate in learning and utilize **critical thinking skills** to test hypotheses, analyze results, and devise creative solutions to problems. This hands-on, **student-directed** approach promotes success in learning by allowing students to interact with learning materials as they seek answers to complex ideas and problems in an engaging environment. Problem-solving enables students to make deeper connections to their learning to enhance understanding, as this strategy prompts them to employ and develop background knowledge. In addition, problem-solving activities allow for collaborative learning in which students can actively engage with peers to build on one another's knowledge and experience, thus enhancing successful learning.

Intellectual Involvement, Active Student Engagement, and Success in Learning

A productive learning environment is composed intellectually involved students that are actively engaged in successful learning. A strong correlation exists between **intellectual involvement**, **active student engagement**, and **success in learning**, and each component is necessary for effective instruction. Effective instruction consists of challenging students based on their abilities and teaching them to think deeply about new ideas and concepts. This ultimately encourages students' intellectual involvement, as it prompts them to utilize their critical thinking skills to build on their background knowledge, consider alternative perspectives, and synthesize their learning to devise creative solutions. When students are intellectually involved in instruction, they become more personally invested and engaged, as learning becomes relevant, interesting, and challenging. Engaged students are active participants in their learning, thus enhancing their overall productivity and academic success.

Effectively Structuring Lessons

When developing instruction, it is imperative that the teacher is knowledgeable on how to effectively structure lessons to maximize student engagement and success. Each lesson must include a clear **objective** and explicitly state the process for achieving it. To initiate engagement, effective lessons begin with an **opening**, or "warm-up," activity to introduce a new topic, diagnose student understanding, and activate prior knowledge. Instruction of new material must be delivered through a variety of teaching strategies that are consciously tailored to students' individual learning needs to enhance participation and ensure comprehension. Direct instruction should be followed by **active learning** activities with clear directions and procedures to allow students to practice new concepts and skills. Throughout a successful lesson, the teacher checks frequently for understanding and comprehension by conducting a variety of **formative assessments** and adjusts instruction as necessary. Including **closure** activities is essential to successful learning, as it gives students the opportunity to reflect, process information, make connections, and demonstrate comprehension. In structuring lessons effectively according to students' learning needs, the teacher establishes a focused and engaging learning environment that promotes academic success.

Example of a Daily Lesson Plan Structure

Flexible Instructional Groupings

Flexible instructional groupings provide the teacher and students with a versatile, engaging environment for successful learning. Skillfully grouping students allows for productive, cooperative learning opportunities in which individual strengths are enhanced and necessary support is provided, thus enhancing motivation and engagement. When working in groups, students' understanding of instruction is strengthened, as they are able to learn and build upon one another's background knowledge, perspectives, and abilities. Instructional groups can include students of the **same** or **varied abilities** depending on the learning objective and task to increase productivity and provide scaffolding as necessary for support. This strategy is effective in enabling the teacher to **differentiate** instruction and adjust groups as needed to accommodate varying learning styles, abilities, and interests to maximize engagement and success in learning.

Effective Pacing of Lessons and Importance of Flexibility to Students' Needs

Effective pacing is imperative to focused and engaging instruction. Teachers must be conscientious of the pace of their instruction and ensure that it is reflective of their students' learning needs and sustains their attention. Instruction that is delivered too quickly results in confusion and discouragement, whereas if instruction is too slow, students will lose interest and become disengaged. A well-paced lesson states clear learning goals and objectives while clearly outlining the means to achieve them to elicit student motivation. The teacher must consider the most **efficient** and **engaging** instructional strategies for presenting new material to establish a steady pace and maintain it by incorporating smooth **transitions** from one activity to the next. It is important that teachers are conscious of the rate of instruction throughout all stages of learning while maintaining **flexibility** in pacing in order to be responsive to their students. As individual students have different learning needs and processing times, they may require a faster or slower rate of instruction to understand new concepts and remain engaged in learning. Frequent checks for understanding and reflection activities are essential strategies in determining if the pace of instruction must be adjusted to accommodate students' needs.

Connecting Content to Students' Prior Knowledge and Experiences

Implementing effective instructional strategies for connecting content to students' prior knowledge and experiences enhances the relevancy of learning and fosters deeper connections that strengthen understanding. To achieve this, teachers must educate themselves on students' backgrounds, experiences, communities, and interests to determine what is important and interesting to them. With this knowledge in mind, teachers can successfully locate and implement **authentic materials** into instruction to enhance relevancy. Additionally, encouraging students to bring materials to class that reflect their backgrounds and including these materials in instruction makes learning relevant by allowing students to make **personal connections** to content. Instructional strategies such as brainstorming, KWL charts, prereading, and anticipation guides allow the teacher to determine what students know prior to learning a new concept, thus enabling them to connect content to students' background knowledge in a relevant way. Incorporating digital resources further enhances relevancy in learning. Teachers can locate videos or audio clips that relate to instruction and reflect students' background experiences and interests. Using digital resources to introduce a new concept is a valuable strategy in developing students' **schema** on a topic to build prior knowledge and make learning meaningful by fostering connections.

MAKING LEARNING RELEVANT AND MEANINGFUL

For learning to be relevant and meaningful, it is essential that teachers present content in a way that connects with students' **prior knowledge** and experiences. When students are able to apply new ideas and information to what they already know through effective instructional techniques, it facilitates strong **personal connections** that make learning relevant and meaningful. In addition, personal connections and **relevancy** are strengthened when teachers consciously incorporate materials to reflect students' individual backgrounds and experiences in instruction. Linking content to students' background experiences enables them to relate instruction to real-world situations, thus establishing a sense of purpose for learning by making it applicable to their lives. Intentionally connecting content with students' prior knowledge and experiences enhances the effectiveness of the instructional process and fosters positive attitudes toward learning.

ENHANCING STUDENT ENGAGEMENT AND SUCCESS IN LEARNING

Engaging instruction employs a variety of instructional strategies and materials to create a relevant, meaningful, and successful learning experience. Effective content establishes a clear and applicable purpose for instruction that increases student participation in the learning process. Presenting relevant and meaningful content enhances understanding and engagement by enabling students to create real-world, **personal connections** to learning based upon their own backgrounds and experiences. In addition, when instruction is tailored to reflect students' unique interests and preferences, content becomes more appealing and students' willingness to learn is enhanced. When students can perceive content through their own frames of reference with instructional materials that reflect their unique differences, they are able to effectively internalize and relate information to their lives, thus increasing engagement. Engaged learning ultimately facilitates academic success in that when students are motivated to learn, they demonstrate positive attitudes toward learning and are more likely to actively participate.

Adapting Instruction to Individual Needs

Evaluating Activities and Materials to Meet Learning Needs

The careful selection of instructional activities and materials is integral to accommodating students' varying characteristics and needs. When evaluating the appropriateness of activities and materials, several considerations must be made. Teachers must consider whether activities and materials align with state and district **academic standards**. Teachers must also evaluate the quality and effectiveness of the activities and materials in supporting students' unique differences as they achieve learning goals and objectives. All materials and activities must be **developmentally appropriate** across domains yet adaptable to individual students' learning needs. In addition, they must be challenging yet feasible for student achievement relative to students' grade levels and abilities to promote engagement and the development of critical and **higher-order thinking** skills. Teachers must evaluate activities and materials for versatility to allow for student choice and differentiation in order to address varying characteristics and needs. Teachers must also ensure that activities and materials are accurate, **culturally sensitive**, and reflective of students' diversities to foster an inclusive learning environment that promotes engagement.

Instructional Resources and Technologies

The implementation of varied instructional resources and technologies is highly valuable in supporting student engagement and achievement. Effective use of resources and technologies requires teachers to evaluate their appropriateness in addressing students' individual characteristics and learning needs for academic success. Teachers must be attuned to students' unique differences in order to seek high quality technologies and resources that address their students' needs and support the achievement of learning goals and objectives. Technologies and resources must be **accurate**, **comprehensible**, easily **accessible** to students, and **relevant** to the curriculum and the development of particular skills. Teachers must also consider the grade-level and **developmental appropriateness** of technologies and resources as well as their adaptability to allow for differentiation. Effective technologies and resources are interactive, engaging, and multifaceted to allow for varying levels of complexity based on students' abilities. This allows teachers to provide appropriate challenges while diversifying instruction to appeal to varied characteristics and learning needs, thus fostering an engaging environment that supports success in learning for all students.

Adapting Activities and Materials to Meet Individual Characteristics and Needs

In effective instruction, activities and materials are adapted to accommodate students' individual characteristics and needs. Teachers must be attuned to students' unique differences and understand how to adjust activities and materials accordingly to facilitate academic success and growth. To achieve this, teachers must incorporate a **variety** of activities and materials that appeal to all styles of learners. Activities and materials should provide **student choice** for engagement in learning and demonstration of understanding. By differentiating instruction, teachers can effectively scaffold activities and materials to provide supports as necessary as well as include extensions or alternate activities for enrichment. **Chunking** instruction, allowing extra time as necessary, and accompanying activities and materials with aids such as graphic organizers, visual representations, and anticipation guides further differentiates learning to accommodate students' learning characteristics and needs. Conducting **formative assessments** provides teachers with valuable feedback regarding student understanding and engagement, thus allowing them to modify and adjust the complexity of activities and materials as necessary to adapt to varied characteristics and learning differences.

Instructional Resources and Technologies

When teachers understand students' individual characteristics and needs, they can adapt instructional resources and technologies accordingly to maximize learning. To do so effectively, the teacher must incorporate a diverse array of **multifaceted** resources and technologies that support and enhance learning through a variety of methods. This ensures that varying learning needs are met, as students of all learning styles are provided with several avenues for building and strengthening understanding. Additionally, the teacher can adapt resources and technologies to accommodate individual students by **varying the complexity** to provide challenges, support, and opportunities for enrichment based on ability level. Supplementing technologies and resources with **scaffolds**, such as extra time, visual representations, or opportunities for collaborative learning, further enables the teacher to adapt to individual learning needs. When effectively implemented and adapted to students' characteristics and needs, instructional technologies and resources serve as valuable tools for differentiating curriculum to enhance the learning experience.

Modifications, Accommodations, and Adaptations

Accommodations and Modifications

Accommodations and modifications are different types of educational supports put in place to help a student participate effectively in school. An **accommodation** changes *how* a student is taught or assessed by providing more time or other supports that remove barriers to the material. Students who receive accommodations are taught and assessed to the same standards as students without accommodations. A **modification** changes *what* is taught or assessed by changing or omitting parts of the materials. Students with modifications may receive fewer problems to solve or lower-rigor versions of the materials compared to other students.

Modifications

Modifications are changes to *what* students are taught or expected to learn. Students with disabilities can receive modifications as determined by their specific needs and as written out in their Individualized Education Programs.

- **Curriculum modifications** allow students to learn material that is different from what their general education peers learn. For example, students with classroom modifications may receive assignments with fewer math problems or with reading samples appropriate for their reading levels. Students with curriculum modifications may receive different grading tiers than their peers. The ways teachers grade their assignments may be different from how the teachers grade their peers' assignments. Students may also be excused from particular projects or given project guidelines that are different and better suited to their individual needs.
- **Assignment modifications** include completing fewer or different homework problems than peers, writing shorter papers, answering fewer questions on classwork and tests, and creating alternate projects or assignments.

Environmental Modifications

Students with disabilities may need environmental modifications in order to be successful in their classrooms, homes, and communities. **Environmental modifications** are adaptations that allow people with disabilities to maneuver through their environments with as little resistance as possible. They allow for more **independent living experiences**, especially for those with limited mobility. Environmental modifications ensure the health, safety, and welfare of the people who need them. Examples of environmental modifications in the home, community, or school include ramps, hydraulic lifts, widened doorways and hallways, automatic doors, handrails, and grab bars. Roll-in showers, water faucet controls, worktable or work surface adaptations, and cabinet and shelving adaptations are also environmental modifications that can be provided if necessary. Other adaptations include heating and cooling adaptations and electrical adaptations to accommodate devices or equipment. Environmental modifications in the home are typically provided by qualified agencies or providers. The Americans with Disabilities Act ensures that environmental modifications are provided in the **community** to help avoid discrimination against people with disabilities.

ACCOMMODATIONS

Accommodations are flexible classroom tools because they can be used to provide **interventions** without time or location boundaries. They remove **barriers** to learning for students with disabilities, and they change how students learn. Accommodations do not change what students are learning or expected to know. Classroom accommodations may be outlined in students' Individualized Education Programs (IEPs) and 504 Plans or simply provided as needed by special educators or general educators. Accommodations are put into place to ensure that students with disabilities are accessing the learning process with the fewest barriers, putting them on the same levels as their peers without disabilities. **Presentation accommodations** include allowing students to listen to oral instructions, providing written lists of instructions, and allowing students to use readers to assist with comprehension. **Response accommodations** include allowing students to provide oral responses, capture responses via audio recording, and use spelling dictionaries or spell-checkers when writing. **Accommodations to setting** include special seating (wherever the students learn best), use of sensory tools, and special lighting.

TYPES OF ACCOMMODATIONS

Timing, schedule, and organizational accommodations change the ways students with disabilities have access to classrooms with the fewest barriers to learning. Students who need these accommodations receive them as written statements in their IEPs, 504 Plans, or as teachers see fit during classroom time.

- **Timing accommodations** allow students more time to complete tasks or tests and/or process instructions. They also allow students to access frequent breaks during assignments or tests.
- **Schedule accommodations** include taking tests in chunks over periods of time or several days, taking test sections in different orders, and/or taking tests during specific times of day.
- **Organizational skill accommodations** include assistance with time management, marking texts with highlighters, maintaining daily assignment or work schedules, and/or receiving study skills instruction.

When accommodations are written in a student's IEP, the student has access to them for state standardized tests. When and how accommodations are put into place is left to the discretion of the teacher unless specifically written in the student's IEP or 504 Plan.

OBTAINING ACCOMMODATIONS

When parents or legal guardians of children with disabilities believe that **accommodations** may help their children, they can arrange to speak with teachers about informal supports. **Informal supports** are strategies teachers can put into place to assist students with their learning processes. These changes do not require paperwork and can be implemented during classroom instruction. Teachers can experiment with informal supports to determine what will be most helpful for removing the barriers to learning students might be experiencing. If it is determined that students need bigger changes to how they learn, **formal evaluations** can take place. Students who do not already have IEPs or 504 Plans may be evaluated to collect data on their needs. For students with IEPs or 504 Plans, accommodations can be included the next time these plans are updated. The IEPs or 504 Plans can also be **amended** if the need for the accommodations is immediate, such as when they need to be put in place before standardized testing time. **Data** supporting the need for the accommodations must be provided and listed in the comprehensive initial evaluations and all versions of IEPs and 504 Plans.

Parents and Legal Guardians Ensuring Accommodations Are Being Provided

Accommodations are changes to the ways children with disabilities learn, not changes to what the children are learning. While parents and legal guardians may only receive **formal updates** on how accommodations are being provided or helping the students during specified reporting times (unless students' IEPs or 504 Plans specifically state otherwise), they can ask for **reports** on goal progress or accommodations for their students at any time. Parents and legal guardians can ensure that accommodations are successfully implemented by using the progress reports and asking the right questions. Parents and legal guardians can ensure that accommodations are being provided in a number of ways. They can **advocate** for their students by making sure the accommodations are being implemented on a regular basis. Parents and legal guardians also have the right to ask if their students are using the accommodations on a **regular basis**. If they are being used on a regular basis, parents and legal guardians can explore additional options that might help their students. Parents and legal guardians can work with special education teachers and the IEP teams to ensure that their students' accommodations are being received and are effective.

Informal Supports vs. Formal Accommodations

Informal supports are generally easier to implement in the classroom setting. They do not necessarily have to be implemented only for students with Individualized Education Programs or students with disabilities. Students who have not been evaluated for special education services can receive **informal supports** to ensure classroom success. Teachers may use informal supports to help students who are struggling with the ways they are learning. They may demonstrate that the students are able to learn with the accommodations in place. Informal supports are often the first step to indicating that students are in need of **special education services**.

Formal accommodations are put in place when students become eligible for IEPs or 504 Plans. Formal supports are written into the IEPs or 504 Plans and then required by law to be provided. Examples of informal supports include frequent breaks, special seating, quiet areas for test taking or studying, teacher cues, and help with basic organizational skills. These informal supports may eventually turn into formal supports if students become eligible for special education services.

Reasonable Accommodations According to ADA

According to the Americans with Disabilities Act (ADA), a **reasonable accommodation** is a change to workplace conditions, equipment, or environment that allows an individual to effectively perform a job. Title I under the ADA requires businesses with more than 15 employees to abide by certain regulations, ensuring that their needs are reasonably met. Any change to the work environment or the way a job is performed that gives a person with a disability access to **equal employment** is considered a reasonable accommodation. Reasonable accommodations fall into **three categories**: changes to a job application process, changes to the work environment or to the way a job is usually done, and changes that enable employee access to equal benefits and privileges that employees without disabilities receive. These effectively level the playing field for people with disabilities to receive the same benefits as their peers. It also allows for the fewest barriers to success in the workplace. Many communities have resources available to help people with disabilities find jobs. They also have resources that help employers make their workplaces accessible for people with disabilities.

Types of Assistive Technology

Assistive technology (AT) tools can be physical objects and devices or online resources that assist students with disabilities in their learning. The purpose of AT tools is to provide students with disabilities **equal access to the curriculum** by accommodating their individual needs to promote positive outcomes. **Personal listening devices (PLDs)**, sometimes called FM systems, are devices that clarify teachers' words. With a PLD, a teacher speaks into a small microphone and the words transmit clearly into a student's headphone or earpiece. **Sound field systems** amplify teachers' voices to eliminate sound issues in classroom environments. **Noise-cancelling headphones** are useful for students who need to work independently and limit distractions or behavioral triggers. **Audio recorders** allow students to record lectures or lessons and refer to the recordings later at their own pace. Some note-taking applications will transcribe audio into written words. Captioning is available to pair visual words with spoken words. **Text-to-speech (TTS) software** lets students see and hear words at the same time. TTS and audiobook technology can help students with fluency, decoding, and comprehension skills.

Voice Recognition Software

Voice recognition software and communication software can assist students who struggle with speaking or communicating. **Voice recognition software** allows people to speak commands into microphones to interact with the computer instead of using a keyboard. This feature helps create a **least restrictive environment** for a student with a disability because it removes the sometimes challenging aspect of using a keyboard while working on a computer. Voice recognition software allows users to carry out actions such as opening documents, saving documents, and moving the cursor. It also allows users to "write" sentences and paragraphs by speaking into the microphones in word processing programs. In order for voice recognition software to be effective, the user must learn to dictate words distinctly into a microphone. This ensures that the correct word is heard and dictated by the voice-to-text software. Some programs collect information and familiarize themselves with people's particular voice qualities. Over time, the systems adapt to people's voices and become more efficient.

Effectively Instructing Students Using Assistive Technology

Assistive technology (**AT**) refers to tools that are effective for teaching students with learning disabilities, as they address a number of potential special needs. The purpose of AT is to level the playing field for students with **learning disabilities**, particularly when they are participating in general education classrooms. AT can address learning difficulties in math, listening, organization, memory, reading, and writing. **AT for listening** can assist students who have difficulties processing language. For example, a personal listening device can help a student hear a teacher's voice more clearly. **AT for organization and memory** can help students with self-management tasks, such as keeping assignment calendars or retrieving information using handheld devices. **AT for reading** often includes text-to-speech devices that assist with students' reading fluency, decoding, comprehension, and other skill deficits. **AT for writing** assists students who struggle with handwriting or writing development. Some AT writing devices help with actual handwriting, while others assist with spelling, punctuation, grammar, word usage, or text organization.

Augmentative and Alternative Communication Systems

Students with communication disorders may require the use of augmentative or alternative communication systems. Communication systems are used to help the students effectively demonstrate **expressive and receptive language** and engage in **social skills**. Teaching appropriate communication skills is a collaborative effort between the students' caretakers, teachers, and other professionals. Typically, **speech services** are written into students' IEPs, and the services are delivered by **speech language pathologists (SLPs)**. Depending on the requirements in the IEPs, the SLPs may work one-on-one with students or work with the teachers to incorporate speech and language skills throughout students' school days. In order for communication systems to work for nonverbal students, measures must be taken to ensure that the particular systems are appropriate for what the students need. It is important for the caretakers, teachers, other professionals, and even classmates to model using the devices so the students can learn how to "talk" appropriately. Students must also have constant access to the systems and receive consistent opportunities to communicate using the systems at home and at school.

Use of Visual Representation Systems with Students with Autism

Assistive technology (AT) helps increase learning opportunities for students with autism by eliminating barriers to learning. AT can help improve students' expressive communication skills, attention skills, motivation skills, academic skills, and more. **Visual representation systems** in the form of objects, photographs, drawings, or written words provide concrete representations of words for students with autism. Visual representations, such as simple pictures paired with words, can be used to create visual schedules for students with autism. Photographs can be used to help students learn vocabulary words and the names of people and places. Written words should be paired with the visual representations in order to create links between the concrete objects and the actual words. The goal is for students to eventually recognize the words without the pictures. Visual representation systems can also help facilitate easier transitions between activities or places, which can be difficult for students with autism.

Communication Systems

Students who are nonverbal may have access to **communication systems** implemented by trained professionals. Teachers, caretakers, and other professionals work with the students to use the communication systems effectively. The goal of a communication system is to teach a nonverbal student how to "talk" and engage in **age-appropriate social skills**. In order for nonverbal students to learn appropriate social interactions, they must spend time learning communication skills, just as they learn academic content. Communication skills can be taught in isolation or as part of students' daily activities. Giving nonverbal students opportunities to foster communication skills in **familiar environments** makes it easier for them to learn appropriate social interactions. Teachers, caregivers, and other professionals must demonstrate how to use communication systems to engage in conversations, make requests, and answer questions. Most importantly, nonverbal students must be instructed to **access** their "words" (communication systems) at all times throughout the school and home environments.

Accessibility Components of a Picture Exchange Communication System

A Picture Exchange Communication System (**PECS**) is a communication system for people with little or no **communicative abilities**. This system is a way for the students to access their environments using **picture symbols** to communicate meaning, wants, and needs. For example, a child may point to a picture symbol to request a book. A PECS provides a way for students with communication disorders to develop their **verbal communication** without actually speaking. It reduces frustration and problem behaviors by providing students with an avenue to express what they want to say. It is commonly used for students with autism spectrum disorder in the form of augmentative communication devices. It can also be used for students with other impairments whose communicative abilities are affected. A PECS focuses on **functional communication skills** and can be practiced in home, school, and community environments.

Supporting Nonverbal Students

Nonverbal students have extra challenges in addition to learning content. These students may need extra instruction in academic areas as well as specialized instruction in the area of communication skills. Students with **nonverbal disabilities** may also need social skills instruction, struggle with abstract concepts, and dislike changes to their routines. Teachers can **facilitate learning** for nonverbal students by making changes to their classroom environments, by teaching strategies for comprehending concepts, and by providing materials to accommodate their needs. Teachers can also provide accommodations or modifications to classwork and tests to make the content accessible to nonverbal students. Using visuals to represent actions, words, or concepts is a helpful instructional strategy for teaching nonverbal students, especially when teaching new material. Additionally, teachers can assist nonverbal students by taking measures to prevent undesirable behaviors from occurring.

Strategies and Accommodations for Students with Working Memory Deficits

Working memory is critical for remembering letters and numbers, listening to short instructions, reading and understanding content, completing homework independently, and understanding social cues. When **working memory skills** are absent or slow to develop, learning may be difficult. This may get worse for children over time. As they fail to develop or retain working memory capabilities, their overall **cognitive abilities** begin to suffer. Working memory deficits vary among people with disabilities, but accommodations can make up for missing or underdeveloped skills. Educators can implement **strategies** like reducing the children's workload; being aware of when children might be reaching memory overload; and providing visual cues, positive feedback, testing alternatives, and extra time. **Accommodations** in an Individualized Education Program for a student with working memory deficits might include frequent breaks, small group instruction, and extended time for tests and assignments.

Social and Functional Living Skills

Targeting and Implementing Social Skills Instruction

Developing good social skills is essential for lifelong success, and people with disabilities often struggle with these skills. Addressing social skill behavior is most effective when specific **social skill needs** are identified, and **social skills instruction** is implemented as a collaborative effort between parents and teachers.

Evaluating **developmental milestones** is helpful in targeting social skills that need to be addressed and taught. If a child with a disability is not demonstrating a milestone, such as back-and-forth communication, the skill can be evaluated to determine if it should be taught. However, meeting milestones is not a reliable way to measure a student's social skill ability, as some children naturally progress more slowly. **Social skill deficits** may be acquisition deficits, performance deficits, or fluency deficits. A student with an **acquisition deficit** demonstrates an absence of a skill or behavior. A student with a **performance deficit** does not implement a social skill consistently. A student with a **fluency deficit** needs assistance with demonstrating a social skill effectively or fluently. Once a student's social skill need is identified, teachers, parents, and other professionals can collaborate to address it by establishing a routine or a behavior contract or implementing applied behavior analysis.

Using Instructional Methods to Address Independent Living Skills

When applicable, goals for independent living skills are included in the **transition section** of students' Individualized Education Programs (IEPs). However, **independent living skills education** should begin well before students reach high school, regardless of whether these skills are addressed in their IEP goals. **Functional skills instruction** is necessary to teach students skills needed to gain independence. Instructional methods used to address independent living skills for students with disabilities include making life skills instruction part of the daily curriculum. An appropriate **task analysis** can be used to determine what skills need to be taught. **Functional academic skills**, especially in the areas of math and language arts, should also be included in the curriculum. Telling time, balancing a checkbook, and recognizing signs and symbols are just some examples of basic skills that students can generalize outside of the classroom environment. The goal of **community-based instruction** is to help students develop skills needed to succeed in the community, such as skills needed when riding a bus or shopping. This type of instruction may be harder to implement than basic social skills training, which should be part of the daily curriculum.

Purposes and Benefits of Social Skills Groups

Social skills groups are useful for helping students with social skill deficits learn and practice appropriate skills with their peers. Social skills groups are primarily composed of similarly aged peers with and without disabilities. An adult leads these groups and teaches students skills needed for making friends, succeeding in school and life, and sometimes obtaining and maintaining a job. Other professionals, such as school psychologists or speech language pathologists, may also lead social skills groups. Social skills groups work by facilitating **conversation** and focusing on **skill deficits**. These groups can help students learn to read facial cues, appropriately greet others, begin conversations, respond appropriately, maintain conversations, engage in turn-taking, and request help when needed.

Evidence-Based Methods for Promoting Self-Determination

Students with disabilities often need to be taught **self-determination** and **self-advocacy** skills. These skills may not come easily to students with specific disorders, like Autism Spectrum Disorder. Self-determination involves a comprehensive understanding of one's own **strengths and limitations**. Self-determined people are **goal-oriented** and intrinsically motivated to **improve themselves**. Teachers can facilitate the development of these skills in a number of ways, starting in early elementary school. In early elementary school, teachers can promote self-determination by teaching choice-making skills and providing clear consequences for choices. Teachers can also promote problem-solving and self-management skills, like having students evaluate their own work. At the middle school and junior high school level, students can be taught to evaluate and analyze their choices. They can also learn academic and personal goal-setting skills and decision-making skills. At the high school level, teachers can promote decision-making skills, involvement in educational planning (e.g., students attending their Individualized Education Program meetings), and strategies like self-instruction, self-monitoring, and self-evaluation. Throughout the education process, teachers should establish and maintain high standards for learning, focus on students' strengths, and create positive learning environments that promote choice and problem-solving skills.

Teaching Self-Awareness Skills

Students engage in private self-awareness and public self-awareness. Some students with disabilities have the additional challenge of needing instruction in **self-awareness skills**. Special educators and other professionals can facilitate the instruction of self-awareness skills by teaching students to be **aware** of their thoughts, feelings, and actions; to recognize that other people have needs and feelings; and to recognize how their behaviors **affect other people**. Students can be taught self-awareness by identifying their own strengths and weaknesses and learning to self-monitor errors in assignments. They can also be taught to identify what materials or steps are needed to complete tasks and to advocate for accommodations or strategies that work for them.

Special educators or other professionals should frequently talk with students about their performance and encourage them to discuss their mistakes without criticism.

Importance of Learning Self-Advocacy Skills

Self-advocacy is an important skill to learn for people entering adulthood. For students with disabilities, **self-advocacy skills** are especially important for success in **postsecondary environments**. Teaching and learning self-advocacy skills should begin when students enter grade school and be reinforced in the upper grade levels. Students with disabilities who have the potential to enter postsecondary education or employment fields need to learn self-advocacy skills in order to **communicate** how their disabilities may affect their education or job performance and their need for supports and possible accommodations. Students with disabilities who graduate or age out of their Individualized Education Programs do not receive the **educational supports** they received at the grade school level. It is essential for students to advocate for themselves in the absence of teachers or caregivers advocating for them, especially when students independently enter postsecondary employment, training, or educational environments. Many colleges, universities, communities, and workplaces offer services to students with disabilities, but it is up to the students to advocate for themselves and seek them out.

Teaching Functional Living Skills

Also known as life skills, functional living skills are skills that students need to live independently. Ideally, students leave high school having gained functional skills. For students with special needs, **functional living skills instruction** may be needed to gain independent living skills. Students with developmental or cognitive disabilities sometimes need to acquire basic living skills, such as self-feeding or toileting. **Applied behavior analysis** is a process by which these skills can be identified, modeled, and taught. Students must also learn functional math and language arts skills, such as managing money and reading bus schedules. Students may also participate in **community-based instruction** to learn skills while completing independent living tasks in the community. These skills include grocery shopping, reading restaurant menus, and riding public transportation. **Social skills instruction** is also important for these students, as learning appropriate social interactions is necessary to function with community members.

Adaptive Behavior Skills Instruction

Adaptive behavior skills refer to age-appropriate behaviors that people need in order to live independently and function in daily life. **Adaptive behavior skills** include self-care, following rules, managing money, making friends, and more. For students with disabilities, especially severely limiting disabilities, adaptive behavior skills may need to be included in daily instruction. Adaptive behavior skills can be separated into conceptual skills, social skills, and practical life skills. **Conceptual skills** include academic concepts, such as reading, math, money, time, and communication skills. **Social skills** instruction focuses on teaching students to get along with others, communicate appropriately, and maintain appropriate behavior inside and outside the school environment. **Practical life skills** are skills needed to perform the daily living tasks, such as bathing, eating, sitting and standing, and using the bathroom. Adaptive behavior assessments are useful in assessing what adaptive behavior skills need to be addressed for each student. These assessments are usually conducted using observations and questionnaires completed by parents, teachers, or students.

Social Skill Deficits

Social skills generally develop alongside language development and emotional development, as they are a major component of communication and awareness. Social skills need to be taught to some students with disabilities, such as students with autism. **Social skills instruction** involves the teaching of basic communication skills, empathy and rapport skills, interpersonal skills, problem-solving skills, and accountability. These are skills that do not come naturally to students with social skill deficits.

- **Basic communication skills** include listening, following directions, and taking turns in conversations.
- **Emotional communication skills** include demonstrating empathy and building rapport with others.
- **Interpersonal skills** include sharing, joining activities, and participating in turn-taking.
- **Problem-solving skills** include asking for help, apologizing to others, making decisions, and accepting consequences.
- **Accountability** includes following through on promises and accepting criticism appropriately.

Instructional Methods for Teaching Students with Social Skill Deficits

Students with social skill deficits may or may not require explicit social skills instruction. These deficits can be addressed in inclusive settings. **Social skills instruction** can be delivered to entire classes or individual students, depending on the needs of the students. Also, **one-on-one** or **small group social skills instruction** can be delivered by professionals like speech-language pathologists. In both settings, it is important to model appropriate manners, hold students responsible for their actions, and have clear and concise rules and consequences. This creates educational environments that are both predictable and safe. Social situations that produce undesired outcomes can be remediated by **role-playing** the situations and teaching students positive responses. **Social stories** are another way to foster social skills growth. Often, these social stories demonstrate appropriate responses to specific social situations. The goal is for the students to generalize learned concepts to their school and home environments.

Life Stage Transitions

Supporting Students Through Transitions

Transitioning to life after high school can be a difficult process, particularly for students with disabilities. It is important for teachers to facilitate and support these **transitions** before students exit their special education programs. **Structured learning environments** that include independent workstations and learning centers provide opportunities for independent learning to occur. **Independent workstations** give students chances to practice previously introduced concepts or perform previously introduced tasks. **Learning centers** provide small group settings where new skills can be taught. Students can also rotate through different learning centers that offer art lessons, focus on academic skills, or provide breaks or leisure activities. **Classroom layout** also plays an important role. Teachers should plan their classroom layouts based on individual student needs in order to create comfortable, predictable environments for students with disabilities. **Visual schedules** help students transition between centers by providing them with concrete schedule references.

Benefits of Vocational Education

Students with disabilities often participate in vocational education in order to gain **independent living skills**. Often, schools and communities offer services that provide vocational training for people with disabilities. These programs offer students **job-specific skills training** and opportunities to earn certifications, diplomas, or certificates. They often involve **hands-on learning experiences** focused on building skills specific to certain occupations. These programs are beneficial to students with disabilities who may struggle with grasping abstract concepts learned in typical classroom environments. Hands-on training in vocational programs can be a meaningful way for students with disabilities to learn academic concepts and gain living skills needed to function in postgraduate life. Vocational education opportunities offer alternatives for students with disabilities who might otherwise drop out of high school. These programs also serve as a viable option for younger students to work towards, as most vocational education programs are offered to students in upper grade levels.

Vocational Skills Needed to Be Successful in Work Environments

Informal vocational training often begins before students even get to high school. Teachers include informal vocational training skills in their classrooms by teaching academic and communication skills. **Academic skills** can both spark and strengthen students' career interests and provide learning platforms to build upon. **Communication skills**, like giving and following instructions and processing information, generalize to work environments. **Social and interpersonal skills**, like problem-solving abilities and participating in phone conversations, are important for performance in workplaces. Students need to learn important **vocational and occupational skills** required by most jobs, such as interacting appropriately with coworkers and keeping track of worked hours. Students also need formal or informal training in completing resumes, cover letters, and tax forms. Training may also include interview practice and job search guidance.

Resources to Promote Successful Transitions to Life after High School

In some states, **statements of transition** should be included in Individualized Education Programs (IEPs) at age 14 for students with disabilities. In most states, the Individuals with Disabilities Education Act mandates that transition plans be put in place for students with IEPs at age 16 and every year thereafter. Some schools and communities have programs and resources available to facilitate students' successful transitions to life after high school. Throughout the transition process, it is important that students and their caregivers participate in any decision-making processes. **Vocational education courses**, sometimes called career and technical education courses, offer academic course alternatives. The courses usually specialize in specific trades or occupations. They can serve to spark or maintain students' interests in vocational fields. Some schools offer **postsecondary enrollment options**, where students can participate in college courses, earning both high school and college credits. **Career assessments**, including interest inventories and formal and informal vocational assessments, serve to gauge students' career interests. These can be worked into students' transitional goals in their IEPs and should be conducted frequently, as students' interests change.

Components of a Transition Plan

Transition plans are flexible but formal plans that help a student identify his or her goals for after school and act as a roadmap to help the support team advocate for the student's future. They generally include postsecondary goals and expected transition services. The four goal areas are vocational training, postsecondary education, employment, and independent living. **Transition goals** must be results oriented and measurable. Goals can be general, but the transition activities need to be quantified to reflect what the student can complete in the IEP year. It is common for interests to change from year to year; therefore, goals and plans may change as well. **Transition services** are determined once the goals are established. Transition services include types of instruction the student will receive in school, related services, community experiences, career or college counseling, and help with adaptive behavior skills. Goals and transition services must be reviewed and updated each year. Academic goals in the IEP can also support transition goals. For example, math goals can focus on money management skills as part of a transition plan.

Factors That Influence Successful Transitions to Postsecondary Life

Parents or legal guardians, teachers, school professionals, community members, and students themselves can all contribute to successful transitions to postsecondary life. Key **factors** that help students successfully transition include the following:

- Participation in standards-based education
- Work preparation and career-based learning experiences
- Leadership skills
- Access to and experience with community services, such as mental health and transportation services
- Family involvement and support

Standards-based education ensures that students receive consistent and clear expectations with a curriculum that is aligned to the universal design for learning standards. Exposure to work preparation and career-based learning experiences ensures that students receive opportunities to discover potential career interests or hobbies. Connections and experiences with community activities provide students with essential postsecondary independent living skills. Family involvement and support ensure that students have advocates for their needs and interests. Families can also help students connect with school and community-based supports that facilitate their career interests.

Instructional Design for Students with Disabilities

Developmentally Appropriate Curriculum

Choosing a developmentally appropriate curriculum is challenging for educators. Special educators have the additional challenge of finding a curriculum that meets the needs of the **individual students with disabilities**. The end result is not usually a one-size-fits-all curriculum because that goes against the intentions of Individualized Education Programs (IEPs) designed to meet the needs of students with special needs. Instead, special educators often pick and choose curriculum components that best meet the needs of differing abilities in the classroom. When selecting an appropriate curriculum, special educators should consider the following:

- Standards and goals that are appropriate to the needs of the students
- Best practices that have been found effective for students
- Curricula that are engaging and challenging
- Instruction and activities that are multimodal
- IEP goals
- Real-world experiences
- Different ways of learning that help teachers understand students' learning processes
- Collaboration with co-teachers to deliver appropriate instruction

In some special education settings, the curriculum is already chosen. In these settings, teachers can collaborate with co-teachers to find ways to provide instruction that meets standards and the individual needs of the students.

Components of Differentiated Instruction

Differentiated instruction is different from individualized instruction. It targets the strengths of students and can work well in both special education and general education settings. **Differentiated instruction** is also useful for targeting the needs of students with **learning and attention deficits**. With differentiated instruction, teachers adjust their instructional processes to meet the needs of the individual students. Teaching strategies and classroom management skills are based largely on each particular class of students instead of on methods that may have been successful in the past. Teachers can differentiate content, classroom activities, student projects, and learning environments. For example, students may be encouraged to choose topics of personal interest to focus on for projects. Students are held to the same standards but have many choices in terms of project topics. **Differentiated content** provides access to a variety of resources to encourage student choice over what and how they learn. **Differentiated learning environments** are flexible to meet the ever-changing needs of the students.

Review Video: Differentiated Instruction
Visit mometrix.com/academy and enter code: 100342

Effectiveness of Differentiated Instruction

Differentiated instruction is effective in general education settings, team-teaching settings, and special education settings because it targets the **strengths** of students. Differentiated instruction is used to target the different ways that students learn instead of taking a one-size-fits-all approach. Differentiated instruction is used in lieu of individualized instruction because it uses a variety of instructional approaches and allows students to use a variety of materials to help them access the curriculum. **Effective differentiated instruction** includes small group work, reciprocal learning, and continual assessment.

Small group work allows for the individual learning styles and needs of students to be addressed. In small groups, students receive instruction by rotating through groups. Group work should be used sparingly or be well-regulated to ensure that all of the students in the group are learning for themselves and contributing to group work sufficiently. Groups may be shuffled or have assigned roles within the group to ensure a good division of labor. In **reciprocal learning**, students play the role of the teacher, instructing the class by sharing what they know and asking content questions of their peers. Teachers who practice **continual assessment** can determine if their differentiated instructional methods are effective or if they need to be changed. Assessments can determine what needs to be changed in order for students to participate in effective classroom environments.

Different Educational Levels and Learning Styles

Learning styles of students differ, regardless of whether or not the students have disabilities. When addressing groups of students in inclusion settings, it is important for teachers to organize and implement teaching strategies that address learning at **different educational levels**. Students generally fall into one or more learning modes. Some are visual learners, some are auditory learners, some are kinesthetic or tactile learners, and some learn best using a combination of these approaches. Teachers can address students' educational levels by creating lessons that allow learning to take place visually, auditorily, and kinesthetically. **Visual learners** prefer information that has been visually organized, such as in graphic organizers or diagrams. **Auditory learners** prefer information presented in spoken words. Lessons that target auditory learners provide opportunities for students to engage in conversations and question material. **Kinesthetic learners** prefer a hands-on approach to learning. These learners prefer to try out new tasks and learn as they go. Lessons that include opportunities for these three types of learning to occur can successfully target different educational levels.

Multiple Modality Instruction and Activities

The purpose of multiple modality instruction is to engage students by offering different ways to learn the same material. **Multiple modality teaching** also addresses students' unique learning styles. Learning modalities are generally separated into four categories: **visual** (seeing), **auditory** (hearing), **kinesthetic** (moving), and **tactile** (touch) modalities. This way of teaching targets students who may have deficits in one or more modalities. It is also helpful for students who struggle in one or more of the learning categories. If a student struggles with understanding content that is presented visually, a lesson that includes auditory, kinesthetic, and tactile components may engage learning. Additionally, presenting lesson material and activities in a multimodal approach helps improve student memory and retention by solidifying concepts through multiple means of engagement. This approach is also useful for students with **attention disorders** who may struggle in environments where one mode of teaching is used. The multiple modality approach ensures that activities, such as kinesthetic or tactile activities, keep more than one sense involved with the learning process.

Review Video: Teaching Through Multiple Modalities
Visit mometrix.com/academy and enter code: 100371

Using Visual Supports to Facilitate Instruction and Self-Monitoring Strategies

Many students learn best when provided with instruction and activities that appeal to multiple senses. A **multimodal approach** is especially important for students with developmental disabilities, who may need supports that match their individual ways of learning. **Visual supports** are concrete representations of information used to convey meaning. Teachers can use visual supports to help students with developmental disabilities understand what is being taught and communicated to them. Visual supports can help students with understanding classroom rules, making decisions, communicating with others, staying organized, and reducing frustrations. **Visual schedules** show students visual representations of their daily schedules. This assists with transitions between activities, which can sometimes be difficult for students with disabilities. Visuals can be used to help students share information about themselves or their school days with their peers and parents. Visual supports can also be used with checklists to help facilitate independence. For example, behavior checklists can be used to help students monitor their own behaviors.

Universal Design for Learning

Universal design for learning (UDL) is a flexible approach to learning that keeps students' individual needs in mind. Teachers that utilize **UDL** offer different ways for students to access material and engage in content. This approach is helpful for many students but particularly those with learning and attention issues. The **principles of UDL** all center on varying instruction and assessment to appeal to the needs of students who think in various ways.

Principles of the Universal Design for Learning	
Multiple means of *representation*	*Instructional content* should be demonstrated in various ways so that students may learn in a mode that is effective for them.
Multiple means of *expression*	*Assessment* should be administered in a variety of ways to adequately allow students to demonstrate their knowledge. This includes quizzes, homework, presentations, classwork, etc.
Multiple means of *engagement*	Instruction should include a variety of *motivational factors* that help to interest and challenge students in exciting ways.

Review Video: Universal Design for Learning
Visit mometrix.com/academy and enter code: 523916

Evaluating, Modifying, and Adapting the Classroom Setting Using the UDL

The **universal design for learning (UDL)** is a framework that encourages teachers to design their instruction and assessment in ways that allow **multiple means** for the student to learn and express their knowledge. The UDL model is most successful when the teacher prepares a classroom setting that encourages the success of students with and without disabilities. Knowledge of the **characteristics** of students with different disabilities, as well as the unique **learning needs** of these students, enables the teacher to address these needs in the classroom setting. Setting clear short- and long-term goals for students is one way to meet the UDL standards. A traditional classroom may offer one assignment for all students to complete, but a UDL-compliant classroom may offer **different assignments** or **different ways** for students to complete assignments. UDL-compliant classrooms often offer **flexible workspaces** for students to complete their classwork and may offer quiet spaces for individual work or group tables for group work. UDL-compliant teachers recognize that students access information differently and provide different ways for students to gain **access** to the information, such as through audio text or physical models to work with. The universal design for learning assumes students learn in a variety of ways, even if those ways have not been clearly identified; it follows that all instruction and assessment can be improved by making it more varied and accessible.

Modifying Classroom Curriculum and Materials for UDL

In order for a **universal design for learning (UDL) model classroom** to be successful, the teacher must evaluate, modify, and adapt the **curriculum** and **materials** to best suit the needs of the individual students. UDL contrasts with a one-size-fits-all concept of curriculum planning, where lesson plans are developed and implemented strictly based on how teachers expect students to learn. Instead, a successful UDL model addresses the many **specific needs** of the students. These needs vary depending on the unique abilities each classroom of students presents. UDL-compliant teachers can evaluate the success of lessons by checking for comprehension throughout lessons instead of only upon lesson completion. Evaluation methods used informally can provide a lot of information about whether students are grasping the concepts. Teachers use the results of the evaluations to modify and adapt classroom instruction to meet the needs of the students. Other means for diversifying the materials include using multiple assignment completion options and varied means of accessing the materials, such as both written, digital, and audio forms of a text. These means of instruction can take place simultaneously. For instance, a UDL-compliant teacher may choose to pair audio output and text for all students during a reading assignment in order to target students with listening or comprehension difficulties.

Principles of the Universal Design for Learning Model

The universal design for learning (UDL) model contains three principles that aim to level the playing field for all learners. **Principle I** of the UDL model primarily focuses on what **representation or version** of information is being taught. This principle aims to target an audience of diverse learners. By providing multiple ways for students to approach content, teachers can ensure that the unique needs of all learners in their classrooms are met. **Principle II** examines how people learn. This principle focuses on the concept that students learn best when provided with **multiple ways** to demonstrate what they have learned. In classrooms compliant with Principle II, students are given more than one option for expressing themselves. **Principle III** focuses on providing multiple ways for students to engage in the learning process. Teachers compliant with Principle III provide options for keeping content **interesting and relevant** to all types of learners. Effective UDL-model classrooms provide multiple ways to present content, engage in learning, and express what was learned.

Specially Designed Instruction

Specially designed instruction (**SDI**) in special education refers to specialized teaching given to students in a co-taught inclusion classroom. While a teacher teaches the class, the special education teacher provides specialized instruction in parallel to a student to help clarify the information. This is distinctive from adaptation and modification, as the content and its medium do not change for SDI. While the general education class engages in instruction, a special education teacher provides SDI to meet the specific needs of learners who may not be successful learning in the same ways as their similar-aged peers. The main purpose of SDI is to provide a student with access to the general education setting without substantially changing the content as it is aligned with state standards.

Diagnostic Prescriptive Method

The diagnostic prescriptive approach to teaching is based on the fact that all students are unique learners. The **diagnostic prescriptive approach** examines factors that impede student learning and how to remedy specific issues. A successful approach begins with a **diagnosis** of what students are bringing to the classroom. This can be completed through careful observations and assessments. Once the skill deficits are clear, **prescriptive teaching** can be put into effect. In this process, teachers examine what will help students the most. It may be switching materials, changing to group settings, or recognizing the need for specialized interventions due to disabilities. In order to address multiple needs in the classroom, lesson plans should be **multimodal**. Developing strategies in advance to address students' needs is also a highlight of this method. Another important part of this method is evaluating results to determine what was effective or ineffective for entire classes and individual students.

Guided Learning

Guided learning is practice or instruction completed by the teacher and students together. The goal of **guided learning** is to help students engage in the learning process in order to learn more about how they think and acquire new information. **Guided practice** occurs when the teacher and students complete practice activities together. The advantage of guided practice is that students can learn ways to approach concepts they have just learned. It allows students to understand and ask questions about lesson-related activities before working independently. Guided practice is useful in classrooms for students with and without disabilities because it helps teachers gauge how students learn and what instructional methods work best for them. Additionally, guided practice allows teachers to understand how students are learning the material. It also allows teachers to revisit concepts that are unclear or fine tune any missed lesson objectives.

How Cooperative Learning Works

Cooperative learning is an interpersonal group learning process where students learn concepts by working together in **small groups**. Cooperative learning involves collaboration among small groups to achieve common goals. With **formal cooperative learning**, an instructor oversees the learning of lesson material or completion of assignments for students in these small groups. With **informal cooperative learning**, the instructor supervises group activities by keeping students cognitively active but does not guide instruction or assignments. For example, a teacher might use a class period to show a movie but provide a list of questions for students to complete during the movie. In the special education classroom, cooperative learning is helpful when students need specific skills targeted or remediated. It is also helpful for separating students who are learning different content at different levels. For example, a cooperative learning activity may involve multiple groups of students with differing levels of mathematic abilities. Group work also promotes development of interpersonal skills as students interact with one another.

Intrinsic Motivation

Intrinsic motivation is a person's inner drive to engage in an activity or behavior. Students with special needs often struggle with intrinsic motivation as a skill. This requires special educators and other professionals to promote and teach intrinsic motivation to students. Teachers can **promote intrinsic motivation** by giving students opportunities to demonstrate **achievement**. This can be done by challenging students with intellectual risks and helping them focus on difficult classwork or tasks. Teachers can build upon students' strengths by providing daily opportunities in the classroom for students to demonstrate their **strengths** instead of focusing on their weaknesses. Offering choices throughout the day provides students with ownership of their decision-making and communicates that they have choices in the classroom environment. Teachers should allow students to **fail without criticism** and should promote self-reflection in order to build students' confidence. Teachers should promote self-management and organizational skills like instructing students on how to **break down tasks**.

Promoting Critical Thinking Skills

Critical thinking is a self-directed thinking process that helps people make logical, reasonable judgments. This is an especially challenging skill for students with **developmental disabilities**, who often demonstrate deficits in logical thinking and reasoning abilities. In order to teach these students **critical thinking skills**, the focus should be on encouraging critical thinking across **home and school environments** and providing opportunities for students to practice this type of thinking. Teachers and parents can encourage critical thinking by implementing teaching strategies focused on fostering **creativity** in students. Instead of providing outlines or templates for lesson concepts, students can use their prior knowledge to figure out the boundaries of the lessons independently and explore new concepts. Parents and teachers should not always be quick to jump in and help students who are struggling. Sometimes the best way to help is by facilitating ways for students to solve problems without doing things for them. Opportunities for brainstorming, classifying and categorizing information, comparing and contrasting information, and making connections between topics are teaching strategies that also facilitate critical thinking skills.

Career-Based Education

During their schooling years, students with disabilities have the additional challenge of determining possible **career options** for life after high school. Fortunately, instruction can be provided during the school day or within after-school programs that address career-based skills. Effective **career-based programs** for students with disabilities should work collaboratively with community and school resources. Students should receive information on career options, be exposed to a range of experiences, and learn how to self-advocate. Information regarding career options can be gathered via **career assessments** that explore students' possible career interests. Students should receive exposure to **postsecondary education** to determine if it is an option that aligns with their career interests. They should also learn about basic job requirements, such as entry requirements for different types of jobs and what it means to earn a living wage. Students should be given opportunities for job training, job shadowing, and community service. It is helpful to provide students with opportunities to learn and practice **work and occupational skills** that pertain to specific job interests. Students need to learn **self-advocacy skills**, such as communicating the implications of their disabilities to employers, in order to maintain success in postsecondary work environments.

Learning Across the Curriculum

Teaching Multiple Subjects in Special Education Settings

Special education classrooms, whether inclusive, self-contained, or resource room settings, often need to deliver instruction in **multiple subject areas**. Students in these settings also represent many **levels of learning**. Therefore, one instructional strategy is not always the most effective way to teach students in these settings. In order to provide quality instruction, special educators can place students with similar skill levels into **small groups** during instruction in the content areas. This way, small groups of students can be working on skills that cater to their specific needs. **Classroom centers** are another way to group students. Classroom centers often feature self-guided instruction in skill or content areas where students can work at their own pace. **Rotating centers** allows teachers to instruct groups of students while the other groups work independently on previously learned skills. **Thematic instruction** is a teaching strategy where multiple subject areas are connected and taught within one lesson unit. Themes are effective in special education classrooms because they tie multiple content areas together. Special educators should also provide **multiple levels** of materials and books for student learning to target different learning levels.

Developmentally Appropriate Math Skills for Young Children

Starting in pre-kindergarten and first grade, children should be able to count to 100, learn how to write numbers, and demonstrate basic addition and subtraction skills. Older students can demonstrate skills associated with counting money and telling time, and they can also understand decimal, place value, and word problem concepts. Students with disabilities may or may not develop what are considered to be **developmentally appropriate mathematics skills** by certain ages or grades. In inclusive special education settings, the needs of these students can be addressed with a number of strategies. **Scaffolding** is the process of breaking down concepts into chunks. Scaffolding addresses the issues that arise when some students are well behind others by allowing students to work at their own pace and helping them connect prior knowledge to new information. This ensures that students have solidified knowledge of concepts before moving on to new concepts.

Teaching Mathematics

Students whose disabilities affect their performances in mathematics require specialized instruction. Eligible students will have Individualized Education Program goals to address their specific needs but are also expected to learn content connected to **state standards**. Additionally, **accommodations and modifications** are available for qualifying students to assist with mathematics instruction. Strategies that can be effective for math instruction for students with disabilities include:

- Using the same instructional strategies in all settings, including the home environment and all school environments
- Using concrete objects to teach math concepts, such as using manipulatives to count out number values
- Providing assistive materials, such as calculators and scrap paper
- Explaining and modeling objectives clearly
- Allowing time for students to check their work
- Activating prior knowledge to assist students with learning new concepts
- Providing opportunities for extra tutoring or one-on-one instruction
- Assisting students with self-monitoring their progress
- Encouraging math games to engage learning and interest in math concepts

Implications of a Mathematics Disability

Disabilities like **dyscalculia** are specific learning disabilities associated with mathematics. Students that have specific learning disabilities in mathematics have trouble with number-related concepts and using symbols or functions. Symptoms of **math disorders** include difficulties with counting numbers, solving math word problems, sequencing events or information, recognizing patterns when adding, subtracting, multiplying or dividing, and understanding concepts associated with time, like days, weeks, seasons, etc. Recalling math facts is also difficult for students with math disabilities. The severity of the disability is impacted when it **coexists** with dyslexia, attention-deficit/hyperactivity disorder, anxiety, or other disabilities. Special educators, math tutors, or other professionals can help students with math deficits by providing multimodal instruction to engage multiple senses and enhance the chances of the students learning the concepts. They may also receive supports according to 504 Plans or Individualized Education Programs that level the educational playing field, such as use of a calculator. Use of concrete examples, visual aids, graph paper, or scratch paper can also assist students with math disabilities.

Components of Direct Reading Instruction

The purpose of direct learning instruction is to specifically target the needs of students with learning disabilities. **Direct learning instruction** can be provided in many educational settings. Direct instruction breaks concept learning into specific tasks and processes, with focus on mastering one skill before moving onto another skill. With **direct reading instruction**, the key components are teaching phonemic awareness, phonics, fluency, vocabulary development, and comprehension. Effective reading programs address all five areas of reading instruction. **Phonemic awareness** focuses on breaking words into sound units (phonemes). **Phonics** focuses on connecting these sound units with letters (graphemes). Phonics instruction allows students to approach decoding by sounding words out instead of attempting to read the whole words. **Fluency** instruction focuses on teaching students to read unfamiliar words and texts quickly and accurately. **Vocabulary development** helps increase familiarity with frequently occurring words in texts. **Comprehension** instruction focuses on helping students to understand what they have read. In comprehension instruction, learners connect prior knowledge to the texts.

Benefits of the Direct Reading Process

Direct reading instruction is an approach to teaching reading which focuses on specific skill development for early readers. Students frequently enter their schooling years with deficits in reading skills, especially when they are identified as having disabilities. Effective **direct reading programs** include the teaching of phonemic awareness, phonics, fluency, vocabulary development, and comprehension. Teachers are generally trained to implement direct reading programs instead of creating direct instruction curriculum. Specific programs ensure that teachers use the same curriculum and methods in order to effectively implement direct reading instruction. Direct reading instruction and programs are especially helpful for **skill remediation** for at-risk students. Efficient direct reading instruction communicates high standards for learning, is replicable or able to be implemented across a variety of settings, and offers support materials, professional development, and implementation guidance. Direct reading instruction is also proven to be effective for the improvement of reading abilities in at-risk students.

Teaching Comprehension with Research-Based Reading Intervention Strategies

Comprehension refers to a person's understanding of something. As it pertains to reading, **comprehension** is the understanding of content that has been read. Students with disabilities often struggle with comprehension, which makes teaching comprehension strategies essential to their learning. Special educators should teach students to **monitor** their comprehension by being aware of what they have read, identifying what they do not understand, and implementing problem-solving strategies to address what they do not understand. Special educators can also teach students to demonstrate **metacognitive strategies**, such as identifying specifically what they do not understand in texts (e.g., identifying the page numbers or chapters where they are struggling), looking back through the texts to find answers to comprehension questions, rereading sentences or sections they do not understand, and putting sentences they do not understand into their own words. **Graphic organizers**, like story maps and Venn diagrams, also allow students to map out the information they have read by laying out important concepts.

Helping Students with Disabilities Become Solid Emergent Readers

Emergent reading refers to the reading and writing abilities of young readers. They precede **conventional literacy**, which refers to older children's reading and writing behaviors, such as decoding, reading comprehension, oral reading fluency, spelling, and writing. Children with learning disabilities may demonstrate discrepancies between emergent literacy behaviors and conventional literacy behaviors. They may flip-flop between the two stages, showing progress one moment or day and then seeming to forget the next. Educators can foster skills in emergent and conventional reading by teaching **phonological awareness** and **written letter/sound recognition**. These are both baseline skills that affect students' future phonological awareness development. Additionally, educators can provide engaging, age-appropriate activities that facilitate connections between emergent literacy and conventional literacy skills. Activities that promote students' print awareness and knowledge of book conventions also help build solid emergent reader skills.

Modifying the Stages of Writing to Assist Students with Learning Disabilities

The **writing process** can be challenging for new learners but especially for students with disabilities. The writing process can be facilitated by special educators and general educators in order to build adequate writing skills. Teachers must first address the needs of their classes before engaging in the pre-writing stage. Getting to know students provides insight into their prior knowledge and abilities. In the **pre-writing (brainstorming) stage**, teachers help students prepare for the writing process by establishing good content or thinking of things that interest them to write about. In the **writing stage**, students should be taught to write their content using graphic organizers or diagrams that assist with using appropriate formatting, grammar, and punctuation. The **rewriting/revising stage** can be facilitated by providing checklists of errors and having students self-check and revise their own work. In the **editing/proofreading stage**, students can self-check their work or exchange their final written projects with other students or their teachers. This can also be facilitated using formatting checklists and/or grammar and punctuation checklists to monitor the writing process.

Teaching Social Studies

Depending on their special education classroom placements, students with **disabilities** receive varying degrees of instruction in other core content areas like social studies and science. Students with mild disabilities, such as learning disabilities, likely participate in inclusive classroom settings or general education classroom settings. Depending on a student's grade level, the student may attend a classroom setting with one or two teachers or switch classes and attend settings with many different teachers. Across all settings, students with mild disabilities receive any **accommodations or modifications** explicitly written in their Individualized Education Programs. Students with mild to moderate disabilities may receive instruction in special education classrooms for part or most of the day. In these instances, general education social studies or science classes may not be the most appropriate educational settings. Special educators then teach the content in the special education classrooms, sometimes connecting it with related tasks or skills. Students with moderate disabilities may receive **indirect instruction** in these content areas that is loosely based on content standards and more appropriate for the ways they acquire knowledge.

Special Education Settings

Least Restrictive Environment

The Individuals with Disabilities Education Act (IDEA) requires a free and appropriate public education to be provided in a student's **least restrictive environment (LRE)**. This means that a student with a disability who qualifies for special education should be educated in a free, appropriate, and public setting and be placed in an instructional setting that meets the LRE principle. IDEA states that LRE means students with disabilities should participate in the general education classroom "to the maximum extent appropriate." **Mainstreaming** and **inclusion** are ways for students with disabilities to participate in general education classrooms while receiving appropriate accommodations, modifications, interventions, and related services. The amount of time students spend in an LRE suitable for their individual needs is stated in their Individualized Education Program (IEP). The accommodations, modifications, interventions, and related services the student should receive are also outlined in the IEP. Students who need special education services for more than 50% of the day may be placed in other instructional settings that meet their LRE needs, such as resource rooms or self-contained classrooms.

Review Video: Least Restrictive Environment
Visit mometrix.com/academy and enter code: 100354

Continuum of Special Education Services

IDEA mandates that school systems educate students with disabilities with students who do not have disabilities to the maximum extent that is appropriate. IDEA also mandates that schools not take students out of regular education classes unless the classes are not benefiting the students. Supplementary aids and support services must be in place before students can be considered for removal. Schools must offer a **continuum of special education services** that range from restrictive to least restrictive. In a typical continuum of services, regular education classrooms offer the **least restrictive access** to students with disabilities. Next on the continuum are resource rooms, followed by special classes that target specific deficits. Special schools, homebound services, hospitals, and institutions are the most restrictive education environments. The number of students at each stage of the continuum decreases as restriction increases. Fewer students benefit more from being educated in hospitals or institutions than in resource rooms.

Inclusion Classroom Setting

The principle of least restrictive environment (LRE) is a right guaranteed under IDEA to protect a student from unnecessary restriction or seclusion from the general population. IDEA does not expressly define an LRE for each specific disability, so it is the responsibility of the IEP team of professionals, including the student's parent or legal guardian, to determine the best **LRE setting** possible for an individual student. **Mainstreaming** or **inclusion** is the practice of keeping students with disabilities in the general education setting for the entire school day. The students may receive supports and services like aides, assistive technology, accommodations, and modifications that are appropriate for their individual needs. These supports and services are intended to help students with disabilities gain access to the general education curriculum with the fewest possible barriers. The principle of LRE also sits on a spectrum and allows for variable inclusion or separation throughout parts of the day depending on a student's particular needs. As this is a student right, any more restrictive setting must be **justified by necessity** in students' IEPs and cannot be determined by convenience or financial considerations of the school or staff.

Collaborative Teaching in an Inclusion Classroom

If determined by an IEP, a student with a disability may participate in an **inclusive setting**. In some classrooms, students participate in **co-taught settings**. In this **collaborative teaching environment**, the general educator and special educator work together to meet the goals of the students with disabilities in the regular education classroom. Students in this setting are all taught to the same educational standards. However, accommodations and modifications may be implemented for students with disabilities. In a successful collaborative teaching model, the special educator and general educator may cooperatively implement the accommodations and modifications for these students. A two-teacher setting also gives students more opportunities to receive individualized instruction, work in small groups, or receive one-on-one attention. Collaborative teaching in the co-taught setting can facilitate differentiated instruction, help teachers follow the universal design for learning framework, and provide individualized learning opportunities.

Implementing Modifications and Accommodations in an Inclusion Classroom

General educators can work with special educators to create an effective **co-teaching model**. In an effective co-teaching model, both general educators and special educators are guided by the **universal design for learning framework**. This helps ensure that the needs of the diverse group of learners are being met. Students' IEPs expressly document any required modifications, such as reduced work. In a co-teaching model, student modifications are communicated to the **general educator**. The **special educator** can work with the general educator to provide the modifications in an inclusive classroom setting. Students' IEPs also expressly document any required **accommodations**. These accommodations may or may not be used in an inclusive setting, depending on the relevancy of the accommodation. For example, the accommodation of using a calculator would be utilized in a math class but not a social studies class. In addition to expressly written accommodations, special educators and general educators can work together in an inclusive setting to provide appropriate accommodations during the learning process. These accommodations may be part of informal assessments used to adjust instruction.

Role of Paraeducators

Paraeducators, sometimes referred to as aides or paraprofessionals, are part of students' education teams. **Paraeducators** work under the supervision of special educators or principals and are key contributors to the learning process for certain students. Their primary role, especially if their positions are funded by the Individuals with Disabilities Education Act, is to provide **educational support** for students. The use of paraeducators is noted in students' IEPs. Paraeducators can facilitate the learning process for students by removing learning barriers, keeping track of goal progress, and organizing goal-tracking activities. Paraeducators cannot introduce new concepts or take over the role of teachers. Paraeducators cannot make changes to what students are learning unless specific modifications are listed in students' IEPs. They cannot provide accommodations unless the accommodations are appropriate for what is written in students' IEPs. Paraeducators may also be instructed by supervising teachers or principals to facilitate and monitor accommodations or modifications for students and reinforce learned concepts.

Self-Contained Classroom Setting

According to the Individuals with Disabilities Education Act, LRE standards require students to spend as much time as possible with their nondisabled peers in the **general education setting**. This means students should receive general education "to the maximum extent appropriate," and special classes, special schools, or removal from the general education classroom should only be considered when students' needs are greater than what can be provided by supplementary aids and services. A **self-contained classroom setting** can be a separate class within a school or a separate school for students with disabilities whose needs are greater than what can be offered in the general education classroom even with educational supports. These settings may provide specialized instruction and support for students with similar needs. Placement in self-contained classrooms must be justified in students' IEPs.

PARTIAL MAINSTREAM/INCLUSION CLASSROOM SETTING

It is generally up to the IEP team of professionals and the parent or legal guardian to determine the LRE that best suits the needs of a student. In a partial mainstream/inclusion classroom setting, a student spends part of the day in the general education classroom and part of the day in a separate, special education classroom. This type of LRE is appropriate when a student's needs are greater than what can be provided in the general education classroom even with educational supports or services in place. For example, a student with severe deficits in mathematical skills may receive math instruction in a separate classroom or receive one-on-one or small group instruction. Placement in partial mainstream/inclusion classrooms must be justified in students' IEPs.

SPECIALIZED EDUCATION SETTINGS

School districts sometimes offer specialized education settings for students with disabilities, such as **special preschools**. Preschools for children with disabilities typically focus on children aged 3–5 years. They are important resources for teaching early learning, communication, and social skills that are essential for children with disabilities. In **life skills settings**, students with disabilities can receive specialized instruction in academic, social, behavioral, and daily-living skills. **Social behavior skills settings** are sometimes called "applied behavior skills settings" or "behavior skills settings." In this setting, the primary focus is on social and decision-making skills. **Transition settings** are available for students making the transition from high school to life after high school. Students with IEPs can stay in high school until the age of 21 or 22, depending on the calendar month they turn 22. Transition settings assist students with work experiences, postsecondary education experiences, and independent living skills.

Behavioral Issues for Students with Disabilities

BEHAVIORAL ISSUES AND INTERVENTION STRATEGIES

Behavior issues occur with students with and without disabilities. However, they may occur more frequently or to a higher degree for some students with disabilities. Behavior issues are often a **manifestation** of a child's disability. For example, students with attention-deficit/hyperactivity disorder may present with attention and focus issues and impulsivity. **Common behavior issues** include the following:

- Emotional outbursts
- Inattention and inability to focus
- Impulsivity
- Aggression
- Abusive language
- Oppositional defiance
- Lying or stealing
- Threatening adults or peers

Other behavior issues may include inappropriate sexual behavior, inability to control sexual behavior, self-harm, or self-harm attempts. Behavior issues can be **avoided** or **remediated** with classroom management skills like setting clear and consistent classroom goals, setting time limits, and providing visuals to assist with transitions or concepts. When a student is in an aggressive state, it is important for the teacher to remain calm, provide choices for the student, and restate the consequences of any aggressive outbursts.

Review Video: Student Behavior Management Approaches
Visit mometrix.com/academy and enter code: 843846

Review Video: Promoting Appropriate Behavior
Visit mometrix.com/academy and enter code: 321015

Managing Students with Emotional Disorders

Managing a classroom of students with emotional disorders can be challenging and unpredictable. Students with emotional disorders have Individualized Education Program (IEP) goals that focus on **controlling** or **monitoring** their daily behavior choices. However, this does not always mean they will engage in meeting these goals. It is important for educators to know how to **manage** issues that students with emotional disorders may bring to the classroom. When creating resources and lesson plans, an educator should do the following:

- Establish a **safety plan**, which includes knowing how to implement a **crisis prevention plan**.
- Maintain an environment that reduces **stimulation** and provides **visual cues** for expected behavior.
- Implement **intervention-based strategies** for managing student behavior.
- Collect and use **data** to identify triggers, track behaviors, and recognize strategies that produce positive outcomes.
- Practice open **communication** about classroom expectations to students, parents, and other teachers.

Special education teachers can be helpful in implementing these guidelines, especially when students with emotional disorders are in inclusive settings.

Supporting Students with Mental Health Issues

Students with disabilities may also have mental health issues. These students may not necessarily be diagnosed with emotional disturbances, as mental health issues can occur concurrently with other disabilities. Students' mental health symptoms may fluctuate on an hourly, daily, or weekly basis. Intervention techniques and supports must be determined by the individual needs of each student. General and special educators across all special education settings can **support** these students by learning how to **recognize mental health issues** in schools. Teachers can use observations and research-based strategies for identifying issues. Training in working with students who have certain mental health disorders may also be useful. Occasionally, training in crisis prevention plans is required of teachers working with students who may become aggressive due to their disorders.

Behavior Assessment and Intervention

Cognitive Behavioral Theory

The cognitive behavioral theory states that people form their own negative or positive concepts that affect their behaviors. The cognitive behavioral theory involves a **cognitive triad** of thoughts and behaviors. This triad refers to thoughts about the **self**, the **world and environment**, and the **future**. In times of stress, people's thoughts can become distressed or dysfunctional. Sometimes cognitive behavioral therapy, based on the cognitive behavioral theory model, is used to help people address and manage their thoughts. This process involves people examining their thoughts more closely in order to bring them back to more realistic, grounded ways of thinking. People's thoughts and perceptions can often affect their lives negatively and lead to unhealthy emotions and behaviors. **Cognitive behavioral therapy** helps people to adjust their thinking, learn ways to access healthy thoughts, and learn healthier or safer behaviors.

Antecedents, Behavior, and Consequences as Stimuli Used in Behavior Analysis

Antecedents and consequences play a role in behavioral analysis, which is important for evaluating the behaviors of students. The purpose of behavior analysis is to gather information about a specific behavior demonstrated by a student. **Antecedents** are the actions or events that occur before the behavior occurs. It is important to recognize antecedents for behaviors to better understand under what circumstances the behavior is occurring. The **behavior** is the undesirable action that occurs as a result of the antecedent. **Consequences** are what happens immediately after the behavior occurs. These can be natural or enforced. A student might desire a certain consequence when engaging in the behavior. Understanding the relationships between antecedents, behavior, and consequences allows a professional to determine how to minimize or eliminate the behavior. In some circumstances, antecedents and consequences can be manipulated, changed, or removed in order to avoid reinforcing the undesired behavior.

Behavior Rating Scale Assessments

Behavior rating scales address the needs of students with emotional disorders who are referred to special education. Problems with behavior are often the reason a student has been referred for special education. These scales are used in determining a student's **eligibility** for special education, and in addressing **undesirable behaviors** demonstrated by students already in special education for reasons other than behavior problems. They are similar to adaptive behavior scales in that teachers or other professionals can administer the scales with little training as long as they are familiar with the students. Behavior rating scales help measure the frequency and intensity of the behaviors for a particular student often by assigning numbered ratings. They serve as a starting point for learning more about a student's behavior so that behavior interventions and management can take place. These scales are **norm-referenced**, so the outcomes of the behavior rating scales are compared to the behaviors of others.

Negative and Positive Reinforcement Related to Applied Behavior Analysis

Part of applied behavior analysis (**ABA**) is applying negative and positive reinforcement strategies, which are forms of conditioning strategies. In behavioral conditioning, the term **reinforcement** refers to trying to increase the frequency of a desired behavior, whereas the term **punishment** refers to trying to decrease the frequency of an undesired behavior. Similarly, when discussing behavioral conditioning methods, the word **positive** refers to the *addition* of a stimulus, whereas the word **negative** refers to the *removal* of a stimulus. These four terms tend to be confused but are very specifically used to denote particular types of behavioral conditioning.

Positive reinforcement works by providing a desired **reward** for a desired behavior. For example, parents may give a child an allowance (the positive reinforcement) for doing chores (the behavior). In contrast, **negative reinforcement** removes an aversive stimulus to encourage a desired behavior. An example of this might be that a parent rewards a child's behavior by taking away some of his chores. Negative reinforcement is different from a punishment because the goal of punishment is to *discourage* an unwanted behavior while the goal of negative reinforcement is to *encourage* a desirable behavior. Although it is not commonly discussed, positive and negative stimuli may be used at the same time in conditioning to effect a greater change.

Term:	Example:
Positive Reinforcement	A teacher *gives* the high-scorers on a test a sticker.
Negative Reinforcement	A teacher *takes away* an assignment if the class performs well on a test.
Positive Punishment	A police officer *gives* a driver a speeding ticket.
Negative Punishment	A parent grounds a student, *taking away* video games for two weeks.
Combination Reinforcement	A physical education teacher *replaces* a workout (negative) with a game (positive) because the class was well-behaved.
Combination Punishment	A student gets low grades and is required to complete extra schoolwork (positive) and is not allowed to participate in sports for a week (negative).

Developing Positive Behavioral Interventions and Supports

Positive behavioral intervention and support (**PBIS**) plans can be implemented in classrooms or schoolwide to encourage specific, positive outcomes in groups of students with and without disabilities. A PBIS plan, such as an anti-bullying campaign, is put in place to encourage **good behavior** and **school safety** and to remove **environmental triggers** of undesirable behavior. The goal of a PBIS plan is for students to learn appropriate behavior just as they would learn an academic subject. Effective PBIS plans are based on research and analysis of data collected on targeted, large-scale behaviors. As with any behavioral plan, the success of PBIS plans is determined by monitoring student progress. PBIS plans should change if they do not work or if they stop working.

Developing a Functional Behavior Assessment

A functional behavior assessment (**FBA**) is a formal process used to examine student behavior. The goal of an FBA is to identify what is causing a specific behavior and evaluate how the behavior is affecting the student's educational performance. Once these factors are determined, the FBA is useful in implementing **interventions** for the behavior. When an FBA is developed, a student's behavior must be specifically defined; then the teacher or other professional devises a plan for collecting data on the behavior. These points of data are helpful in determining possible causes of the behavior, such as environmental triggers. The teacher or other professional can then implement the most appropriate plan for addressing the student's behavior. Often, this means implementing a **behavior intervention plan**, which includes introducing the student to actions or processes that are incompatible with the problem behavior. It is important to monitor the plan to ensure its effectiveness or remediate certain steps.

Review Video: Functional Behavior Assessments
Visit mometrix.com/academy and enter code: 783262

Developing Behavior Intervention Plans

A behavior intervention plan (**BIP**) is based on a functional behavior assessment. The purpose of the BIP is to teach the student actions, behaviors, or processes that are incompatible with the problem behavior. The BIP may be included in an Individualized Education Program (IEP) or 504 Plan, or components of the BIP may be written out as IEP goals. Once an FBA is conducted, a BIP is put in place that describes the target behavior, lists factors that trigger the behavior, and lists any interventions that help the student avoid the behavior. The interventions include problem-solving skills for the student to use instead of demonstrating the target behavior. If the interventions fail to target the problem behavior or are no longer effective for targeting the behavior, then the FBA must be revisited and a new BIP developed.

Positive Classroom Discipline Strategies

A core element of effective classroom management, positive classroom discipline is a means of holding students accountable for their actions, and it starts with establishing clear and consistent **consequences** for poor choices. Students learn to predict consequences and self-correct their behaviors. It is helpful to give students **reminders** about behavior and rules instead of immediately resorting to consequences. **Pre-reminders** about expectations can be given before starting a lesson. **Nonverbal reminders** such as looks, touches, silence, or removal are possible ways to discourage students from engaging in poor choices. Removal as a consequence involves sending the student out of the classroom either to protect the other students from harm or to prevent a student from impeding the course of instruction. Removal laws vary between states and local districts, but removal is generally mandatory whenever a student is being violent. **Spoken reminders** can be used to further encourage self-management skills and should be used as precursors for reminding students about expectations instead of delivering immediate consequences.

Promoting Appropriate Behavior in Inclusive Learning Environments

Effective classrooms have good management strategies in place that promote good learning environments and minimize disruptions. Teachers with effective classroom management strategies demonstrate good leadership and organization skills. They also promote positive classroom experiences, establish clear expectations for behavior, and reinforce positive behaviors. In **inclusive learning environments**, it is important for teachers to keep all students on track with their learning. When it comes to students with disabilities, planning classroom management strategies presents different challenges. Effective teachers understand how students' special needs come into play with expected classroom behaviors. General and special educators can demonstrate effective classroom management strategies by figuring out what is causing students to act out or misbehave. They should collaborate with other professionals and students' parents to ensure the success of students with special needs in their classrooms. Lastly, effective classroom management includes setting goals for inclusive classrooms to achieve. Clear goals help establish good rapport with students with special needs because they know what is expected of them.

Crisis Prevention and Management

Crises and Crisis Prevention and Management Plans

Crises

A **crisis** is generally defined as a situation that is so emotionally impactful that an individual is not able to cope with the situation by normal means and is at risk of harming themselves or others. Crises can arise from either developmental changes that happen throughout life, such as going through puberty or graduating from school, or they can be situational and arise at any time. Examples of situational crises include sickness, losses, family deaths, and any other kind of unpredictable situation that comes up throughout life. Students with disabilities often have particular difficulty coping with stressful life situations and may need the help of a **crisis prevention plan** as a result. Crisis prevention and management goals generally focus on coping mechanisms and healthy anticipation of unavoidable situations to help the individual understand and safely navigate their way through a crisis.

Crisis Prevention Plans

Crisis prevention plans essentially serve to help with early identification of a crisis and to provide the necessary support to help the individual through a crisis to an effective resolution. These plans are often put together with the help of various members of an individual's support team, taking into account past behaviors, health, and other factors of his or her life. Some organizations, such as the Crisis Prevention Institute, specialize in crisis prevention and intervention training for professionals. Crisis prevention plans should take into account principles of least restrictive environment to support individuals in their normal environments, while also removing or being aware of any known **behavioral triggers** that may be problematic. In the event that the individual in crisis becomes physically violent or harmful to themselves, stronger emergent response may be warranted. The ultimate goal is to keep the individual and others safe until his or her emotional state has been normalized. There is no specific duration of time for a crisis, but any intervention should be treated as short-term to prevent restricting the individual's rights through unnecessary intervention. It is important to provide the individual with clear structures and expectations to help understand direct consequences for undesired choices prior to entering a crisis. Crisis prevention plans should also provide clear processes that professionals and family members can use when students do enter a crisis in order to de-escalate the situations.

Review Video: Crisis Management and Prevention
Visit mometrix.com/academy and enter code: 351872

Chapter Quiz

Ready to see how well you retained what you just read? Scan the QR code to go directly to the chapter quiz interface for this study guide. If you're using a computer, simply visit the online resources page at **mometrix.com/resources719/iltslbsi290** and click the Chapter Quizzes link.

Working in a Collaborative Learning Community

Transform passive reading into active learning! After immersing yourself in this chapter, put your comprehension to the test by taking a quiz. The insights you gained will stay with you longer this way. Scan the QR code to go directly to the chapter quiz interface for this study guide. If you're using a computer, simply visit the online resources page at **mometrix.com/resources719/iltslbsi290** and click the Chapter Quizzes link.

Collaborating with IEP Team Members

It is important for Individualized Education Program (IEP) team members to **collaborate** with each other in order to ensure that students are receiving educational plans that are suitable to their needs in the least restrictive environments. **IEP team members** include special education teachers, general education teachers, parents or legal guardians, students, school district representatives, and others knowledgeable about the students' performances. Each member brings a valuable piece of information about the students for instructional planning and IEP planning meetings. It is important for special educators to establish good relationships and collaborate with the students and parents or legal guardians in order to gauge the students' strengths and weaknesses. Collaboration is essential between the general and special educators in order to ensure that students' IEP goals and needs are being met in the appropriate settings. Collaboration with district team members or others like school psychologists is helpful for gaining insight on special education procedures or assessment results.

Review Video: Collaborating with Other Professionals
Visit mometrix.com/academy and enter code: 100351

Communicating with Service Members Across All Special Education Settings

In order to provide the best educations possible for students with disabilities, it is important for special educators and related service members to **communicate** effectively. Communication is important due to the degree of collaboration required between the special educators and the related service members. Related service members are often IEP team members and help students meet their IEP goals and objectives. **Related service members**, like speech pathologists and occupational therapists, also work on a consultation basis with special educators. They may also consult with general education teachers to ensure that students receive required related services in the general education or inclusive classroom settings. Special educators and related service members must collaborate in order to ensure the needs of the students are met, especially when IEP goals or objectives are out of the scope of the special educators' knowledge bases. For example, a speech pathologist might help a teacher address a student's fluency goal.

Communicating with Parents of Students with Disabilities

It is good practice to communicate with parents outside of progress reporting times and Individualized Education Program meetings. This is especially important for students with **communication deficits** who may not be able to communicate with their parents or legal guardians. Communication also helps prevent potential crises or problem behaviors and alerts parents or legal guardians before any major issues arise. Special educators should find methods of communication that work best for parents or legal guardians, such as phone calls, emails, or writing in daily communication logs. Email is beneficial for creating paper trails, especially for any discussions about educating students. However, email lacks tone and body language and can sometimes be misunderstood. Phone calls fulfill an immediate need to speak with a parent or legal guardian. However, there are no paper trails with phone calls, and they can also lead to misunderstanding. Phone calls may be time consuming, but they can be conducted on special occasions or when behavioral issues need to be discussed. Written communication logs are useful for writing brief summaries about students' days. With any mode of communication, it is essential to **document** what is communicated between the parents or legal guardians and the educators.

The Roles and Rights Families have in the Education of Children with Disabilities

Under the Individuals with Disabilities Education Act, parents and legal guardians of children with disabilities have **procedural safeguards** that protect their rights. The safeguards also provide parents and legal guardians with the means to resolve any disputes with school systems. **Parents and legal guardians** may underestimate their importance to IEP teams. However, they are important members of IEP teams and integral parts of the decision-making processes for their children's educational journeys. Parents and legal guardians often work more closely with their children than other adults. Therefore, as part of IEP teams, they serve as **advocates** and can often provide insight regarding the children's backgrounds, educational and developmental histories, strengths, and weaknesses. Parents and legal guardians are also important decision-makers in transition meetings, when students with disabilities move from one level of school to another. Their input in transition meetings helps ensure that appropriate services and supports are in place at the next levels of school so that students can succeed.

Roles of Parents/Legal Guardians and the School District During Evaluation

If parents or legal guardians suspect their children have disabilities, they can request that the school districts **evaluate** the children for special education. A parent or legal guardian can send a **written evaluation request** to the child's school, principal, and the school district's director or director of special education services. In some states, parents and legal guardians may be required to sign a school district form requesting the evaluation. Parents should follow up on the request and/or set a time frame for the school district to respond. The school district may choose to implement the **Response to Intervention (RTI) pre-referral process**. RTI is a process by which the school gives the student special academic support before determining whether or not to move forward with the evaluation process. Not all states or school districts have the same method for applying RTI. Under the Individuals with Disabilities Education Act, the time frame for completion of RTI is 60 days. However, some states can set their own timelines. RTI should not be the only means by which the school district collects data on the student and should be part of a comprehensive evaluation conducted by the student's school.

Speech Language Pathologist

Speech language pathologists (**SLPs**) provide interventions for children with communication disorders. They can assist, evaluate, prevent, and diagnose a variety of **speech issues**, from fluency to voice disorders. Before children reach grade school age, it is important that they receive early interventions for suspected communication disorders. SLPs are helpful with targeting speech or language issues, identifying at-risk students, or providing interventions for children and adults. SLPs also play a role in helping children develop good reading and writing skills, especially when deficits are evident. SLPs work collaboratively with special educators to deliver **interventions** to children with speech and language disorders in grade school. In schools, SLPs play a role in prevention, assessment, intervention, program design, data collection and analysis, and Individualized Education Program compliance. SLPs work with special educators, parents, students, reading specialists, occupational therapists, school psychologists, and others in order to provide effective services to students who require them.

Occupational Therapist

Students with special needs may need **occupational therapy services**. The number of services students receive is defined on their IEPs. **Occupational therapists (OTs)** may help students on IEPs refine their fine motor skills, improve sensory processing deficits, improve visual skills, and improve self-care skills. OTs can also assist with behavior management, social skills, and improving attention and focus. When a student is identified as possibly needing occupational therapy, the OT spends time observing the student in a variety of settings where the skill or skill deficit will be demonstrated. Prior to the student's IEP meeting, the OT typically meets with the student's teachers, parents, and other professionals in order to discuss observations, assessment results, and determinations. **Determinations** are then put into the IEP and implemented as related services. Fine motor skill instruction begins with the OT instructing the student on a particular skill. OTs can set up regimens for teachers and parents to generalize using the fine motor skills in the classroom and home environments.

Paraprofessional

The US Department of Education requires paraprofessionals to have high school diplomas or the equivalent under Title I law. Paraprofessionals (paras), sometimes called **paraeducators**, assist classroom teachers with classroom activities and help students with special needs. In a special education setting, a para works with a certified teacher to help deliver **instruction** and help students meet **Individualized Education Program goals and objectives**. Paras are not responsible for teaching new skills or introducing new goals and objectives to students. In this respect, special educators generally work alongside the paras and students to introduce new skills, goals, or objectives. At times, paras may be responsible for helping students maintain behavior plans, working with students who may be aggressive or violent, and providing physical assistance if necessary. Training is usually provided by the school district for situations when physical assistance is a possible necessity. Paras can also help take notes on students' progress toward meeting their goals or objectives. They can also discuss how students are progressing with behavior plans.

Learning Environments for Students with Disabilities

Determining the Special Education Setting Placement

Special education setting placement is determined in a student's Individualized Education Program (IEP), as specified by the Individuals with Disabilities Education Act (IDEA). IDEA requires that students be placed in **general education classrooms** to the maximum extent possible. Students should be placed in environments that are most appropriate for them, known as the **least restrictive environment**. If students can be educated in general education classrooms (**inclusion**) when provided with appropriate accommodations, they can be placed in general education classrooms. When students with disabilities need modifications to curriculum that are significantly below grade level or different than their peers, the students may be placed in **resource rooms** for remedial instruction. However, the students may also participate in the general education curriculum with modified work that meets their current abilities. For example, a student who struggles in math can use a calculator accommodation in the inclusion setting. A student whose math skills are two grade levels below the skills of same-aged peers may be placed in an inclusion setting with modifications or receive instruction in a resource room.

Full or Partial Inclusion Settings vs. Self-Contained Classrooms

Students with mild to moderate disabilities are often placed in **inclusion** or **partial inclusion classrooms**. The responsibilities of the special educator include assisting and collaborating with the general education teacher to create a curriculum with **modifications** that meets the learning styles and needs of the students with disabilities. The special educator may circulate during lessons or classwork to help students when needed and provide modifications to the general education curriculum to best meet the individual needs of each student.

The role of a special educator in a **self-contained classroom** is much different. Students in a self-contained classroom typically have disabilities that significantly limit their ability to receive quality education in inclusion or partial inclusion settings. Students with moderate disabilities in self-contained classrooms receive **modified instruction** with accommodations. The special educator is usually assisted by teaching assistants or paraprofessionals who help the educator meet the needs of individual students.

Special educators in inclusion, partial inclusion, and self-contained classrooms share some similar **responsibilities**. These responsibilities include monitoring IEP data on annual goals for each student, giving standardized pre-tests and post-tests, facilitating parent-teacher conferences, completing annual IEP reviews, and developing curriculum.

Structured Learning Environments

A structured learning environment is an important component of good **classroom management**. Teachers that create environments that are conducive for teaching and learning create environments where students feel safe. In **effective structured learning environments**, teachers create solid relationships with students by getting to know them and their interests. Often, this information can be used to implement learning activities based on students' interests. Another way to promote effective structured learning environments is to consistently follow implemented rules and maintain **consistency** in procedures in order to communicate what to expect to students. Transitioning students appropriately between activities increases time spent learning. Additionally, teachers create solid environments for their students by spending time designing effective lesson plans that anticipate student behaviors. Teachers can also establish good learning environments by promoting target behaviors. This means promoting standards of behavior and clear consequences for breaking rules. Students that have clear expectations learn in effective structured learning environments.

Non-Traditional Classroom Seating Arrangements

Seating arrangements are part of good classroom management strategies, especially for students with disabilities. Special education settings and inclusion settings often require flexibility with instruction and versatility with **seating arrangements**. The traditional setting includes rows of desks facing the area where the teacher conducts instruction. More **student-centered arrangements** include a horseshoe seating arrangement, a group pod arrangement, or a paired arrangement. A **horseshoe seating arrangement** is conducive to student-centered instruction because it allows the students to face each other and the instructor to move around the classroom easily. This setup facilitates classroom discussions and encourages interactions between instructors and students and among peers. The **group pod** or **paired-pod arrangement** is useful for student-centered instruction like small group work. This arrangement is also helpful when students need to rotate through lesson stages or work in small groups on projects. Effective teachers do not use one seating arrangement for the entire year. Best practices indicate that seating arrangements should change and be tied to the intent of lesson objectives.

Inclusive Learning Environments That Meet Unique Needs

Effective inclusive environments abide by the **universal design for learning (UDL) framework**. Special educators and general educators can work together to create learning environments that are accessible to students with unique language or physical needs. This can be done by providing **multiple ways** for students to access lesson concepts, express learned concepts, and engage in the learning process. For students with language barriers, signs, symbols, pictures, and learning concepts may have different meanings than they do for students without language barriers. Keeping this in mind, teachers can address UDL guidelines for students with **language barriers** by providing diverse ways to activate prior knowledge, emphasizing key learning elements, and using visuals to guide the learning process. For students with **physical barriers**, teachers can level the learning process by making their physical classroom environments accessible and providing different ways for students to express what they have learned. In general, teachers abiding by the UDL framework would have these supports in place in order to ensure that the needs of diverse learners are met.

Positive and Inclusive Learning Environments

Whether in the general education classroom or special education classroom, the UDL model should foster **positive and inclusive learning environments**. General education and special education teachers can take measures to ensure the UDL concept is implemented to address the unique needs of students with **cognitive or behavioral needs**. Since each student presents different needs, a one-size-fits-all approach to learning is not suitable or UDL compliant for these students. Special educators and general educators should openly communicate about students' unique learning or cognitive needs. General strategies include receiving regular **input from special educators** on how to best meet the needs of the students in the classroom. This includes sharing information with any **paraprofessionals and aides** regarding how to assist the students in the general education classroom. UDL-based strategies include the general educators providing multiple means by which students can complete the assignments. Students with cognitive disabilities may also benefit from the use of concrete examples and instruction, especially when addressing abstract concepts.

Learning Environments that Support Students with Behavioral Needs

The **UDL concepts** can be implemented to reduce challenging behavior in the classroom. They can also be used to help students with behavioral needs find success in the general education classroom. **Lack of student engagement** is compatible with the presentation of **challenging behaviors**. When UDL concepts are demonstrated appropriately, engagement can improve. Providing **multiple means of representation** is one UDL strategy for improving engagement and challenging behavior. This means the classroom teacher provides multiple ways of presenting the teaching material in order to engage as many students as possible. Teachers that provide multiple means of representation look to activate prior knowledge and help students make sense of the current content. UDL-compliant strategies also include providing **multiple means of expression**. Teachers applying UDL principles recognize that differentiating activities and assignments addresses a variety of abilities and learning styles. UDL-compliant teachers should also provide **multiple means of engagement**. Successful engagement in learning can often offset challenging behaviors by helping students focus on lesson material. Offering both challenging and simplistic work options and making engaging, solid connections to past and/or future lesson content can minimize the possibility of problems arising in the classroom.

Classroom Strategies Promoting Social-Emotional Development and Growth

Classroom environments should emanate **positivity** and **growth**. Classrooms that promote **social-emotional development and growth** provide security for students and create environments where learning takes place. Teachers can promote social-emotional development and growth by creating predictable classroom routines with visual reminders, keeping classrooms free of dangerous objects and materials, and arranging for learning to take place in large and small groups. They can also rotate activities and materials to keep students engaged, provide appropriate materials for learning centers, and create opportunities for children to engage socially. Teachers can act as nurturing adults by encouraging social interactions and problem solving, modeling appropriate language and social skills, encouraging and validating children's thoughts and feelings, and using clear signals to indicate transitions between activities. Teachers should build community environments in their classrooms, build appropriate relationships with students by getting to know their strengths and weaknesses, and demonstrate good conflict resolution and problem-solving abilities.

Effect of Emotional and Psychological Needs of Students with Disabilities

When a child is diagnosed with a disability, educators often primarily focus on the educational implications. However, students with disabilities also have **emotional needs** associated with their disabilities. These needs vary by student and disability. Generally, students with disabilities struggle emotionally. Symptoms may include low self-esteem, anxiety, acting out, reduced intrinsic motivation, and physical effects, like headaches. Educators, parents, and other professionals can manage the emotional needs of students with disabilities by talking with them about the disability diagnoses and educational implications. Educators can increase their **awareness** of how students might be feeling about the diagnoses and identify situations that may cause anxiety or acting out. Educators can also help by praising students consistently, even for small actions, which can help with confidence. Parents, educators, and other professionals can also work together to ensure that the students receive instruction in the most appropriate educational environments for their disabilities.

Lifting Guidelines for Students Who Require Physical Lifting

Teachers and paraprofessionals may encounter students with physical disabilities who require **assisted transfers**. In some circumstances, students must be **lift-assisted** from their wheelchairs in order to participate in physical therapy or floor activities. While this practice is more common in low-incidence classrooms and not always a job requirement, it is important to know school guidelines for **lifting techniques** to keep staff and students safe. Knowing school guidelines for lifting can also help prevent back injuries from occurring. Physical therapists working with the students should be consulted before attempting student lifts. They are trained professionals who know specific procedures for lifting students in order to keep the students and staff members safe. Every school district has policies for lift-assisted student transfers. Each student should be evaluated to determine if a one-person lift or two-person lift is needed. Two-person lifts are for heavier students, and some school districts do not allow two-person lifts for safety reasons.

Managing Distractions That May Affect Learning and Development

Managing distractions is a part of good teaching practices. Special educators demonstrate good **classroom management strategies** when they do the following:

- Create positive learning environments by getting to know students' individual emotional, intellectual, social, and physical needs.
- Remove or accommodate environmental triggers specific to students.
- Remove or accommodate behavioral triggers.
- Encourage students to help with classroom jobs and small tasks.
- Create lesson plans with anticipated behaviors in mind.
- Attempt verbal de-escalation first when behavioral issues arise.

- Set clear, consistent rules.
- Set and follow through with consequences for breaking the rules.
- Take time to get to know students and their triggers.
- Create seating arrangements that minimize distractions, such as placing distractible students closer to the teacher.
- Teach social, thinking, test-taking, problem-solving, and self-regulation skills alongside academic content.
- Use visual aids in lessons.
- Utilize peer-instruction opportunities.
- Provide opportunities for breaks.
- Incorporate computer-based programs, which can hold the attention of students with disabilities like autism.

Effect of Home Life Factors on Learning and Development

Students' home lives are interconnected with their school lives. **Home life factors**, especially negative ones, are difficult for students to avoid generalizing to the school environment. **Home stressors** can often develop into dysfunction at school. Factors that affect the learning and development of students with disabilities include academic, environmental, intellectual, language, medical, perceptual, and psychological factors. **Academic factors** include developmental delays in core content areas, lack of basic skills, and apparent inconsistency of learning in certain stages of development. **Environmental factors** occur when children are exposed to home life trauma, such as divorce, drug abuse, alcoholism, parental fighting, or family illness. **Intellectual factors** include limited intellectual abilities or unnoticed gifted abilities. **Language factors** include issues with language barriers or language acquisition, such as aphasia, bilingualism, expressive language disorder, and pragmatic language disorder. **Medical factors** include attention-deficit/hyperactivity disorder, muscular problems, and hearing problems. **Perceptual factors** include any factors that affect or slow down students' processing of information. **Psychological factors** include depression, anxiety, and conduct disorders.

Team Teaching Models

Components of a Successful Team-Teaching Model

A successful team-teaching model is one where the teachers involved set clear, effective, specific **goals** for performance. These goals must demonstrate clarity. All team-teaching members must be clear on the components of the goals and their potential outcomes. Clear goals allow team members and students to know what they are working towards as a classroom. Goals should be specific and measurable. **Goal criteria** should be qualified in percentages or quantities. This provides hard evidence for how effectively the team-teaching classroom is meeting the goals. Challenging goals set high expectations for what the team needs to work towards. Challenging goals ensure that team members and classroom students are working to achieve goals right outside their ability levels. Goals that are too challenging can be frustrating for all team members and students. A successful team-teaching model also reflects **commitment** from team members and any other professionals involved in the classroom.

Function of a Multidisciplinary Team-Teaching Model

The three disciplinary team models include a multidisciplinary team, an interdisciplinary team, and a transdisciplinary team. The **multidisciplinary team** is usually composed of the special educator, general education teacher, parents, paraprofessionals, principal, and school psychologist. As a whole, this team presents a comprehensive group of expertise, qualifications, and skills. In the multidisciplinary team model, these professionals do not collaborate but instead work alongside each other to pursue a **common goal** for the individual student with special needs. The multidisciplinary team model is effective for evaluating a student for referral for special education, completing pre-referral testing, and completing an Individualized Education Program or Evaluation Team Report. Sometimes this team is referred to as the child study team or student support team. In this model, professionals usually pull out students to work with them individually. Parents and legal guardians are a part of this process. Professionals working with the student should openly communicate their processes and the results of any evaluations or informal observations.

Interdisciplinary Team Model

An interdisciplinary team model features the **general education teacher** providing all curriculum and accommodations for a student with an Individualized Education Program (IEP). In this model, the special educator and other professionals relevant to the education of the student collaborate to ensure that the curriculum meets the needs of the student and the accommodations are appropriate. This model is not a team-teaching model. Advantages of this model include the collaboration of all IEP team members towards a common goal and the student's needs being addressed by one teacher instead of several different teachers or professionals. The disadvantages of this model include difficulties with collaboration between professionals and issues with delivering related services to students who need them. Related service provision sometimes includes one-on-one instruction, which requires the student to be pulled out for a certain amount of time during general education instruction. This model may also not be appropriate for students with intense needs, as they often require **individualized education** in order to meet IEP goals. They may also require specific accommodations and modifications not suitable for the general education classroom.

Transdisciplinary Team-Teaching Model

In this model, professionals working with the student work together collaboratively to ensure the individual needs of the student are met. The **special educator** may teach in the general education classroom, delivering instruction to both students with and without disabilities. This model features a team-teaching experience for classroom students, where the special educator and general educator may take turns teaching. The presence of the special educator in the general education setting means the special educator can offer advice for **accommodating** the students with special needs in the classroom. Additionally, this model provides opportunities for teachers and other professionals to communicate consistently about students' progress, share ideas, and work collaboratively to solve any issues that arise. The effectiveness of this model relies heavily on the collaboration of the special educator and the general educator in addressing the major features of this team-teaching model.

Advantages and Disadvantages of Team-Teaching Models

Students with and without disabilities present a variety of **learning abilities** in the general education classroom. One advantage of team-teaching models in this setting is being able to target the unique abilities, learning methods, and skills that each student brings to the classroom. Another advantage is effective classroom management. In an **effective team-teaching model**, one teacher provides the instruction, while the other practices classroom management skills to minimize disruptions and promote a safe learning environment. This model encourages class participation, facilitates group activities, and provides multiple means of engagement for learning content. One disadvantage is there may be an offset between the teachers sharing a class. When one teacher is not open to multiple methods of delivering instruction, the team-teaching approach is ineffective. Planning and making group decisions regarding curriculum can be time consuming and stressful in a team-teaching environment.

Chapter Quiz

Ready to see how well you retained what you just read? Scan the QR code to go directly to the chapter quiz interface for this study guide. If you're using a computer, simply visit the online resources page at **mometrix.com/resources719/iltslbsi290** and click the Chapter Quizzes link.

Foundations and Professional Practice

Transform passive reading into active learning! After immersing yourself in this chapter, put your comprehension to the test by taking a quiz. The insights you gained will stay with you longer this way. Scan the QR code to go directly to the chapter quiz interface for this study guide. If you're using a computer, simply visit the online resources page at **mometrix.com/resources719/iltslbsi290** and click the Chapter Quizzes link.

Disability Education Laws

Individuals with Disabilities Education Act

The Individuals with Disabilities Education Act (**IDEA**) includes six major principles that focus on students' rights and the responsibilities public schools have for educating children with **disabilities**. One of the main principles of IDEA is to provide a **free and appropriate public education** suited to the individual needs of a child with a disability. This requires schools to provide special education and related services to students identified as having disabilities. Another purpose of IDEA is to require schools to provide an appropriate **evaluation** of a child with a suspected disability and an **Individualized Education Program (IEP)** for a child with a disability who qualifies under IDEA. Students with IEPs are guaranteed **least restrictive environment**, or a guarantee that they are educated in the general education classroom as much as possible. IDEA also ensures **parent participation**, providing a role for parents as equal participants and decision makers. Lastly, **procedural safeguards** also serve to protect parents' rights to advocate for their children with disabilities.

Review Video: Development of the Individuals with Disabilities Education Act
Visit mometrix.com/academy and enter code: 100350

People Protected by Parts B and C of IDEA

Early intervention services are provided to children with special needs from birth to age three under **IDEA Part C**. Children from birth to age 3 who are identified as having disabilities and qualify under IDEA receive **Individualized Family Service Plans (IFSPs)**.

Special education and related services are provided to children with disabilities from ages 3 to 21 under **IDEA Part B**. Children ages 3 to 21 who are identified as having disabilities and qualify under IDEA receive educational documents **IEPs**.

Individualized Education Programs vs. Individualized Family Service Plans

IFSPs and IEPs are both educational documents provided under the Individuals with Disabilities Education Act to service the rights of children with disabilities and their families. The major differences between IEPs and IFSPs, aside from the ages they service, is that **IFSPs** cover **broader services** for children with disabilities and their families. IFSP services are often provided in the children's homes. **IEPs** focus on special education and related services within the children's **school settings**.

Purpose of IEPs and Function of the PLOPs

An IEP is a written statement for a child with a disability. Its primary purposes are to establish **measurable annual goals** and to list the **services** needed to help the child with a disability meet the annual goals.

The Individuals with Disabilities Education Act mandates that a statement of the child's academic achievement and functional performance be included within the IEP. This statement is called **Present Levels of Performance**. It provides a snapshot of the student's current performance in school. Present Levels of Performance should also report how a student's disability is affecting, or not affecting, progress in school.

IDEA mandates that an **Annual Goals section** be provided within the IEP. Annual goals outline what a student is expected to learn within a 12-month period. These goals are influenced by the student's PLOPs and are developed using objective, measurable data based on the student's previous academic performance.

Review Video: 504 Plans and IEPs
Visit mometrix.com/academy and enter code: 881103

Child Find Law

Child Find is part of the Individuals with Disabilities Education Act and states that schools are legally required to find children who have **disabilities** and need **special education** or other services. According to the **Child Find law**, all school districts must have processes for identifying students who need special education and related services. Children with disabilities from birth to age 21, children who are homeschooled, and children in private schools are all covered by the Child Find law. Infants and toddlers can be identified and provided with services so that parents have the right tools in place to meet their children's needs before they enter grade school. The Child Find law does not mean that public schools need to agree to evaluate students when evaluations are requested. Schools may still refuse evaluation if school professionals do not suspect the children of having disabilities.

Steps to Implementing IEPs

The five most important steps in the IEP process are the identification via "Child Find" or the referral for special education services; evaluation; determination of eligibility; the first IEP meeting at which the IEP is written; and the ongoing provision of services during which progress is measured and reported. The referral can be initiated by a teacher, a special team in the school district, the student's parent, or another professional. The evaluation provides a snapshot of a student's background history, strengths, weaknesses, and academic, behavioral, or social needs. An IEP team of professionals as well as the student's parents/guardians use the evaluation and any other reports regarding a student's progress to determine if the student is eligible for special education services. Once a student has been found eligible for special education, the first IEP meeting is held during which an IEP is written by a special education teacher or other specialist familiar with the student. The IEP meeting, either initial or annual, is held before the new IEP is implemented. Once the IEP meeting has occurred, services will be provided as detailed in the written IEP, during which the student's progress will continually be measured and reported. The IEP team includes the student, parents/guardians, special education teacher, general education teacher, school psychologist, school administrator, appropriate related service professionals, and any other professionals or members that can comment on the student's strengths.

Manifestation Determination

Manifestation determination is a process defined by IDEA. The **manifestation determination process** is put into effect when a student receiving special education needs to be removed from the educational setting due to a suspension, expulsion, or alternative placement. Manifestation determination is the process that determines if the **disciplinary action** resulted from a **manifestation of the student's disability**. This is important because if the action was a manifestation of the disability, the outcome of the disciplinary action may change. During the initial part of this process, relevant data is collected about the student and the circumstances of the offending behavior. The student's Individualized Education Program team determines whether or not the student's behavior was related to the disability. If they determine that the behavior was not related to the disability, the disciplinary action is carried out. If the behavior is determined to be related to the disability, the student is placed back into the original educational setting.

Provision of Title III of the Americans with Disabilities Act

Title III of the Americans with Disabilities Act (ADA) prohibits discrimination against people with disabilities in **public accommodations**. Title III seeks to level the playing field of access for people with disabilities participating in public activities. Businesses open to the public, such as schools, restaurants, movie theaters, day care facilities, recreation facilities, doctor's offices, and restaurants, are required to comply with **ADA standards**. Additionally, commercial facilities, such as privately-owned businesses, factories, warehouses, and office buildings, are required to provide access per ADA standards. Title III of the ADA outlines the general requirements of the **reasonable modifications** that businesses must provide. Title III also provides detailed, specific requirements for reasonable modifications within businesses and requires new construction and building alterations to abide by ADA regulations. Title III also outlines rules regarding **enforcement of ADA regulations**, such as the consequences for a person or persons participating in discrimination of a person with a disability. Title III provides for **certification of state laws or local building codes**. This means that a state's Assistant Attorney General may issue certification to a place of public accommodation or commercial facility that meets or exceeds the minimum requirements of Title III.

Larry P. v. Riles

The *Larry P. v. Riles* (1977) court case examined possible **cultural discrimination** against African-American students. The court case questioned whether an intelligence quotient (IQ) test was an accurate measurement of a student's true intelligence. The case argued that a disproportionate number of African-American students identified as needing special education services; the term at the time was "educable mentally retarded" (EMR) program services. The court plaintiff, Larry P., argued that IQ tests were **biased** against African-American students, which resulted in their placements in limiting educational settings. The defendant, Riles, argued that the prevalence of African-American students in the EMR classes was due to genetics and social and environmental factors. The court ultimately ruled that the IQ tests were discriminatory and resulted in the disproportionate placement of African-American students in the EMR setting. It was determined that these particular assessments were **culturally biased**, and the students' performances would be more accurately measured using adaptive behavior assessments, diagnostic tests, observations, and other assessments.

Diana v. State Board of Education

Diana v. State Board of Education (1970) was a court case involving a student who was placed in special education after results of the Stanford-Binet intelligence test indicated she had a mild case of "mental retardation." This class-action lawsuit was developed on behalf of nine **Mexican-American children**, arguing that IQ scores were not an adequate measurement to determine special education placement. The case argued that Mexican-American children might be at a disadvantage because the IQ tests were written and administered in English. This might possibly constitute **discrimination**. The plaintiffs in the case argued that IQ scores were not a valid measurement because the children might have been unable to comprehend the test written in English. In the conclusive results of this case, the court ordered children to be tested in their primary language, if it was not English. As a result of this case, IQ tests were no longer used as the sole assessments for determining **special education placement**. There was also increased focus on **cultural and linguistic diversity** in students.

Winkelman v. Parma City School district

This court case began as an argument against a **free and appropriate public education** (FAPE) as required by IDEA. The parents of Jacob Winkelman believed their son was not provided with a FAPE in his special education setting in Parma City Schools. The disagreement became about whether or not children can be **represented by their parents** per IDEA in federal court. The U.S Court of Appeals for the Sixth Circuit argued that IDEA protected the rights of the children and not the parents. In the end, the District Court ruled that parents could represent their children within disputes over a free and appropriate public education as constituted by IDEA. Ultimately, this settled the question of whether or not **parents have rights under IDEA**, in addition to their children. The court case determined that parents play a significant role in the education of their children on IEPs and are IEP team members. Therefore, parents are entitled to litigate *pro se* for their children.

Honig v. Doe

Honig v. Doe (1988) was a Supreme Court case examining the violation of the **Education for All Handicapped Children Act** (EAHCA, an earlier version of the Individuals with Disabilities Education Act) by the California School Board. The offense occurred when a child was suspended for a violent behavior outburst that was related to his disability. The court case centered on two plaintiffs. Both were diagnosed with an emotional disturbance and qualified for special education under EAHCA. Following the violent incident, the school suspended the students and recommended them for expulsion. The plaintiff's case argued that the suspension/expulsion went against the **stay-put provision of the EAHCA**, which states that children with disabilities must remain in their current educational placements during review proceedings unless otherwise agreed upon by both parents and educational representatives. The defendant argued that the violence of the situation marked an exception to the law. The court determined that schools are able to justify the placement removal of a student when maintaining a **safe learning environment** outweighs a student's right to a free and appropriate public education.

Pennsylvania Association for Retarded Children v. Commonwealth of Pennsylvania

The Commonwealth of Pennsylvania was accused by the Pennsylvania Association for Retarded Children (PARC 1971), now known as the Arc of Pennsylvania, of denying a **free and appropriate public education** to students with disabilities. The Commonwealth of Pennsylvania was accused of refusing to educate students who had not reached the "mental age of 5." The groups argued before the District Court of the Eastern District of Pennsylvania. This case was significant because PARC was one of the first institutions in the country to challenge the **placement of students with special needs**. The plaintiffs argued that all children should and would benefit from some sort of educational instruction and training. Ultimately, this was the beginning of instituting the state requirement of a free and appropriate public education (**FAPE**) for all children in public education from ages 6–21. The Commonwealth of Pennsylvania was tasked with providing a FAPE and sufficient education and training for all eligible children receiving special education. They could no longer deny students based on their mental ages. This triggered other state institutions to make similar decisions and led to the creation of similar federal policies in the **Education for All Handicapped Children Act** (1974).

1990 Amendments to IDEA

The Individuals with Disabilities Education Act (IDEA) replaced the Education for All Handicapped Children Act in 1990. IDEA amendments changed the **age range** for children to receive special education services to ages 3–21. IDEA also changed the language of the law, changing the focus onto the **individuals with disabilities** rather than the **handicapped children**. Therefore, the focus shifted from the conditions or disabilities to the individual children and their needs. IDEA amendments also **categorized** different disabilities. IDEA 1997 increased the emphasis on IEPs for students with disabilities and increased parents' roles in the educational decision-making processes for their children with disabilities. Part B of the 1997 amendment provided services to children ages 3–5, mandating that their learning needs be outlined in **IEPs** or **Individualized Family Service Plans**. Part C of IDEA provided **financial assistance** to the families of infants and toddlers with disabilities. Part C states that educational agencies must provide **early intervention services** that focus on children's developmental and medical needs, as well as the needs of their families. Part C also gives states the option to provide services to children who are at risk for developmental disabilities.

Disabilities Education Improvement Act of 2004

In 2004, the Individuals with Disabilities Education Act (IDEA) implemented the **Individuals with Disabilities Education Improvement Act**; IDEA was reauthorized to better meet the needs of children in special education programs and children with special needs. As a result of these changes:

- Special educators are required to achieve **Highly Qualified Teacher status** and be **certified in special education**.
- Individualized Education Programs must contain measurable **annual goals** and descriptions of how progress toward the goals will be **measured and reported**.
- Schools or agencies must provide science or research-based **interventions** as part of the evaluation process to determine if children have specific learning disabilities. This may be done in addition to assessments that measure achievement or intelligence.

The changes made to require science or research-based interventions resulted in many districts implementing **Response to Intervention procedures**. These procedures meet IDEA 2004 requirement of providing interventions in addition to achievement reports or intelligence tests on the Individualized Education Programs for children with disabilities.

Development of Educational Laws Like Goals 2000 and No Child Left Behind

President Bill Clinton signed the **National Educational Goals Act**, also known as Goals 2000: Educate America Act, into effect in the 1990s to trigger standardized educational reform. The act focused on **outcomes-based education** and was intended to be completed by the year 2000. The goals of this act included ensuring that children are ready to learn by the time they start school; increasing high school graduation rates; demonstration of competency by students in grades 4, 8, and 12 in core content areas; and positioning the United States as first in the world in mathematics and science achievement. Goals 2000 was withdrawn when President George W. Bush implemented the **No Child Left Behind Act (NCLB)** in 2001. The NCLB also supported standards-based reform, and it mandated that states develop more **skills-based assessments**. The act emphasized state testing, annual academic progress, report cards, and increased teacher qualification standards. It also outlined changes in state funding. The NCLB required schools to meet **Adequate Yearly Progress (AYP)**. AYP was measured by results of achievement tests taken by students in each school district, and consequences were implemented for school districts that missed AYP during consecutive years.

Every Student Succeeds Act of 2015

The NCLB was replaced in 2015 by the Every Student Succeeds Act (**ESSA**). The ESSA built upon the foundations of NCLB and emphasized **equal opportunity** for students. The ESSA currently serves as the main K–12 educational law in the United States. The ESSA affects students in public education, including students with disabilities. The purpose of the ESSA is to ensure a **quality education** for all students. It also aims to address the achievement of **disadvantaged students**, including students living in poverty, minority groups, students receiving special education services, and students with limited English language skills. The ESSA determined that states may decide educational plans as long as they follow the government's framework. The ESSA also allows states to develop their own educational standards and mandates that the curriculum focus on preparing students for postsecondary educations or careers. The act requires students to be tested annually in math and reading during grades 3–8 and once in high school. Students must also be tested in science once in elementary school, middle school, and high school. **School accountability** was also mandated by the ESSA. The act requires states to have plans in place for any schools that are underperforming.

ESL Rights for Students and Parents

As public schools experience an influx of English as a Second Language (ESL) students, knowledge of their **rights** becomes increasingly important. The **Every Student Succeeds Act (ESSA)** of 2015 addresses funding discrepancies for ESL students and families. The ESSA allocates funds to schools and districts where low-income families comprise 40 percent or more of the enrollment. This is intended to assist with ESL students who are underperforming or at risk for underperforming. The ESSA also provides funding for ESL students to become English proficient and find academic success. However, in order for schools and districts to receive this funding, they must avoid discrimination, track ESL student progress, assess ESL student English proficiency, and notify parents of their children's ESL status. Avoiding discrimination includes preventing the over-identification of ESL students for special education services. The referral and evaluation process must be carried out with caution to ensure that students' perceived disabilities are actual deficits and not related to their English language learning abilities.

Rehabilitation Act of 1973

The Rehabilitation Act of 1973 was the law that preceded the Individuals with Disabilities Education Act of 1975. The Rehabilitation Act protects the rights of people with disabilities in several ways.

- It protects people with disabilities against discrimination relating to **employment**.
- It provides students with disabilities equal access to the **general education curriculum** (Section 504).

Americans with Disabilities Act of 1990 (ADA)

The Americans with Disabilities Act (1990) also protects the rights of people with disabilities.

- The ADA provides **equal employment** for people with disabilities. This means employers must provide reasonable accommodations for people with disabilities in their job and work environments.

- It provides **access** for people with disabilities to both public and private places open to the public (e.g., access ramps and automatic doors).
- It provides **telecommunications access** to people with disabilities. This ensures people with hearing and speech disabilities can communicate over the telephone and Internet.

ELEMENTARY AND SECONDARY EDUCATION ACT (ESEA)

The Elementary and Secondary Education Act (ESEA) also protects the rights of people with disabilities.

- Passed by President Johnson in 1965, the ESEA was part of the president's "War on Poverty." The law sought to allow **equal access to a quality education**.
- The ESEA extended more funding to secondary and primary schools and emphasized high **standards and accountability**.
- This law was authorized as the **No Child Left Behind** (2001) under President Bush, then reauthorized as the **Every Student Succeeds Act** under President Obama.

SECTION 504

A Section 504 Plan comes from the civil rights law, Section 504 of the Rehabilitation Act of 1973, and protects the rights of individuals with disabilities. A 504 Plan is a formal plan or blueprint for how the school will provide services to a student with a disability. This essentially removes barriers for individuals with disabilities by ensuring that **appropriate services** are provided to meet their special needs. A 504 Plan includes:

- **Accommodations**: A 504 Plan includes accommodations a student with a disability may need to be successful in a regular education classroom. For example, a student with ADHD may need to sit near the front of the room to limit distractions.
- **Related Services**: A 504 Plan includes related services, such as speech therapy or occupational therapy, a student may need to be successful in the general education classroom.
- **Modifications**: Although it is rare for a 504 Plan to include modifications, sometimes they are included. Modifications change what the student is expected to do, such as being given fewer homework assignments.

504 PLANS VS. INDIVIDUALIZED EDUCATION PROGRAMS

- A 504 Plan and an IEP are similar in that they serve as a blueprint for a student with a disability. However, a 504 Plan serves as a blueprint for how the student will have **access to school**, whereas the IEP serves as a blueprint for a student's **special education experience**.
- A 504 Plan helps level the playing field for a student with a disability by providing services and changes to the **learning environment**. An IEP provides individualized special education and related services to meet the **unique needs of a student with a disability**. Both IEPs and 504 Plans are provided at no cost to parents.
- The 504 Plan was established under the **Rehabilitation Act of 1973** as a civil rights law. The Individualized Education Program was established under the **Individuals with Disabilities Education Act** (1975 and amended in 2004).
- Unlike an IEP, a 504 Plan does **not** have to be a planned, written document. An IEP is a **planned, written document** that includes unique annual learning goals and describes related services for the student with a disability.

Informed Parental Consent

IDEA requires that parents be **informed** before a student is evaluated for special education services. IDEA mandates that a school district receive **parental consent** to initiate an evaluation of a student for special education services. Consent means the school district has fully informed the parent of their intentions or potential reasons for evaluation of the student. Legally, the request must be written in the parent's native language. This consent does not mean the parent gives consent for a student's placement in special education. In order for a student to be initially placed in special education or receive special education services, parental consent must be given for this issue separately. At any time, parents can withdraw consent for special education placement or special education services. Schools are able to file **due process** if they disagree with the parental withdrawal of consent. Parents also have a right to consent to parts of a student's IEP, but not necessarily all of the IEP. Once parental consent is granted for all parts of the IEP, it can be implemented.

Tiers of the Response to Intervention Model

- **Tier 1: High Quality Classroom Instruction, Screening, and Group Interventions**: In Tier 1, **all students** are screened using universal screening and/or the results of statewide assessments. Students identified as at risk receive supplemental instruction. Students who make adequate progress are returned to their regular instruction. Students who do not make adequate progress move to Tier 2.
- **Tier 2: Targeted Interventions**: These interventions are designed to improve the progress of the students who did not make adequate progress in Tier 1. Targeted instruction is usually in the areas of reading and math and does not last longer than one grading period. This is applied generally to smaller groups and not the full classroom as in Tier 1.
- **Tier 3: Intensive Interventions and Comprehensive Evaluation**: Students who are not successful in Tier 2 move on to Tier 3. They receive intensive interventions that target their specific deficits. Students who do not meet progress goals during intensive interventions are referred to receive comprehensive evaluations and are considered to be eligible for special education under the Individuals with Disabilities Education Act.

Stakeholders in Special Education

Stakeholders that play roles in educating students with disabilities include the students, parents, general educators, administrators, and community members. Students should receive an educational **curriculum** based on strict standards, such as the Common Core Content Standards. This ensures that they receive good educational foundations from which to grow and expand upon during their school careers. Parents, legal guardians, and sometimes agencies act in the best interests of their children. If they do not think the IEPs suit the needs of their children, they can request **due process hearings** in court. Requirements for a free and appropriate public education and least restrictive environment ensure that students are educated alongside peers in general education classrooms by general educators. General educators collaborate with special educators to create **successful inclusion classrooms**. When inclusion is done successfully, the students with disabilities meet their IEP goals.

Multi-Factored Evaluations or Evaluation Team Reports

Multi-Factored Evaluations (MFEs) are processes required by the Individuals with Disabilities Education Act to determine if a student is eligible for special education. When a student is suspected of having a disability, the parent or school district can initiate the evaluation process. **Student information** that is evaluated in an MFE includes background information, health information, vision testing, hearing testing, social and emotional development, general intelligence, past and current academic performance, communication needs, gross and fine motor abilities, results of aptitude or achievement tests, academic skills, and current progress toward IEP goals. Progress reporting on IEP goals is only appropriate during an annual MFE when a student has already qualified for special education services. The purpose of an MFE is to provide **comprehensive information** about a student for professionals working with the student. An MFE also helps determine what academic or behavioral **goals** or related services might be appropriate for a student with disabilities.

Free and Appropriate Public Education Components

IDEA defines free and appropriate public education (FAPE) as an educational right for children with disabilities in the United States. FAPE stands for:

- **Free**: All students found eligible for special education services must receive free services, expensed to the public instead of the parents.
- **Appropriate**: Students are eligible for educations that are appropriate for their specific needs, as stated in their IEPs.
- **Public**: Students with disabilities have the right to be educated in public schools.
- **Education**: An education must be provided to any school-aged child with a disability. Education and services are defined in a student's IEP.

Ideally, FAPE components are put in place in order to guarantee the best education possible that also suits the individual needs of a student with a disability. FAPE should take place in the least restrictive environment, or the environment with the fewest barriers to learning for the individual student with a disability.

Review Video: Legal and Ethical Issues in Special Education
Visit mometrix.com/academy and enter code: 934372

Multi-Factored Evaluation or Evaluation Team Report

A Multi-Factored Evaluation (**MFE**), sometimes referred to as an Evaluation Team Report (**ETR**), serves as a snapshot of a child's abilities, strengths, and weaknesses. An MFE is conducted to determine a student's eligibility for special education. Once a student with a disability qualifies for special education, an MFE is conducted at least every three years after the initial MFE date. MFEs are conducted for students ages 3 to 21 who are on IEPs. The purpose of the MFE is to influence a student's IEP. An MFE reports on a student's **current abilities** and how the disability may affect **educational performance**. MFEs can also determine if a student qualifies for related services, such as occupational therapy or speech-language therapy. An MFE can be requested by a parent or school district when a child is suspected of having a disability. The school district typically has 30 days or less to respond to a parental request to evaluate a student, giving consent or refusal for an evaluation. While initial MFEs are conducted as a means to determine special education qualification, annual MFEs are conducted to address any changes in the needs or services of a student already receiving special education services.

Least Restrictive Environments to Deliver Special Education Services

Special education services are delivered to students that qualify with a **disability** defined by IDEA. IDEA also requires that students who qualify for special education must receive special education services in **least restrictive environments** that provide the fewest barriers to their learning. A student's most appropriate instructional setting is written out in the **IEP**. Some special education instructional settings include:

- No instructional setting
- Mainstream setting
- Resource room
- Self-contained classroom
- Homebound instruction

With **no instructional setting**, students participate in the general education curriculum but may receive related services, such as speech-language therapy or occupational therapy. In the **mainstream setting**, students are instructed in the general education classroom for most or part of the day and provided with special education supports, accommodations, modifications, and related services. A **resource room** is an environment where students receive remedial instruction when they cannot participate in the general curriculum for one or more subject areas. A **self-contained classroom** is a setting for students who need special education and related services for more than 50 percent of the day. **Homebound instruction** is for students who are homebound or hospitalized for more than four consecutive weeks.

Due Process Rights Available to Parents and Legal Guardians

When parents or legal guardians and school districts cannot agree on components of IEPs for students with disabilities, parents and legal guardians have a right to **due process**. Due process is a legal right under IDEA that usually involves the school district violating a legal rule. Examples of these violations include a school district not running an IEP meeting, failing to conduct a triannual evaluation, or failing to implement a student's IEP. Disputes often involve a student's instructional placement, appropriate accommodations or modifications, related services, or changes to IEPs. School districts' due process policies vary depending on the district. IDEA, however, mandates that a **due process legal form** be completed by the parent or legal guardian in order to move forward. This form must be completed within two years of a dispute. **Mediation**, or the process of coming to an agreement before filing due process, can be a solution to the dispute. IEP meetings, even when it is not time for an annual review, are also appropriate options for resolving a dispute before filing due process.

Purpose of Mediation in Lieu of a Parent or Legal Guardian Filing for Due Process

Mediation is a process used to address a dispute prior to a parent or legal guardian filing for due process. The purpose of mediation is to **resolve a dispute** between the parent or legal guardian of a student with a disability and the school district. Disputes occur when the parent or legal guardian does not agree with an IEP component, such as what related services are provided or the way a student's IEP is being implemented. Mediation is not a parent or legal guardian's legal right, but school districts often support mediation to offset a **due process filing**. Mediation involves the attempt to resolve a dispute and includes a meeting between the parent or legal guardian, school district member, and a neutral third party, such as a mediator provided by the state. States have lists of **mediators** available for these situations. Agreements that come out of the mediation process are put into writing and, if appropriate, put into a student's IEP. Disagreements can continue to be mediated, or the decision may be made to file due process. Prior to mediation, parents or legal guardians and school districts have the option of holding IEP meetings (outside of annual meetings) to resolve disputes.

Maintaining Confidentiality and Privacy of Student Records

Similar to the Health Insurance Portability and Accountability Act of 1996 (HIPAA), the **Family Educational Rights and Privacy Act (FERPA)** is a law that protects privacy. However, the FERPA is specific to the privacy of students. The FERPA law applies to any school or agency that receives funds from the US Department of Education. This ensures that schools or agencies cannot share any confidential information about a student without a parent or student's written consent. **Student educational records** can be defined as records, files, documents, or other materials which contain a student's personal information. **IEPs** and **ETRs** are examples of private documents under the FERPA law. The responsibility of a school covered by the FERPA is to maintain confidentiality and privacy. The members of an IEP team, such as special educators, related service professionals, general educators, or other professionals, cannot share any identifying, private information about a student. Information addressing the needs of individual students found on an IEP, ETR, or other identifying document must remain confidential unless express written consent is given by the parent or legal guardian.

Pre-Referral/Referral Process for a Student with a Disability

The purpose of a pre-referral process for a child with a suspected disability is to attempt **reasonable modifications and accommodations** before the child is referred for special education services. Schools often have **pre-referral teams** whose purpose is to identify the strengths and needs of a child, put reasonable strategies into action, and evaluate the results of this pre-referral intervention. If the results do not show any change, another intervention can be attempted, or the student can be referred for a special education evaluation.

If a child is suspected of having a disability and did not succeed with pre-referral interventions, the school or parent can request an **evaluation**. During the evaluation process, the school compiles information to see if the student needs special education or related services. This information is used to determine if the student's disability is affecting school performance and if the student qualifies for special education. The evaluation lists and examines the student's strengths, weaknesses, and development and determines what supports the student needs in order to learn. An evaluation must be completed before special education services can be provided.

Role of a School Psychologist in Special Education

School psychologists are certified members of school teams that **support the needs of students and teachers**. They help students with overall academic, social, behavioral, and emotional success. School psychologists are trained in data collection and analysis, assessments, progress monitoring, risk factors, consultation and collaboration, and special education services. In special education, school psychologists may work directly with students and collaborate with teachers, administrators, parents, and other professionals working with particular students. They may also counsel students' parents, participate in the Response to Intervention process, and perform initial evaluations of students who are referred for special education services. School psychologists also work to improve academic achievement, promote positive behavior and health by implementing school-wide programs, support learning needs of diverse learners, maintain safe school environments, and strengthen and maintain good school-parent relationships.

Overrepresentation of Students from Diverse Backgrounds

Disproportionate representation occurs when there is not an equal representation of students from different **cultural and linguistic backgrounds** identified for special education services. Students from different cultural and linguistic groups should be identified for special education services in similar proportions. This ensures that no one group is **overrepresented** and **overidentified as having special needs** due to their cultural or linguistic differences.

Disproportionality can occur based on a child's sex, language proficiency, receipt of free and reduced lunch, or race and ethnicity. Historically, most disproportionality has been a civil rights issue and due to a child's cultural or linguistic background. Recently, the focus has been on the disproportionate number of students who spend time in special education classrooms instead of being educated alongside regularly educated peers.

The referral process, **Response to Intervention (RTI)**, provides safeguards against disproportionality. The RTI process requires instruction and intervention catered to the unique, specific needs of the individual student. The purpose of RTI is not the identification of a disability or entitlement to services. Instead, it focuses on data used to make educational decisions about individuals, classrooms, schools, or districts. Models like RTI address disproportionate representation, but they are not perfect.

Special Education Models

Purpose of Special Education

Special education is specially designed instruction delivered to meet the individual needs of children with disabilities. Special education includes a free and appropriate education in the least restrictive environment. In the past, a special education model might consist of a self-contained classroom of students with special needs whose needs were addressed in that setting. Today, students who qualify for special education must receive instruction in **free and appropriate settings**. This means they receive special education services in settings that provide the **fewest barriers** to their learning. The most appropriate setting varies, depending on the student and the disability. The purpose of special education is to ensure that the unique needs of children with disabilities are addressed. In the public-school setting, the Individuals with Disabilities Education Act mandates that students with disabilities receive free and appropriate public educations. The goal of special education is to create **fair environments** for students with special needs to learn. Ideally, the settings should enable students to learn to their fullest potential.

Co-Teaching Models

Co-teaching models are utilized in collaborative, inclusive teaching settings that include students with and without disabilities. General educators teach alongside special educators and hold all students to the same educational standards. In the **one teach/one support model**, one instructor teaches a lesson while the other instructor supports students who have questions or need assistance. A **parallel teaching model** involves a class being split into two groups, with one instructor teaching each group. The **alternative teaching model** may be appropriate in situations where it is necessary to instruct small groups of students. In this model, one instructor teaches a large group of students while the other provides instruction to a smaller group of students. In **station teaching**, students are split into small groups and work in several teaching centers while both instructors provide support. Teachers participating in **team teaching** collaboratively plan and implement lesson content, facilitate classroom discussions, and manage discipline. Successful co-teaching uses all of these models as appropriate to meet the needs of diverse groups of learners in the inclusive classroom setting.

Remedial Instruction vs. Special Education

Though the terms are sometimes used interchangeably, remedial instruction does not always equal special education. The difference between remedial instruction and special education has a lot to do with the intellectual levels of the students. In **remedial instruction**, a student has average or better-than-average intellectual abilities but may struggle with **skills** in one or more content areas. Remedial instruction provides one-on-one instruction to students who are falling behind. Remedial programs are often mainstreamed into general education classrooms to address the varying learning abilities of students. Remedial instruction can be delivered by general education teachers. **Special education** programs address the needs of students who may have lower intellectual abilities and require individualized instruction. Students in special education have **disabilities** specified by the Individuals with Disabilities Education Act and use Individualized Education Programs. Unlike remedial instruction, special education requires qualified and credentialed special educators to decide how to best provide interventions in classroom settings for students with disabilities.

Remedial Instruction vs. Compensatory Approaches to Intervention

Compensatory interventions can be offered in the form of programs or services that help students with special needs or students who are at risk. The compensatory approach is different from remedial instruction because remedial instruction involves the breaking of concepts or tasks into smaller chunks and reteaching information. The **remedial approach** focuses on repetition and developing or reinforcing certain skills. The **compensatory approach** is implemented when a remedial approach is not working. It focuses on building upon students' strengths and working with or around their weaknesses. Tools such as audiobooks, text-to-speech software, speech recognition software, and other types of assistive technology are compensatory accommodations that help provide a free and appropriate education for students with disabilities who might otherwise continue to demonstrate skill deficits without these tools. Compensatory approaches and remedial instruction can and should be delivered at the same time to help ensure that students with disabilities are meeting their potential.

Chapter Quiz

Ready to see how well you retained what you just read? Scan the QR code to go directly to the chapter quiz interface for this study guide. If you're using a computer, simply visit the online resources page at **mometrix.com/resources719/iltslbsi290** and click the Chapter Quizzes link.

ILTS Practice Test #1

Want to take this practice test in an online interactive format?
Check out the online resources page, which includes interactive practice questions and much more: **mometrix.com/resources719/iltslbsi290**

1. Which of the following describes the purpose of an intelligence test?

a. To measure a student's ability to think abstractly
b. To measure a student's ability to understand spoken language
c. To measure a student's ability to convey ideas through oral language
d. To measure a student's ability to retain visual information

2. Which one of the following disability categories is likely to have the greatest impact on individuals across their life span?

a. Developmental delays
b. Speech or language impairments
c. Multiple disabilities
d. Specific learning disabilities

3. Which of the following is the most common disability in children aged 5-21 according to the IDEA annual reports to Congress?

a. Specific learning disability
b. Speech or language impairment
c. Intellectual disability
d. Emotional disturbance

4. Having a print-rich environment includes all of the following except:

a. Writing classroom labels in only one language to avoid confusion
b. Making sure print is at the children's eye level
c. Displaying the students' work around the classroom
d. Having the teacher prepare materials in front of the students to model writing

5. Which of the following learning theories views motivation as extrinsic and intrinsic?

a. Behaviorism
b. Cognitivism
c. Constructivism
d. Humanism

6. How can the interpretation of curriculum-based assessments be valuable in determining the growth of a student?

a. By comparing the student's score to others in the district
b. By comparing the student's score to their grade in the class
c. By comparing the student's score to the average score
d. By comparing the student's score to their previous scores

7. Mrs. Stroud's pupil Janet has delayed language development and reading difficulties. Mrs. Stroud discovers that Janet's mother does not help her with reading at home. It turns out that Janet's mother is not unwilling; rather, she lacks confidence in her own reading skills and has been embarrassed to admit this. How can Mrs. Stroud help in this situation?

a. Refer Janet's mother to a reading teacher for free adult education sessions in the community and have a few group practice sessions with Janet, her mother, and both teachers.
b. Schedule private sessions herself with Janet's mother to improve her reading skills and teach her how to help Janet at home with her reading and her homework.
c. Schedule more time with Janet to work on her reading skills and assignments, since her mother is not able to help Janet at home with reading-related activities.
d. Arrange for a tutor to make home visits to work with Janet on her reading assignments, since her mother does not have the necessary reading skills to do this.

8. Behavioral management should include specific techniques for students who have difficulty staying on task. Which one of the following would not be appropriate?

a. Allowing such students to walk around to look at the materials that pertain to the lesson
b. Assigning specific tasks to be completed
c. Using response cards so that all students feel compelled to be aware and involved
d. Not allowing peer helpers because they might harm more than help by distracting the students who have trouble staying on task

9. Joel lived for many years at an institution and has now been placed in a group home. He has profound intellectual disabilities and a number of obsessive-compulsive behaviors. He has certain habits; for example, at meals he tends to sit sideways at the table with his legs crossed, with the result that he drops a great deal of food on the floor. What should the houseparent do?

a. Put Joel in time-out for the rest of the meal when this occurs.
b. Direct Joel to clean up the floor after the meal is over.
c. Meet with Joel's IEP team to write training objectives.
d. Place a drop cloth on the floor under Joel's chair.

10. Which of the following models used in planning instruction for students with disabilities is described as an example of student-directed planning?

a. The model and process of Group Action Planning (GAP)
b. The Choosing Outcomes and Accommodations for Children (COACH) model
c. The model and process of Making Action Plans (MAPs)
d. The Planning Alternative Tomorrows with Hope (PATH) model

11. According to Piagetian theory, how does learning occur?

a. Naturally
b. Through discrete and predictable stages
c. Through repetition
d. With a good teacher

12. Peyton is a new student at Harbor Light High School. He is a ninth-grade student with a specific learning disability in the area of math problem solving. How can a diagnostic assessment be used to best guide his math instruction?

a. Assessing which accommodations he can access
b. Assessing which math class is most appropriate
c. Assessing which goals to develop in his IEP
d. Assessing which modifications need to be made

13. In the first week of school, a resource teacher asks her high school students to make lists of things they know how to do well. How is this activity most useful to the teacher?

a. It establishes a feeling of success in her students from the start
b. It is an informal assessment of their writing skills and gives the teacher an idea of each student's interests and abilities
c. It is a formal assessment of prior knowledge
d. It invites further discussion of each student's unique contributions and will help the class bond with mutual respect

14. Which of the following instructional strategies would be most appropriate when teaching a science lesson to a third-grade class?

a. Reciprocal teaching
b. Socratic questioning
c. Direct instruction
d. Learning centers

15. Clyde is 16 years old, has visual impairment, and reads on a first-grade level. What would be a good choice of materials for his teacher to provide him?

a. Large-print books on subjects relevant to teens
b. Children's books, which have large print and simple text
c. Regular library books with a magnifying glass
d. Large-print books with subjects geared to teens but with simplified text

16. Regarding teaching strategies to improve reading fluency, teachers can encourage students to read independently by providing books with suitable difficulty levels that students find interesting. Which is true about these additional strategies?

a. Timed exercises should be avoided for creating undue pressure
b. Repetition is a very effective technique to build reading fluency
c. Readers' theatre is good for showing progress but not making it
d. Reading in pairs assists reading comprehension but not fluency

17. A special education teacher shows parents of a dyslexic child a study that examined brain scans of dyslexic and non-dyslexic readers. The study demonstrated that dyslexics use (the) ________ side(s) of their brains, while non-dyslexics use (the) ______ side.

a. Both, the left.
b. Both, the right.
c. Left, right.
d. Right, left.

18. Which of the following is not true with regard to the role of parental participation in the IEP process?

a. Parents are members of the IEP team.
b. Parents can call an IEP meeting.
c. Parents can run an IEP meeting.
d. Parents can help develop IEP goals.

19. Which of the following community services would be most appropriate for a group of high school students with specific learning disabilities?

a. Job skills trainers
b. Independent living agencies
c. College recruiters
d. Mental health services

20. Samuel is a student with a specific learning disability in the area of oral expression. What kind of assessment would be most appropriate in order to evaluate his continued eligibility?

a. Expressive language
b. Receptive language
c. Auditory discrimination
d. Verbal intelligence

21. Which of the following is the best example of an independent living skills goal for a high school student with a specific learning disability?

a. The student will be able to access the city bus.
b. The student will live with a roommate in an apartment.
c. The student will live in a group home.
d. The student will attend community college.

22. A student with disabilities does not demonstrate certain adaptive life skills such as cleaning up a work area at school, but his parents report that he has done so at home for years. An ecological assessment finds he does not demonstrate these skills in any other settings. Which instructional procedure is most appropriate for this student?

a. Re-teaching him these skills
b. Teaching skill generalization
c. Teaching skill maintenance
d. Teaching skill discrimination

23. Mr. Ivanov has several students in his class whose parents have recently immigrated to the United States and who are not comfortable conversing in English. The parents' native language is Spanish, and Mr. Ivanov does not speak Spanish. In order to ensure that these parents can participate in the upcoming parent-teacher conferences, which of the following steps should Mr. Ivanov take first?

a. He should ask the Spanish-speaking students if they would be willing to serve as translators for the conferences
b. He should send a note to the parents informing them that they will need to hire a translator if they want to participate in the conferences
c. He should inform the school principal that he cannot hold the conferences if he is not supplied with a translator
d. He should find someone to help him write a note to the parents in Spanish explaining that he will help them find a volunteer translator if they do not have a friend or family member who could translate for them

24. A special education teacher assigns his students a collaborative group project. Which strategy would be most effective to benefit all students in the group?

a. Assigning one student the task of compiling and presenting the group's work
b. Allowing students to volunteer to make contributions to the project
c. Leading the activities himself and directing what the students do
d. Assigning each student an equal number of duties related to the project

25. Which of the following is most likely to be true about students with learning disabilities and their families?

a. Families that have children with disabilities typically bond closer.
b. Parents can sometimes be the cause of a learning disability.
c. Parents will often suspect a disability before the school does.
d. Families often seek out information about disabilities.

26. Ms. Winslow has a class with many LD students. She consistently calls her students' attention to features in their textbooks such as boldface headings, illustrations, tables, charts, indexes, and chapter summaries. Which is most accurate regarding this practice?

a. Doing this helps her students to organize what they read and learn.
b. She does this because none of her students ever reads a textbook.
c. It enhances her presentation but does not really facilitate learning.
d. This helps her LD students but is a waste of time for other students.

27. When working with a group of eighth-grade students with writing deficiencies who struggle to stay on topic when writing, which of the following intervention strategies would be most appropriate?

a. Providing a graphic organizer for the students to use
b. Modeling the writing for the students
c. Providing opportunities for the students to practice
d. Allowing students to collaborate with peers

28. When selecting a functional curriculum for a high school class focusing on independent living skills, what would be the MOST essential to include in the curriculum?

a. Cooking
b. Laundry
c. Personal hygiene
d. Shopping

29. Nina is a student who has severe hearing impairment. She wears a hearing aid and has a low level of hearing. She can communicate verbally but speaks very loudly. Nina visited the public library in the past, but the local librarian was upset at the disruption created by her loud speech. The librarian now does not like Nina and does not want her in the library. What does Nina's special education teacher do?

a. She tells Nina that the school library is just as good and that she should do all her library activities at school instead of aggravating the local librarian and putting up with her rejection.
b. She supervises Nina during visits to the public library and teaches her to control her voice while there; she also helps establish a friendly relationship between Nina and the librarian.
c. She complains to the school principal about the local librarian, saying she is discriminating against Nina because of her disability.
d. She sends Nina to the school psychologist for counseling to console her after her feelings have been hurt by the local librarian's disapproval.

30. Which teacher behaviors reflect strategies for supporting education through partnering with the families of students?

a. Inviting parents by building rapport at the beginning of the year
b. Being considerate of parents by only contacting about problems
c. Respecting parents by not giving advice about the home settings
d. Respecting family privacy by not prying into their lives and needs

31. Which of the following is not true about the referral process for special education eligibility?

a. Parental consent is required to start the evaluation.
b. The evaluation must be completed in 30 days.
c. The evaluation must be conducted by a multidisciplinary team.
d. The referral may be initiated by a parent.

32. What would be the MOST effective instructional strategy in teaching a reading lesson to students with dyslexia?

a. Using a whole-word approach
b. Using multisensory strategies
c. Using modeling
d. Using graphic organizers

33. Students with LD characterized by deficits in memory typically have:

a. More difficulty with short-term than long-term memory
b. More difficulty with long-term than short-term memory
c. Equal difficulties with short-term and long-term memory
d. No clear pattern of difficulty with either type of memory

34. Which of the following methods of collecting observational data of student behavior is most indicated for a behavior which seems to occur constantly?

a. Event recording
b. Duration recording
c. Latency recording
d. Interval recording

35. A special education teacher is working to create an IEP for one of her students. To complete her IEP, she needs to record when the student reached certain developmental and academic milestones. Who is the best person to reach out to in order to get this information?

a. The student's pediatrician
b. The student's previous teachers
c. The school counselor
d. The student's parent or guardian

36. Which of the following teacher behaviors impedes rather than promotes school-home communication?

a. Listening to the parents and/or families of students
b. Mutually exchanging teacher and family expertise
c. Instructing parents and/or families in what to do
d. Brainstorming supportive strategies together

37. Which of the following is the best example of how to interpret the results of a diagnostic assessment?

a. To determine the instructional level that students are at
b. To determine the disability that a student may have
c. To determine the kind of special education services that a student needs
d. To determine the amount that a student has learned

38. Which of the following is a disadvantage of an externally facilitated IEP meeting?

a. The discussion can often get off topic.
b. It can be difficult to resolve conflicts.
c. It can make certain members feel left out.
d. It takes more time to prepare.

39. Part of the emotional environment of a classroom is the relationships between the teacher and the children. Children learn and develop well in a nurturing relationship that includes all the following except:

a. Remaining consistent in the teacher's interactions with and expectations of the children
b. Rigidly ensuring compliance with rules and routines
c. Empowering children with choices
d. Providing feedback in a positive manner

40. Rob is a second-grade student with a hearing impairment. Which of the following characteristics would not be included in the criteria for his continued eligibility?

a. His hearing impairment is fluctuating.
b. Amplification improves his hearing.
c. He also has a visual impairment.
d. His educational performance is adversely affected.

41. Miguel is a second grader with a specific learning disability that began exhibiting some behaviors that have never arisen before. What would be the best strategy in communicating these issues to Miguel's parents?

a. Calling the parents immediately to try to resolve the issue
b. Waiting a week or two to see if the behavior improves
c. Setting up a meeting for the parents to come in and discuss it
d. Holding an Individualized Education Program (IEP) meeting to gather the entire team

42. Which of the following best describes when it would be necessary for a teacher to create their own assessment?

a. When students do not have access to the curriculum
b. When testing students with intellectual disabilities
c. When providing accommodations to students
d. When the academic standards are modified

43. Ms. Loomis is a teacher of LD (Learning Disabilities) students in Texas. This term she has had a new group of students referred to her for reading difficulties. She realizes that all of these students are English language learners (ELLs). Which statement about these referrals is most likely to be true?

a. These students will have reading problems regardless of which language they are reading.
b. The language acquisition process may well be the cause of these students' reading problems.
c. These students' reading problems are most likely the result of their learning disabilities.
d. These students' reading problems and their ESL status are most likely a coincidence.

44. Ms. Kincaid has sent home a note with her fourth grade students asking their parents to sign up for parent-teacher conferences, but after a week, only about ten percent of the students' parents have done so. Ms. Kincaid is concerned that if a student's parents fail to attend a conference this will negatively impact the student's academic achievement. What is the first step that she should take in order to increase the number of parents who attend conferences?

a. Take the students whose parents have not scheduled conferences aside and ask them whether or not they gave their parents the note about parent-teacher conferences
b. Call the parents directly and notify them about the upcoming conferences
c. Give the students another note to take home that emphasizes the importance of conferences to the students' academic development
d. Tell the students that their grades will suffer if they don't convince their parents to attend the conference

45. A kindergarten teacher has a new student who will not make eye contact with anyone, so she doesn't appear to be listening. She often rocks back and forth and does not stop when asked or give any indication she has heard. She avoids physical contact. Sometimes the teacher must take her arm to guide her from one place to another. Occasionally the student erupts, howling in terror and fury. The most likely diagnosis is:

a. Conduct Disorder
b. Obsessive-Compulsive Disorder
c. Autism
d. Oppositional Defiant Disorder

46. Joseph is a fourth-grade student being evaluated for special education services as a student with a specific learning disability in the area of math problem solving. Which of the following would be the best interpretation of his assessment results that show he is within one standard deviation of the mean in math problem solving?

a. Joseph would likely be determined eligible for special education services.
b. Joseph would likely need more testing in order to determine his eligibility.
c. Joseph would likely be determined ineligible for special education services.
d. Joseph would likely be determined eligible for a 504 plan instead.

47. Which one of the following instructional strategies allows students to move around the room while still learning?

a. Embodied learning
b. Inquiry-based learning
c. Blended learning
d. Service learning

48. Josh is a preschooler who is just starting school for the first time. Which of the following would be atypical social development for a child of his age?

a. Showing some separation anxiety
b. Cooperating with other children
c. Exploring things independently
d. Wanting to be like his friends

49. When transitioning from one subject to another and when she becomes anxious, a student always taps her front tooth 5 times then opens and closes her eyes 11 times before leaving her desk. The child most likely has:

a. Tic Disorder
b. Obsessive Compulsive Disorder
c. Anxiety Disorder
d. Depression

50. Jaden is a second-grade student with a diagnosis of ADHD. When conducting a special education evaluation, which of the following behavior rating scales would be most appropriate?

a. Single-domain scales
b. Self-report scales
c. Multidomain scales
d. Observer/informant scales

51. When holding an Individualized Education Program (IEP) meeting with stakeholders, which method would be least effective in establishing rapport?

a. Facilitated meetings
b. Slide show meetings
c. Student-led meetings
d. Scripted meetings

52. When teaching a new group of students, which one of the following strategies is most productive in creating a supportive classroom environment?

a. Including community-building activities
b. Allowing the students to negotiate
c. Posting student work in the room
d. Establishing authority as the teacher

53. What legislation gives students and families increased protection in regard to the confidentiality of student records?

a. No Child Left Behind Act
b. Americans with Disabilities Act
c. Family Educational Rights and Privacy Act
d. Human Equity Act

54. Andrea was transitioned from a residential facility for the developmentally disabled to a group home. Her medications contribute to bladder control problems. She was successfully trip-trained in toileting at the residential facility. After moving to her new home she began having episodes of enuresis at night. What should her team do?

a. Reinstitute trip-training at the group home.
b. Search for another strategy in this setting.
c. Have her wear adult diapers to bed.
d. Have her wear absorbent underwear to bed.

55. What is an example of a modification of the curriculum?

a. Access to textbooks with larger print
b. Access to a computer to type assignments
c. Access to manipulatives
d. Access to alternative books

56. Andrea is a first-grade student with a developmental delay. Which formative assessment can be implemented to best monitor her progress throughout the school year?

a. Interviewing her each week
b. Giving her academic probes
c. Observing her in class
d. Monitoring her test scores

57. Stephen has a very high IQ, but he must use a wheelchair and is almost completely immobilized except for limited use of one hand, with which he can only press buttons. His paralysis affects his vocal cords so he cannot speak. Stephen excels in all academic subjects, most notably the sciences and expressive and receptive language skills. His communication is limited by his disabilities. Which would be the most appropriate adaptive equipment for him in the classroom and elsewhere?

a. An adaptive pencil holder and paper holder both attached to his wheelchair
b. A computer with a voice synthesizer that he can program to speak for him
c. An electrolarynx he can use for speech in place of his paralyzed vocal cords
d. A communication board with buttons he can press to select various words

58. Alex is a ninth-grade student who receives services as a student with a traumatic brain injury. In order to be eligible to receive services under this disability category, which of the following causes of the injury can be ruled out?

a. Birth trauma
b. Combat injuries
c. Violence
d. Sports-related injuries

59. Of the following criteria for defining intellectual disabilities, which one was widely used only from 1961 on?

a. Mental deficiency/incomplete development
b. Originates during the developmental period
c. Associated with impaired adaptive behavior
d. A condition manifested at maturity

60. Which of the following strategies can a special education teacher implement to best ensure that inclusion is successful in their school?

a. Articulating the need for inclusion to the school administrators
b. Collaborating with general education teachers
c. Developing new assessments to measure student growth
d. Providing professional development to staff

61. Comparing a student's performance on a test to a national average for age/grade level is a(n)...

a. Norm-referenced test
b. Criterion-referenced test
c. Performance-based test
d. Ipsative measure/test

62. Mr. John and Ms. Deere are team-teaching a special education class of high school students who are deaf or hard of hearing. Mr. John has written a lesson plan of multimodal activities based around a scenario involving a boys' basketball team. Ms. Deere is recommending some changes to this lesson plan as she feels it is biased. Which of the following is the most likely basis for her objections?

a. Mr. John's lesson plan is not likely to be one to which the female students can relate.
b. Mr. John's lesson plan is not likely to appeal to students with hearing impairments.
c. Mr. John's lesson plan did not include any input from Ms. Deere when he wrote it.
d. Mr. John's lesson plan focuses on a physical education activity with no academics.

63. When having a parent-teacher conference, who should generally open the conference and state its main purpose?

a. The administrator or school counselor should be the one who starts the conference.
b. The parents should begin the conference because they know what their child needs best.
c. The person who asked for the conference should start the meeting and establish its focus.
d. The teacher should begin the conference because it is the teacher's responsibility.

64. Which of the following is accurate regarding federal and state public health services?

a. The federal government funds and controls every state's delivery of public health services.
b. The federal government funds but delegates the states to organize and deliver services.
c. In all states, public health agencies are freestanding agencies that function on their own.
d. In all states, public health is under the umbrella of the US Health & Human Services Department.

65. Introducing each of the stages of career development for students with disabilities should be determined *most* by which of the following?

a. The student's developmental level
b. The student's grade level in school
c. The student's level of experience
d. The student's chronological age

66. Which of the following strategies would likely be most beneficial in preparing a student with a specific learning disability for adulthood?

a. Incorporating a postsecondary goal in the student's IEP
b. Incorporating money management skills in the student's class
c. Incorporating transition services into the student's IEP
d. Incorporating job application writing in the student's class

67. Which of the following strategies would be least effective in communicating to parents as the new case manager of a student?

a. Calling them with an introduction
b. Setting up a meeting to discuss the IEP
c. Sending home a note for the student to deliver
d. Meeting them in person when they pick up their child

68. When advertising and other media use the word "LOOK!" with the two O's depicted as eyes, this association mimics which of Ehri's (1995) phases of sight word recognition?

a. Partial alphabetic
b. Pre-alphabetic
c. Full alphabetic
d. Consolidated

69. When working with students who struggle with managing their own behavior, which of the following would not be considered a positive behavior intervention?

a. Social-emotional strategies
b. Consequences
c. Self-regulatory strategies
d. Coping skills

70. Which of the following is true regarding alternate curriculum programs?

a. These programs are the first choice for students identified with disabilities
b. A student's eligibility for these programs is determined by his/her IEP team
c. They are preferable to general curricula with accommodations/modifications
d. Students are still assigned to general education classrooms in these programs

71. The school psychologist is explaining assessment results to Clifford's parents and other IEP team members. She says that Clifford has difficulties with planning, organizing, keeping track of time, relating a current lesson to earlier learning, and that he talks out of turn in class. These all relate most to deficits in:

a. Executive function
b. Self-regulation
c. Sequencing
d. Memory

72. Oscar is a young adult living in the community and attending a day habilitation training program. He has Down syndrome and his IQ tests yield very low scores. However, he is cooperative and can follow directions. Due to his level of cognitive functioning he needs intensive training and repeated prompting to complete any task with multiple steps. He also requires prompting to continue to work; he is not lazy, but he loses focus and forgets what to do. Oscar does not display maladaptive behaviors. He is normally passive and does not initiate many activities, but he is quite willing to do many tasks given the direction to do so. His caregivers and the team planning his IEP want to help Oscar gain some independence by learning employment skills. Which training program would be most suitable for him?

a. A sheltered workshop where he assembles product sample kits along with other disabled students, with periodic group supervision
b. A special warehouse program for people with disabilities doing a packing job with 1:1 supervision and ongoing verbal prompts to complete each step
c. A special education classroom where he applies labels to products and is monitored along with many other students by one teacher with occasional verbal prompts
d. A special education classroom where the teacher gives academic lessons and quizzes on job skills to the whole class

73. Which one of the following challenges is least likely to arise when collaborating with parents at IEP meetings?

a. Differences with regard to IEP goals
b. Differences with regard to accommodations
c. Differences with regard to attendance issues
d. Differences with regard to service delivery

74. Stephanie is a middle school student with a variety of maladaptive behaviors. The nature of these behaviors is disruptive to the classroom. Her IEP team is meeting to address these. What should their first step be?

a. Remove Stephanie from the classroom to stop these disruptions.
b. Differentially reinforce alternative behaviors.
c. Conduct a functional behavior assessment to learn why she behaves as she does.
d. Write a different instructional plan to address her needs better.

75. Among the following, a child with which type of disability is likely to be best at focusing attention on one thing for a long time?

a. Down syndrome
b. Developmental delay
c. Attention deficit disorder
d. Autism spectrum disorder

76. When does current federal legislation (IDEA 2004) require transition planning for students with disabilities to begin?

a. At age 18
b. At age 22
c. At age 14
d. At age 16

77. The emotional balance of a classroom can be upset by conflict. Appropriate methods for a teacher to use in handling conflict do not include:

a. Gathering information and re-capping the situation
b. Allowing children to come up with a solution themselves
c. Letting the issue drop once a solution has been agreed upon
d. Dealing with the conflict calmly and with a quiet voice

78. Which of the following is LEAST descriptive of the purpose of the co-teaching model applied to teaching English to seventh-grade students?

a. Co-teaching increases the amount of attention that students receive.
b. Co-teaching helps to share control of the classroom.
c. Co-teaching increases the amount of differentiation in instruction.
d. Co-teaching helps to provide multiple areas of expertise.

79. A student displays a slight learning disability, which mostly effects reading and writing development. He is removed from the general student body to receive special education. While this student's disability has put him behind in his English class, he is not behind in any other class. What has the school violated in removing this student from the general student body?

a. Individual Education Plan
b. Human Rights Act
c. Americans with Disabilities Act
d. Least Restrictive Environment (LRE)

80. Which of the following was one of the main purposes of the Individuals with Disabilities Education Act (IDEA) of 2004?

a. To provide opportunities for students with disabilities to learn
b. To protect the rights of students with disabilities
c. To afford students with disabilities protection from expulsion
d. To initiate new programming for students with disabilities

81. Of the following criteria for defining intellectual disabilities, which was NOT used before 1961?

a. IQ score
b. Social incompetence
c. Impaired adaptive behavior
d. Essentially incurable

82. Which of the following is the best example of how the results of an adaptive behavior scale can drive instruction?

a. To determine which problem behaviors the student engages in
b. To determine whether or not a student needs a behavior plan
c. To determine which independent living skills a student needs to work on
d. To determine how to adapt the curriculum to a student's needs

83. Zachary is a 10th-grade student who receives special education services as a student with an other health impairment due to his ADHD, and he struggles to sit still for long periods of time. Which of the following strategies would be most effective in providing opportunities for Zachary to move around?

a. Giving Zachary a pass to move around when he needs to
b. Giving Zachary a timer to get up and stretch every 10 minutes
c. Organizing the classroom so that Zachary has his own area
d. Incorporating movement activities for the entire class

84. Which of the following is NOT a good practice to incorporate for students who have difficulty finishing routine assignments?

a. The teacher should teach self-discipline about staying on task.
b. The teacher should avoid incorporating games into the materials because they might add too much time to the task.
c. The teacher should remove segments of the task, such as requiring the student to copy word problems before calculating the answer.
d. The teacher should divide the task into segments and allow the student to work on the parts throughout the day.

85. Justin is a fourth-grade student who receives special education services as a student with deaf-blindness. Which of the following collaborative approaches would be most effective at the beginning of the new school year?

a. Giving the general education teacher access to the IEP to review
b. Allowing the general education teacher to teach the student as they see fit
c. Asking the district for advice on working with this student
d. Meeting with the general education teacher to develop a plan

86. A kindergarten teacher has received a community outreach referral. She asks the school's speech-language pathologist to evaluate a preschool child for delayed language development, as the parents cannot afford to pay a private practitioner's fees. The parents bring their child to the school. The speech-language pathologist assesses the child and privately has a strong suspicion that this child is displaying many signs of early autism. The speech-language pathologist takes the appropriate action. What does she do?

a. Tells the parents what she suspects and recommends treatment.
b. Refers the parents to a free community clinic for a complete behavioral assessment.
c. Asks the referring kindergarten teacher to tell the parents that she suspects autism.
d. Recommends that the parents take their child to their pediatrician for a checkup.

87. How would the use of a supplementary curriculum be most appropriate for a group of high school students in a social studies class?

a. Providing the students with accommodations to access the curriculum
b. Providing the students opportunities to explore careers
c. Providing the students use of assistive technology
d. Providing the students extra credit for additional assignments

88. What most reflects factors that can interfere with diverse parent and family communication and participation in the education of their children?

a. Language barriers rarely stop parents/families from communicating.
b. Parents with unsuccessful school histories try harder to participate.
c. Families can be alienated from school processes because of culture.
d. Poor past school experiences induce parents to help their children.

89. Stewart is a student who uses a wheelchair. This year he will be placed in Ms. Joplin's class, where all of the other students are ambulatory. He will be the only student in a wheelchair. Stewart's IEP team is meeting to discuss his placement. Regarding concerns about the wheelchair, what is the best recommendation?

a. Stewart should not be placed in this class because his wheelchair will stand out, making both him and the other students feel uncomfortable about it.
b. Someone should accompany Stewart to transfer him from his wheelchair to a regular student desk/chair and then back to his wheelchair when it is time to leave the classroom.
c. Stewart should only be placed in a class that has other students who use wheelchairs.
d. School staff should ensure that the classroom is wheelchair-accessible and that Stewart can navigate it; they should also show other students how to adjust to the situation.

Refer to the following for question 90:

Christina is an 11th-grade student who receives special education services due to an emotional disturbance and has a hard time completing any work due to frustration. When Christina becomes frustrated enough, she tends to lash out verbally to nearby people.

90. Which of the following would be the most appropriate strategy to include in her behavior plan to help her calm down when frustrated and complete her schoolwork?

a. Teaching her stress management techniques
b. Allowing her to complete work in a separate setting
c. Provide rewards for completing work
d. Giving her choices about what work she does

91. What is the *primary* purpose of universal newborn hearing screenings?

a. Educational planning
b. Disability diagnosis
c. Early identification
d. IDEA eligibility

92. Of the following instructional strategies used, which is most likely to support LD students in taking risks during reading lessons in a large group/class setting?

a. Assigning students to pairs to discuss teacher questions about the lesson
b. Asking students to give summaries reviewing the main points of a lesson
c. Having students complete reminder worksheets at the end of the lesson
d. Inviting students to ask "who," what," or "where" questions on a lesson

93. A teacher notices that the majority of students in his class failed an assignment despite demonstrated effort. Which of the following is the best course of action?

a. Lower the expectations of the students and design easier assignments.
b. Provide additional scaffolding and teaching while maintaining expectations
c. Do not make any changes, as students should be operating outside of their comfort zones.
d. Remove expectations and allow students to work at their own paces and skill levels, facilitating a more natural approach.

94. Ms. Ross introduces new vocabulary words to her class daily. She then assigns reading that includes these words, uses those words in her speech as she presents lessons, and points them out when they appear in other contexts. Which instructional method does this represent?

a. Appropriate word choice
b. Teaching of word analysis
c. Using contextual analysis
d. Multiple word exposures

95. Which of the following is not one of the components of a free appropriate public education (FAPE)?

a. Parents must participate in IEP meetings.
b. Schools must provide the best possible education.
c. Schools must notify parents of changes to the IEP.
d. Parents are allowed to request an outside evaluation.

96. Which of the following is not one of the purposes of the prereferral process when evaluating students for special education services?

a. To evaluate student strengths and weaknesses
b. To put accommodations and interventions into place
c. To evaluate accommodations and interventions
d. To obtain consent to begin the evaluation process

97. Mr. Stewart's students show good reading comprehension of any given paragraph in any chapter of their textbook, but they have trouble organizing, recalling, or applying the main points of a chapter. Which of the following is the simplest, most direct, and efficient way to help?

a. Point out and explain the text's informational structure and features.
b. Create separate handouts with simplified organization of main points.
c. Identify, select, procure, duplicate, and distribute graphic organizers.
d. Create and deliver a slide show presentation for each text chapter.

98. Bart is not only graduating from elementary/middle school and entering high school; he is also being mainstreamed from a special education class and school to a general education class in a regular high school. All of his teachers, therapists, and other team members as well as his parents agree he has developed the skills needed to be successful in this new placement. Despite his accomplishments, Bart is very anxious about the move. What can his teacher do?

a. Recommend that he be medically evaluated for an anti-anxiety prescription medication.
b. Advise against the move until such time as his anxiety abates.
c. Teach Bart coping skills to help him to manage the transition.
d. Disregard his anxiety and move him; he will get over it.

99. Bobby is an 11th-grade at-risk student with a specific learning disability who rarely sees either of his parents. Which of the following instructional strategies is likely to be most effective for Bobby long term?

a. Helping Bobby research colleges he might want to attend
b. Giving Bobby extra support to pass all of his classes
c. Teaching Bobby executive functioning skills
d. Assisting Bobby in applying and interviewing for jobs

100. William is autistic and is very proficient at computer programming. His teacher helped him to find a part-time computer job while he was still in high school. William has always lived at home with his parents. He will be attending community college classes following graduation from high school and continuing to work at his part-time job. He is interested in living on his own but is unsure about what he will need to know to accomplish this. How might his teacher best help him reach this goal?

a. Advise him to take a class in independent living skills along with his other classes.
b. Tell him about a free resource network's website that helps people make such transitions.
c. Tell him to try getting an apartment with a roommate and see how he likes it.
d. Advise him to stay at home with his parents until he is more prepared to move.

Answer Key and Explanations for Test #1

1. A: The purpose of an intelligence test is to measure a student's ability to reason and solve problems, which includes thinking abstractly. Intelligence tests can provide valuable information in deciphering the reasons that a student may struggle in particular areas. These tests can be beneficial for students of all grades and disabilities for gathering information. Answer B is incorrect because measuring a student's spoken language abilities would be considered a processing assessment. Answer C is incorrect because measuring a student's ability to convey ideas through oral language would be considered a communication assessment. Answer D is incorrect because visual information assessments would typically fall under the visual-spatial assessment categories.

2. C: Although all of these choices may impact students throughout their lifetimes, students with multiple disabilities are likely to be impacted the most. Students with multiple disabilities have two or more disabilities that severely impact their access to education. One of these disabilities is typically an intellectual disability, which impacts students throughout their life. Answer A is incorrect because developmental delays typically impact younger students and may or may not last throughout a person's lifetime. Answer B is incorrect because students that have just speech or language impairments may end up learning to overcome these disabilities eventually. Answer D is incorrect because although specific learning disabilities may impact students in different ways, these are less likely to have an impact on a person than someone with multiple disabilities.

3. A: The IDEA annual reports to Congress consistently show that specific learning disability is the most common disability. The 2024 46th Annual Report to Congress illustrates that the second most common disability was speech or language impairment, followed by other health impairment.

4. A: Making labels in more than one language is not confusing to the children. Rather, it is supportive of their home language (if it is not English), and bilingual or multilingual labels send the message that writing comes in a variety of shapes and languages. A print-rich environment includes labels to identify objects and work areas, print that is at a child's eye level so it can be seen easily, and print that was created by the children themselves so that they can make the connection between print and their own work. That connection between individual creation and print is reinforced when the teacher models writing by preparing posters and other written materials in front of the children.

5. C: The constructivism theory states that learning motives are determined by the learner and by outside rewards from the community. Motivation comes not just from the learners themselves based on their knowledge but also through communicating with others. It is important to understand which approach to take when motivating students to achieve their highest potential. Answer a is incorrect because the behaviorism theory states that motivation is extrinsic. Answer b is incorrect because the cognitivism theory states that motivation for learning is intrinsic. Answer d is incorrect because the humanism theory states that motivation comes from inside the learner and is therefore intrinsic.

6. D: Curriculum-based assessments can be beneficial in determining how much progress a student is making on their goals. It is important to monitor the progress a student is making by giving them curriculum-based assessments that are directed toward their IEP goals. These data can help to guide instruction and determine if any changes need to be made so that the student makes continued progress toward that goal. Answer a is incorrect because comparing a student's score to others in the district would be a norm-referenced or standardized assessment. Answer b is incorrect because comparing a student's score to their grade in the class would likely be a summative assessment. Answer c is incorrect because comparing a student's score to the average score would likely be a norm-referenced assessment.

7. A: Referring the mother to a free reading teacher is a way to improve her reading skills and increase her confidence so that she can participate in her daughter's education. Having a few practice sessions in which Janet's mother gets to participate with both teachers as well as her daughter will further boost her confidence at the beginning and give her ideas about how to work with Janet at home. Therefore option A is correct.

For Mrs. Stroud to work with the mother herself is unrealistic given the constraints on a teacher's time. If Mrs. Stroud knows of free adult education, this would be more practical. Therefore option B is incorrect.

There are two disadvantages in Mrs. Stroud scheduling more time to work with Janet. First, Mrs. Stroud's schedule may make this impossible. Second, it does not involve Janet's mother as an active participant in her daughter's education. Even if this plan were possible, if Mrs. Stroud took on extra work it would result in a missed opportunity to involve Janet's mother. It would also preclude the opportunity to improve an adult's education. Therefore option C is incorrect.

Arranging home tutoring for Janet has several disadvantages. First, tutors normally charge fees. If Mrs. Stroud knows of a free tutoring program, there is no reason to cause Janet's mother the financial burden that would come from hiring a private tutor. Second, the tutor would be filling a role that, given some help, Janet's mother could assume. Third, tutoring would not promote the mother's active participation in Janet's education. Fourth, not helping Janet's mother improve her reading skills misses an opportunity to improve an adult's education, which benefits both mother and daughter. Therefore option D is incorrect.

8. D: Peer helpers are more likely to keep the restless student on task than to distract that student; therefore, peer helpers are a good idea. Allowing a student who has trouble staying on task to do a "gallery walk"; that is, to expend some energy by walking around to examine the lesson materials that are on display, is a good practice because once the student has seen the materials s/he is less likely to be distracted by wondering about them. A student who has trouble staying on task is helped by being assigned specific tasks to accomplish because breaking up the assignment into smaller jobs seems more achievable. Using response cards catches the attention of the student who has trouble staying on task and pulls that student into the lesson with the others.

9. C: Joel has odd behaviors but many can be remedied by training. Time-out will not change his behavior in this case. Punishment is inappropriate. He has not been taught proper mealtime behavior. Therefore option A is incorrect.

Having Joel clean up the floor is another type of punishment. With an individual who has profound intellectual disabilities, this is unlikely to change his sitting and eating behavior. Therefore option B is incorrect.

The houseparent should meet with the IEP team to plan IEP objectives. The team can write objectives for Joel to sit facing forward with his legs under the table and to eat over the table. The behavior specialist can write a task analysis for the houseparent to implement in training him to perform these behaviors, with reinforcement of proper execution. Therefore option C is correct.

Placing a drop cloth under Joel's chair would make it easier for the houseparent to clean up after meals, but Joel will not learn anything. If he eats in other settings, he will still make a mess. If he learns to sit and eat properly at home, this will transfer to other places. It would be impractical and inappropriate to put a drop cloth under him wherever he eats. Therefore option D is incorrect.

10. B: The COACH model (Giangreco, Cloninger and Iverson, 1998) is a collaborative approach described by educational researchers as student-directed planning, which they claim goes "beyond person-centered planning" (Wehmeyer et al, 2002) by making the student central in the process. Person-centered planning typically centers more on family and social support systems. GAP (Turnbull & Turnbull, 2002) (A); MAPs (Pearpoint, Forest, & O'Brien, 1996) (C); and PATH (D), which extends the MAPs process to develop "a more definitive plan of action," are all examples of person-centered planning.

11. B: According to Piaget's theory, there are four stages of development that occur in sequence and result in learning. These stages begin at birth with the sensorimotor stage, which continues until the child is approximately 2 years old. During this stage, an infant learns about himself or herself and the environment through motor reflexes. The preoperational stage, which begins when the child is 2 years old and ends when he or she is approximately 6 years old, includes language development. The next stage is the concrete operational stage, which begins at approximately 6 years old and continues into early adolescence. During this stage, learning continues, and the ability for abstract thought begins to develop. Finally, in adolescence, a person enters the formal operational stage. At this point, according to Piaget, abstract thought is fully functional, and individuals are able to utilize deductive reasoning skills.

12. C: A diagnostic assessment is used to identify a student's specific strengths and skill gaps so that meaningful, individualized IEP goals can be developed. Assessment data shows exactly which math problem-solving skills Peyton has mastered and which ones he still needs to learn. This information best guides his math instruction because the IEP team can write targeted goals. Answer A is incorrect because accommodations are determined through the IEP process, not by the diagnostic assessment alone. Answer B is incorrect because class placement is not the primary goal for Peyton. Answer D is incorrect because modifications are typically based on comprehensive IEP decisions, not diagnostic results alone.

13. B: It is an informal assessment of their writing and also gives the teacher an idea of each student's interests, abilities and skills. This assignment gives the teacher an idea of her students' writing abilities at the beginning of the year. She can return to this piece of writing during the school year to assess progress.

14. D: When teaching a science lesson to a group of third-grade students, it is important to incorporate hands-on learning activities. Learning centers can provide opportunities for these students to do activities and learn about different topics. Learning centers are most appropriate for younger students, such as a group of third graders. Answer A is incorrect because reciprocal teaching would be most appropriate for older students who are capable of teaching each other rather than younger students. Answer B is incorrect because Socratic questioning would be most appropriate for higher level questioning based on thoughtful dialogue between the teacher and student and is a skill that third graders likely would not have. Answer C is incorrect because direct instruction may be more appropriate for a more abstract topic such as reading or math, as it does not promote hands-on exploration and investigation.

15. D: Large-print books are a good idea for Clyde's visual impairment and subjects relevant to teens are appropriate for his age, but not for his first-grade reading level. Therefore, option A is incorrect.

Children's books have the large print and simple subject matter Clyde needs but are not appropriate to his age. Therefore, option B is incorrect.

With the availability of large-print textbooks, a magnifying glass is not the easiest way for Clyde to read. Having one would certainly expand the types of media he could see, and it would be beneficial for him to have it if he should want or need to see the small print in everyday media like newspapers and phone books. But for reading, it would not be as easy on his eyes as large print. Also, many books with regular size print will be beyond Clyde's first-grade level of reading comprehension. Therefore, option C is incorrect.

Books in large print and on teen-related topics but with simplified text are the ideal combination for Clyde's visual impairment, age, and reading comprehension level. Therefore, option D is correct.

16. B: The only true choice is (B): Repetition is very effective for building reading fluency. The teacher can have the student read a passage aloud repeatedly until s/he achieves the desired fluency, and then progress to a harder selection. Timing this exercise also promotes fluency, which includes speed as well as accuracy; therefore (A) is incorrect: Timed exercises should not be avoided in remediating fluency problems. Teachers can also use timing by giving students "speed drills" for individual words. A non-timed exercise can be having a student repeatedly read a familiar book out loud, giving feedback and direction as needed. Another technique is a readers' theatre; it is not true that this is good for showing progress but not making progress (C). The practice and feedback component of this exercise aids with improvement, even as it showcases progress in fluency. It is not true that reading in pairs increases comprehension but not fluency (D); partner/paired reading promotes both.

17. A: Both, the left. Research using MRIs shows dyslexics use both sides of their brains for activities such as reading, while non-dyslexics use only the left side.

18. C: Although parents have many rights with regard to their child's IEP, running the IEP is not one of those rights. Typically, the IEP meeting will be run by a special education teacher or administrator. Parents are encouraged to be highly involved in the IEP meeting, but they are not responsible for facilitating the meeting. Answer a is incorrect because parents are important members of the IEP team. Answer b is incorrect because parents can call an IEP meeting if they believe their child's needs must be addressed. Answer d is incorrect because parents can help to develop IEP goals.

19. A: Although all of these choices may potentially be beneficial for students with specific learning disabilities, job skills trainers would likely benefit all of these students. Students with specific learning disabilities will often need to improve their job seeking, interview, and career interest abilities in order to pursue a career after high school. Job skills trainers can help them in each of these areas and provide them with the support they will need to be confident in their career. Answer b is incorrect because the majority of students with learning disabilities will not need independent living assistance. Answer c is incorrect because although many of these students may attend colleges and universities, more will likely attend community colleges and vocational programs. Answer d is incorrect because although many of these students will need mental health services, more will likely benefit from job skills training.

20. A: In order to assess a student for oral expression abilities, a test to measure their expressive language abilities is most appropriate. Students who struggle with oral expression tend to struggle expressing themselves orally due to many factors. This kind of assessment can guide the data collection needed for classroom instruction and skills to work on. Answer B is incorrect because receptive language assessments are more appropriate for students who struggle with language input rather than output. Answer C is incorrect because auditory discrimination tests are used for students who struggle with different sounds. Answer D is incorrect because this kind of assessment would be more appropriate in measuring a student's cognitive abilities.

21. A: Independent living skills goals focus on functional, teachable behaviors that support daily life after high school. Being able to access public transportation is a specific, measurable skill that can be taught and practiced. Answer B is incorrect because living with a roommate is a life outcome rather than a skill-based goal. Answer C is incorrect because living in a group home is a placement decision, not an instructional goal. Answer D is incorrect because attending community college is an educational outcome, not an independent living skill.

22. B: This student has learned to perform the skills at home but has not generalized them to other settings. It is superfluous to re-teach him the skills (A) because he has demonstrated their acquisition at home. Teaching skill maintenance (C) is unnecessary as the parents report he has performed the skills for years, so he has achieved maintenance but not generalization. Teaching skill discrimination (D) does not apply to this example as there was no mention of the student having any problems separating one skill or skill set from another or applying skills to the wrong tasks.

23. D: Mr. Ivanov should find someone to help him write a note to the parents in Spanish explaining that he will help them find a volunteer translator if they do not have a friend or family member who could translate for them. Since parent-teacher communication is very important to students' development, Mr. Ivanov should make every reasonable effort to ensure that the parents can participate in conferences. Simply telling the parents or his principal to find a translator would create an unnecessary barrier to the parents' participation in the conferences. Asking fifth-graders to serve as translators for their own parent-teacher conferences would be inappropriate since students of this age are not usually present during these conferences, and their presence could prevent a frank discussion between the teacher and the parents from occurring.

24. D: Assigning one student to compile and present the group's work could result in that student doing more of the project than the others. This would not be truly collaborative, so option A is incorrect.

Allowing students to volunteer to contribute to the project will result in some students doing most or all of the work while others end up doing little or none. This is not collaboration, so option B is incorrect.

The teacher leading the activity and directing what the students do would not be a collaborative group project. The students should be learning to cooperate with one another and to be more independent in conducting the project. The description in this option is a traditional teacher-led activity, so option C is incorrect.

Assigning each student an equal number of duties related to the project is a way to ensure that they all do equal amounts of work. The students will still be conducting the project themselves and working cooperatively together, but the teacher's initial assignment will prevent unequal distribution of participation, so option D is correct.

25. C: Although some of these choices may be true in certain situations, parents of students with disabilities will typically see some of the signs before the child is evaluated at school. The parents likely spend a good deal of time with these children, so they are aware of what they can and can't do. They may not know for certain whether or not a student has a disability, but they can determine what they struggle with at home. Answer A is incorrect because families of children with disabilities are more likely to experience issues than they are to come together. Answer B is incorrect because parents are not the cause of the learning disability and also cannot be the cure. Answer D is incorrect because while some families do often seek out information to learn more about disabilities, this is not as consistently seen as families suspecting a disability is present in a child before the school does.

26. A: Answer choice A is the most accurate. Doing this helps Ms. Winslow's students to organize what they read and learn from the textbooks. While many teachers are familiar with students never reading their textbooks (B), this is not Ms. Winslow's main reason for her practice. The textbook items listed in the question as being features she regularly points out to her students are all specifically organizational devices. Thus, answer C is incorrect: This practice may or may not enhance her presentation, but it does facilitate learning. Answer D—that this helps LD students but is a waste of time for other students—is also incorrect, since all students can benefit from being reminded to use these features in their textbooks as aids to effective learning.

27. A: Although all of these choices may be beneficial to certain students, providing a graphic organizer would be most beneficial for students who struggle with organizing their writing because it gives them a framework for how to set it up. Many students struggle to organize their writing and stay on topic, and the graphic organizer is designed to help with this. Answer B is incorrect because simply modeling the writing likely is not enough support for many students. Answer C is incorrect because practice without organizational support does not address the underlying difficulty. Answer D is incorrect because peer collaboration may support idea development, but it does not directly teach students how to structure and focus their writing.

28. C: When selecting a curriculum for functional skills, it is important to focus on tasks that will occur the most often. Personal hygiene is a skill that people do every single day and is a crucial skill to work on. Answer A is incorrect because although cooking is important, personal hygiene is more useful and vital. Answer B is incorrect because laundry is something that should be learned after personal hygiene skills have been mastered. Answer D is incorrect because people must be able to care for themselves and their bodies before they can go out shopping in the community.

29. B: Telling Nina simply to avoid the public library does not help to fulfill the goal of inclusion. It puts additional limits on a student who already has a disability. Restricting her library activities to the school does not give Nina the least restrictive environment. Therefore option A is incorrect.

The special education teacher should know how to foster respectful, beneficial relationships with professionals in the community. By supervising Nina she can aid her in using the public library while keeping her from disturbing the quiet and annoying the librarian. Teaching her to control the volume of her voice when she is in the public library may enable Nina to visit the library by herself in the future without disturbing the peace. Acting as a facilitator can change the librarian's negative attitude toward Nina and establish more friendly relations. This will eliminate the librarian's discrimination against Nina and will promote a more positive relationship between a student with a disability and a community professional. Therefore option B is correct.

Complaining to the principal is not taking responsibility as a teacher for collaborating with members of the community. Though the librarian is discriminating, complaining to the principal is a negative action. The school principal could not do anything beneficial unless he supervised Nina's library visits, which is a better role for the teacher to take. If he simply insisted to the librarian that she allow Nina to visit, the librarian would be further antagonized. Therefore option C is incorrect.

Sending Nina to the school psychologist for consolation would not change the situation itself. Counseling would be more appropriate for a situation that cannot be changed (i.e., to accept the fact that she has a disability). Therefore option D is incorrect.

30. A: Building rapport with parents at the beginning of the school year is a teacher strategy inviting parental involvement and partnership by showing that teachers value the importance of parental contributions, rather than only contacting/meeting with parents about problems (B). Rather than avoid all advice, teachers should offer all families information for positive home learning environments (C), e.g., homework spaces, homework-checking plans, scheduling homework, limiting TV, etc. While some topics are private, teachers usually should ask families (D) about expectations for students, current homework support, emotional impacts of hardships, student home responsibilities, and how teachers and schools can help.

31. B: Special education evaluations are required to be completed within 60 days or parent consent, not 30. Districts are required to comply with the 60-day limit in order to determine eligibility for special education services. It is important to understand that although the evaluation needs to consider all of the needs of the student and be in-depth, it must also occur in a timely manner. Answer a is incorrect because parental consent is required before the evaluation process can begin. Answer c is incorrect because a multidisciplinary team, including special services providers, special education teachers, general education teachers, parents, and the student, must be involved. Answer d is incorrect because a parent can request that their child be evaluated for special education services.

32. B: Multisensory strategies, including the use of touch in manipulating letters or tapping the letters with their fingers, can be effective strategies for students with dyslexia. This sensory approach allows them to break down words and memorize them in different ways. Answer A is incorrect because the whole-word approach does not tend to be as effective for students with dyslexia. Answers C is incorrect because, while it may be useful, modeling is not as effective for addressing reading skills as using multisensory strategies. Answer D is incorrect because graphic organizers typically help students with comprehension and idea organization rather than with the reading challenges typically associated with dyslexia.

33. A: Students with LDs characterized by memory problems typically have (A) more difficulty with short-term memory than with long-term memory. This appears related to problems with retrieval more than with storage. (LD students with reading disabilities may also have difficulty storing new information if they have deficits in linking old knowledge to new.) Therefore, answer (B) is backwards. Answer (C) is incorrect as the difficulties are not equal with both types of memory, but more with short-term than long-term, meaning that answer (D), no clear pattern, is also incorrect.

34. D: Interval recording is best for a behavior which seems constant or nearly so. By marking whether a behavior occurs during specified short time intervals (e.g., 10 seconds, 30 seconds, one minute, or two minutes) on a data sheet, the observer can provide an estimate of how many times a high-frequency behavior occurs. Event recording (A) is better suited for less frequent behaviors of shorter duration. The observer counts the number of times the behavior occurs during a specified period, such as a 30-minute lesson. Duration recording (B) is best for determining how long a behavior continues (for example, out-of-seat behavior) using a stopwatch or clock. Latency recording (C) can be used for measuring how long a student takes to respond to teacher instructions.

35. D: The parent/guardian is the best person to consult for this information. Parents and guardians have been with their children for their entire lives and would have much more information than any other source. They should have access to the student's medical records and will have information from before their children started attending school. Previous teachers and school counselors likely would not have access to most developmental milestones and would likely be missing other pertinent information.

36. C: Teacher behaviors that promote school-home communication include devoting equal time to listening to parents/families (A), mutually exchanging teacher and family expertise (B) with each other, and brainstorming with families to find strategies supporting individual students (D). However, when teachers limit their behaviors with families to telling them what to do (C), this impedes school-home communication.

37. A: Diagnostic assessments are primarily used to determine a student's current instructional level and identify areas of strength and need. Diagnostic data can influence instructional decisions, but specific decisions about disability identification and special education services require more comprehensive evaluations beyond a single diagnostic assessment. Answer B is incorrect because the diagnostic assessment alone would not be able to determine what disability a student may have. Answer C is incorrect because although the diagnostic can assist in determining the special education services for a student, it likely would not be the only measure used. Answer D is incorrect because a summative assessment would be more appropriate to determine how much a student has learned.

38. D: Although there may be many benefits to holding an externally facilitated IEP meeting, it typically takes a little longer for the special education teacher to prepare. The purpose of the externally facilitated IEP meeting is to include everyone in the conversation using an outside facilitator who may or may not know the student. The external facilitator will need to meet with the special education teacher beforehand in order to get an understanding of the student, which tends to take extra time. Answer A is incorrect because the facilitated IEP is designed to be focused and handle one issue at a time. Answer B is incorrect because part of the facilitator's role is to ensure that they can problem solve whenever a conflict does arise. Answer C is incorrect because everyone on the IEP team will be included in the discussion at a facilitated IEP meeting.

39. B: While setting rules and establishing routines is important to classroom management, the teacher should not be so firm that there is no room for flexibility and adjustments. A teacher's relationship with a child must remain consistent in terms of the teacher's interactions with the child and the expectations set for the child; a moody or fickle teacher can frustrate and anger the children. Teachers should respond to children positively and avoid negativity for the relationship to be constructive and nurturing. Although the teacher is the ultimate decision-maker in the classroom and must establish authority, sharing power with the children by guiding them into making responsible choices gives the children a sense of empowerment and a stake in the classroom situation.

40. C: According to IDEA, students with a dual diagnosis of a hearing and visual impairment are considered deaf-blind and receive services under that category. Students who have one diagnosis of a hearing impairment would be eligible under that category instead. It is important to under each of the areas of impact for students so they can receive all of the services they are eligible for. Answer a is incorrect because students with fluctuating hearing can still be eligible for the "hearing impairment" category. Answer b is incorrect because amplification is expected to improve a student's hearing. Answer d is incorrect because if Rob's educational performance is adversely affected by his hearing loss, he would be eligible for the category.

41. C: It is likely best to try to have this conversation in person with the parents as there may be something going on at home or elsewhere. Answer A is incorrect because calling the parents immediately may catch them off guard and they may think their son is in trouble. Answer B is incorrect because it is possible the behavior continues to worsen, and more issues arise if no action is taken. Answer D is incorrect because an IEP meeting likely isn't warranted until more information is discussed with the parents and student to see what might be going on.

42. D: Although all of these choices may provide instances to change the test or the format of the test, it is likely most beneficial to create a new test when the standards are modified. When students are unable to access the regular academic standards, it is often necessary to create a new assessment to meet the needs of these students are assess what they know. Although the majority of students can access these regular standards with accommodations or modifications, some students need to work with modified standards due to their disability. Answer A is incorrect because students who do not have access to the curriculum would likely not be assessed at all. Answer B is incorrect because students with intellectual abilities may or may not be able to access the standards with accommodations or modifications. Answer C is incorrect because accommodated tests typically do not involve a new test being created.

43. B: The only way to identify a true learning disability with reading would be to test these students in reading both English and their native language. Without ruling out English as a second language being the source of their reading difficulties, it is impossible to assume they all have learning disabilities regardless of language. Therefore, option A is incorrect.

Because these students are all English language learners, it is more likely that this is the true source of their reading difficulties rather than learning disabilities. Therefore, option B is correct.

Since English is a second language for these students, it cannot be assumed that the first or most likely cause of their reading difficulties is a learning disability. Therefore, option C is incorrect.

It is so common for ELLs to perform less well in reading English than native English speakers that it is highly unlikely for reading problems and ESL status to be a complete coincidence with every student in the group. Therefore, option D is incorrect.

44. B: Ms. Kincaid should call the parents who have not responded to notify them directly about the conferences. When one strategy (sending notes) does not appear to be effective, the teacher should shift her strategy accordingly. Answer D is inappropriate because it is unfair to place the responsibility of getting parents to attend conferences on fourth grade students. Asking students directly (A) would also be inappropriate because it would not necessarily yield reliable information and it could also make students feel uncomfortable or "singled-out" on the basis of their parents' behavior.

45. C: The most likely diagnosis is autism. Autistic children are typically very withdrawn, avoid eye contact, and are not responsive to verbal or physical attempts to connect. Some autistic children fall into repetitive behaviors that are very difficult to arrest or prevent. These behaviors include rocking, spinning and handshaking.

46. C: When students fall within one standard deviation of the mean, this is most often considered in the average range, and a student would not be eligible. Students being evaluated for a specific learning disability must have a score that is considered statistically significant in order to be eligible. It is important to understand where one standard deviation falls in order to determine where the student scores. Answer A is incorrect because the student would likely not be eligible unless they were outside one standard deviation. Answer B is incorrect because although it is possible that more testing could be considered, this score shows that the student is within the average range. Answer D is incorrect because there is likely not enough information to determine whether or not a 504 plan would be appropriate for Joseph.

47. A: Embodied learning allows students to participate in activities that get the whole body involved. It allows students to move while still learning the content. Many students struggle to sit and learn all day, so this kind of instruction allows them to get up and move. It is important to provide a variety of learning activities in order to meet the needs of all of the students in the class. Answer B is incorrect because inquiry-based learning involves having students ask questions in order to learn. Answer C is incorrect because blended learning involves a combination of online and traditional learning. Answer D is incorrect because service learning typically involves students going out into the community to learn.

48. D: Although some children may want to start being more like their friends at Josh's age, this is an aspect of social development that typically comes later. This is a behavior that would likely occur after a child has spent more time with friends in order to learn more about them. This typically happens as children make friends and spend the majority of their time with them. Answer a is incorrect because showing some separation anxiety is typical of a student in preschool. Answer b is incorrect because cooperating with other children is expected from a child of this age. Answer c is incorrect because exploring independently is also to be expected.

49. B: Obsessive Compulsive Disorder (OCD). Children and adults with OCD typically engage in a series of highly ritualized behaviors that are rigidly performed when they feel stressed. Behaviors include tapping, snapping fingers, blinking, counting and so forth.

50. A: Although all of these choices may be beneficial in targeting specific student behavior, single-domain scales tend to be most beneficial for students with ADHD. Single-domain scales are designed to assess a specific area of concern such as executive functioning. Many students with ADHD will have one main area of concern that the evaluators will focus on. Answer b is incorrect because self-report scales tend to be more beneficial for older students who can accurately report their behavioral concerns. Answer c is incorrect because multidomain scales may make it difficult to target one specific area of concern in students. Answer d is incorrect because observer/informant scales tend to be for students with multiple areas of concern in order to determine the cause of the behavior.

51. D: If the IEP meeting is already scripted, it does not provide each of the stakeholders with an opportunity to provide input and share their side of the story. Answer A is incorrect because facilitated meetings are a great way to make everyone feel included and have a say. Answer B is incorrect because a slide show presentation can be more entertaining than simply reading from the IEP. Answer C is incorrect because a student-led meeting heavily includes the student and allows him or her to truly be the center of the meeting.

52. A: Although all of these choices may have their own benefits in helping students feel welcome, community building is likely the best long-term strategy in ensuring that the students feel supported. When students have opportunities to get to know each other and the teacher, they will be more likely to feel welcome and needed. If students do not feel welcome in the class, they may not feel safe and may start to distance themselves from the rest of the class. Answer B is incorrect because if there is too much room to negotiate, the students will not clearly understand the rules. Answer C is incorrect because although posting work in the room can make some students feel welcome and important, other students may be embarrassed. Answer D is incorrect because although it is important to establish authority, it is also important that the students feel like they are involved in the process as well.

53. C: The Family Educational Rights and Privacy Act of 1974 protects student records. Under this legislation, parents (and eligible students once rights transfer at age 18 or upon attendance at a postsecondary institution) have the right to inspect and review the student's education records, and schools generally may not disclose these records to others without written consent, except in specific circumstances allowed by law (e.g., to school officials with a legitimate educational interest). Additionally, students have the opportunity to review their academic records and if necessary, make amendments in the instance of incorrect information. Information pertaining to the students' social security number, grades, GPA, and academic performance are protected by this legislation, as well as information about behavioral issues such as suspensions, academic dishonesty, and probation.

54. A: Trip-training was successful in the previous, more restrictive setting. Even in the case of a less restrictive community setting, something that worked before will work again. The stress of the change and the decrease in structure probably contributed to the reemergence of Andrea's enuresis. Reapplying a technique familiar to her will remedy it. With her prior training she will soon be getting up and going to the bathroom every two hours on her own. Therefore option A is correct.

Trying to find a different strategy is unnecessary. This would only be indicated if trip-training had never been successful. Also, trip-training is not too restrictive a strategy for the group home. It is a technique that works well in any setting. Therefore option B is correct.

Wearing adult diapers would be a step backward for Andrea. It is more restrictive and makes her less independent. It does not teach, remind, or encourage her to use constructive methods for bladder management. Therefore option C is incorrect.

Wearing absorbent underwear seems more grown-up than diapers, but this still does not make use of Andrea's capacity to use techniques for bladder management, whereas trip-training does. Therefore option D is incorrect.

55. D: Modifications of the curriculum alter the curriculum that is being taught, and these students are expected to complete assessments that are different from those their peers complete. Access to alternative books changes what the student is learning and therefore would change the expectations for the assignment. Answers A, B, and C are all accommodations that allow students to access the same curriculum as their peers with alterations to how the material is presented. Textbooks with large print, computers for typing, and manipulatives are all accommodations to allow students to access the curriculum.

56. C: Although all of these choices may be examples of some kind of formative assessment, observing her in class is most likely to provide the best data. Formative assessments are designed to assess what the student knows as the learning occurs. In order to monitor progress using formative assessments, it is important to take a look at the areas the student struggles in and if she is improving. Answer A is incorrect because interviewing a first grader like Andrea may not always provide the most accurate data. Answer B is incorrect because giving her academic probes would not show how she is developing on her overall social and behavioral skills as well as observation would. Answer D is incorrect because simply monitoring how she does on tests may not provide the whole picture in how she is developing overall.

57. B: Adaptive pencil and paper holders would not help Stephen, as he can only press buttons with one hand. He could not manipulate a writing implement with his paralysis. Therefore, option A is incorrect.

A computer with a built-in voice synthesizer would let Stephen program all the words in his vocabulary into it. He could express himself despite his paralyzed vocal cords. He has excellent expressive and receptive language skills and a high IQ, so this would be the best solution for him. Therefore, option B is correct.

An electrolarynx is used by some laryngectomy patients whose larynxes have been surgically removed because of laryngeal cancer. It is an alternative to learning esophageal speech. This device is hand-held. Stephen could not hold it up to his throat as required. It also requires the speech system's muscles to work. It emits a tone, and the user manipulates the tongue, lips, cheeks, and throat, as in normal speech, to modulate the tone into recognizable speech sounds. Stephen could not use this device with his paralysis. Therefore, option C is incorrect.

A communication board would not be the best choice for Stephen, as it would afford simpler communication of basic needs and feelings. With Stephen's high IQ and advanced academic skills, he can program a computer with more complex ideas and complete sentences. He would undoubtedly find the communication board limited and would be frustrated. Therefore, option D is incorrect.

58. A: According to IDEA, birth trauma would not be considered one of the causes of traumatic brain injury. Students with birth trauma would likely be considered under a different eligibility category. Students who receive services under the traumatic brain injury category will typically have a medical diagnosis of a traumatic brain injury. Answer B is incorrect because combat injuries can be one of the causes of traumatic brain injuries, even at a young age. Answer C is incorrect because violence is often associated with students who are impacted by traumatic brain injuries. Answer D is incorrect because sports-related injuries can also cause damage to the brain and cause traumatic brain injuries.

59. B: James M. Baldwin used the term "mental deficiency" in 1901. In 1937, Tredgold referred to "a state of incomplete mental development," so option A is incorrect.

The criterion that intellectual disabilities originate during the developmental period, defined as from birth to age 16, was used by Heber for the AAMD's 1961 definition. It does not appear in earlier definitions, so option B is correct.

The association of intellectual disabilities with impaired adaptive behavior appears as early as 1937. In Tredgold's definition, he states "...that the individual is incapable of adapting himself to the normal environment of his fellows..." Therefore, option C is incorrect.

Contrary to Heber's 1961 AAMD definition, which states that intellectual disabilities originate in the developmental period, or Grossman's 1973 AAMD definition, which extends the developmental period to age 18, Edgar A. Doll's 1941 definition includes as one of his six criteria that intellectual disabilities "obtains at maturity." Therefore, option D is incorrect.

60. B: Although all of these choices can be helpful in ensuring that inclusion programs are successful, collaboration between teachers can best help students with disabilities access the general education curriculum. This collaboration can allow teachers to develop lesson plans and strategies to promote student growth. Without this collaboration, students with disabilities may not be as successful in their classes as they otherwise could have been. Answer a is incorrect because just meeting with the administrators may or may not change the inclusion programs at the school. Answer c is incorrect because although new assessments can help to measure growth, these may not always ensure successful inclusion. Answer d is incorrect because professional development in itself likely will not improve the inclusion model.

61. A: Norm-referenced tests compare the student's score to norms, such as national averages of scores for students of the same age or grade level. These are standardized tests, such as national achievement tests including the SAT, ACT, GRE, etc. Criterion-referenced tests (B) do not compare students' scores to other students' scores, but rather measure students' performance against a criterion, standard, or objective previously determined and given to students before testing. Class quizzes, exams, oral reports, presentations, experiments, and performance-based tests (C) are examples of criterion-referenced tests. Ipsative measures or tests (D) compare the student's performance to his/her own previous performance.

62. A: Mr. John's lesson plan is based around a boys' basketball team. Ms. Deere objects to this because their class is coeducational, and girls are less likely to relate to scenarios about an all-boy team. Girls can also play basketball. The female students will probably feel left out when considering this scenario. Therefore option A is correct.

There is no reason students with hearing impairments could not play basketball with some accommodations, so they could relate to this scenario. Even if none of them has ever played basketball, they have probably all seen a basketball game by the time they are in high school (on TV if not live). Therefore option B is incorrect.

It is possible that Ms. Deere could resent Mr. John having written the lesson plan without her input. But this is not the most valid reason for her objection. If it were, the question would not state specifically that Ms. Deere feels the lesson is biased. Therefore option C is incorrect.

While the lesson plan does involve a physical education/sport activity, this does not mean that no academics are involved. The question states that the plan is for multimodal activities. The students will thus be doing a variety of activities using different media and modes of learning and expression. So academic exercises such as writing essays and taking quizzes or tests could easily be parts of the lesson plan. Therefore option D is incorrect.

63. C: The person who requested the conference should be the one who starts the conference so they are able to establish the purpose of the meeting. This could be a teacher, counselor, administrator, parent, or (in some cases) even the student. This allows everyone in attendance to know the purpose of the meeting so they are better able to focus their discussion and not waste valuable time. Administrators, school counselors, parents, and teachers can all request meetings, and if they are the ones to request the meeting, they should generally be prepared to be the ones that will open the meeting. However, it is important to note that in some instances when a parent requests a conference, it may still be best for a staff or faculty member to introduce and organize the discussion to help establish clear lines of communication.

64. B: The federal government funds and supports public health systems, but it does not control the states' organization and delivery of public health services. Therefore, option A is incorrect.

The federal government gives funding and support, but it delegates authority to each state to organize and deliver public health services, as dictated by the Constitution. Therefore, option B is correct.

All states do not have freestanding public health agencies operating on their own. Some states do have such agencies and some do not. Therefore, option C is incorrect.

All states do not have umbrella organizations known as departments of health and human services. Some states do and some do not. Therefore, option D is incorrect.

65. A: With students who have disabilities, the time to introduce each career development stage depends more on the individual student's developmental level, which often is not commensurate with the student's grade level (B) or chronological age (D) in some or all domains. While the student's experiential level (C) is important for selecting instructional materials and methods, the developmental level has more impact on whether a student will be able to learn the skills acquired in each stage.

66. B: Although all of these choices would be helpful in preparing these students for adulthood, money management skills would be most likely to translate into life after high school. Students will need to be able to manage money throughout their entire lives. It is important to give them the tools to be successful in navigating specific scenarios in which they will need to manage their money. Answer a is incorrect because simply including a goal will not automatically prepare a student for adulthood. Answer c is incorrect because not all students are eligible for transition services after high school. Answer d is incorrect because although applying for jobs is important, managing money is something that adults do on a daily basis.

67. C: Although it may be a good idea to send home a note for some students, many times a note will get lost in the transition from school to home. It is important to make a good first impression, and it is not the best idea to take a chance on the note not making it to the parents. The first meeting or introduction as case manager is important due to the nature of the relationship that will occur with the student. Answer A is incorrect because calling them with an introduction is a great way to establish a connection with the parents. Answer B is incorrect because setting up a meeting, if done in a positive manner, can allow the parents and the teacher to get on the same page at the start. Answer D is incorrect because meeting them in person can always be an effective way to first get to know someone.

68. B: In Ehri's pre-alphabetic phase of sight word recognition, children recognize words by associating their visual appearance with their meaning, as in the "LOOK" example, or with their sound. The association is not between letters and sounds and is thus termed pre-alphabetic. This phase is in the earliest stage of reading. The successive partial alphabetic (A), full alphabetic (C) and consolidated (D) alphabetic phases occur later and all involve letter-sound associations, albeit incomplete in the partial alphabetic phase.

69. B: The use of consequences would be considered a negative behavior intervention because it is a reaction to a student's poor behavior. Positive behavior interventions typically include strategies for the student to use when they might be experiencing frustration. These tend to be strategies for the student or teacher to use before the event takes place, rather than after. Answer a is incorrect because social-emotional strategies can be beneficial in helping the student to stay calm in certain situations. Answer c is incorrect because self-regulatory strategies can also help a student avoid negative behavior. Answer d is incorrect because coping skills are valuable in handling stress.

70. B: A student's IEP team does determine his/her eligibility for an alternate curriculum program. These programs are not the first choice for students with disabilities (A) and are not preferred over general curricula with accommodations and/or modifications (C). Rather, if an individual student still finds the general education curriculum too demanding even with accommodations and modifications provided, then an alternate curriculum program is a placement to consider. Students typically are not still assigned to general education classrooms in these programs (D); usually they are assigned to a special education classroom, but have general education classes and enrichment activities throughout their school day where they can interact with students without disabilities.

71. A: Executive function includes planning, organizing, keeping track of time, keeping track of multiple things, relating earlier learning to current learning, and other higher cognitive activities. Self-regulation (B) relates only to talking out of turn in class and is just one component of executive function. Sequencing (C) involves arranging items in the correct order (chronological, logical, etc.) and is also one specific aspect of executive function. Memory (D), or retaining and retrieving information, requires using mental strategies that are included in executive function.

72. B: A sheltered workshop could be a good initial setting for a disabled individual to learn job skills if there is future transitioning. But in this option Oscar would be assembling product sample kits, which involves multiple steps, and he would have only periodic group supervision. He would have trouble remembering all the steps and would be likely to stop working without more direct, continuous supervision. Therefore option A is incorrect.

The warehouse packing job also has multiple steps, but in this option Oscar would have 1:1 supervision with constant verbal prompts to complete each step. This would keep him on task. The repetition and constant reinforcement would help him learn a useful job skill. Packing is also larger-scale, more physical work than the seated manual work of assembling sample kits or applying labels. This is more suitable for Oscar as he has Down syndrome with low IQ scores and is normally passive. The combination of physical activity and using more gross motor skills than fine motor skills could benefit him. Therefore option B is correct.

Applying labels is a repetitive task without many steps, so it could be easier. But Oscar requires repeated prompts to stay on task. The classroom described would not afford him this; he would only get occasional prompts from the teacher, who has many students. And as a young adult Oscar may not be able to stay in a classroom indefinitely. Therefore option C is incorrect.

A class with only academic lessons and quizzes about job skills is not the most useful exercise for someone with Oscar's level of intellectual disabilities. He needs intensive training in actually doing a job to make a transition to real work. In his case, the real work would also need to be supervised on an ongoing basis. Therefore option D is incorrect.

73. C: Although parents may discuss some of the issues they have with their child's attendance at the IEP meeting, this is not typically discussed at the meeting. Differences that arise from the IEP meeting will be typically stem from the IEP itself. Because there is no section in the IEP that specifically discusses attendance issues, this is the least likely issue to arise. Answer A is incorrect because it is common for the parents and teacher to have differences with regard to the student's IEP goals. Answer B is incorrect because parents may disagree about some of the accommodations that their child has access to. Answer D is incorrect because some parents may also have differences of opinion regarding the service delivery section of the IEP.

74. C: Removing Stephanie from the classroom is not the answer. This would deprive her of an education in the least restrictive setting. None of the given information indicates that her behaviors only occur in the classroom, so they could very well continue outside of class. Therefore option A is incorrect.

Differential reinforcement of low behavior (DRL), of alternative behavior (DRA), or of other behavior (DRO) is a behavior modification technique that could be effective depending on the types of behaviors and why Stephanie is engaging in them. But the types of behaviors are not specified in the question. Without knowing why they are occurring it is impossible to know if this is an appropriate intervention plan or not. Therefore option B is incorrect.

Conducting a functional behavioral assessment is a way to find out the purposes of Stephanie's behaviors. Only when her team members know why she is doing what she does can they plan appropriate and effective intervention. The functional behavioral assessment should be their first step. Therefore option C is correct.

Maladaptive behaviors have many different etiologies and serve many different purposes. It cannot be assumed from the information given that Stephanie's instructional plan is the reason for her behaviors. In the behavioral aspect, her IEP is not optimally meeting her needs or she may not have had an IEP written for her yet; this information is not given. In fact, the reason her IEP team is meeting may be to write her first IEP. It would do no good to write a different plan, or a new one, without first doing a functional behavior assessment to uncover the reasons behind Stephanie's behaviors. Therefore option D is incorrect.

75. D: Children with autism spectrum disorders often have deficits in social skills, communication skills, and joint or shared attention. They tend to prefer focusing individual attention on one activity or subject for sustained periods and may have difficulty with transitions. Children with attention deficit disorder (C) have difficulty focusing and sustaining their attention, are easily distracted, have short attention spans and tend to jump from one thing to another. Children with intellectual disabilities secondary to Down syndrome (A) and those with overall developmental delays (B) are likely to have shorter attention spans and less ability to focus.

76. D: The 1997 version of IDEA required transition planning to begin when the student was 14 years old (C). The 2004 reauthorization of this law changed the age to 16. Some students with disabilities, such as those with autism spectrum disorders, often need extended time periods for transition planning, so many special educators still advocate beginning at age 14. Some individual states also specify age 14. The later age in the current reauthorization may reflect considerations related to developmental levels. Some students with disabilities need more time to complete secondary education. However, others will graduate at age 18 (A), so this can be too late for transition planning. (Under IDEA, legal rights to transition planning and services generally transfer from parents to students when students reach the age of majority as defined by state law, which is often 18.) Students with disabilities have the legal right to attend school until they graduate or reach the age of 22 (B), so transition planning must start before this.

77. C: There should be follow-up to the conflict resolution to make certain that the children are sticking to their agreed-upon solution and to ensure that the conflict does not re-occur. Some teachers might feel that dropping the issue will help everyone forget the conflict, but that usually is not the case. Conflicts are best handled with calmness and a quiet voice as the teacher gathers information about the conflict in order to get a complete and fair picture of the situation. Then the teacher should review the conflict with the children and ask for their ideas for ways the problem could have been prevented and ways to solve the conflict. Involving the children in the resolution of the problem teaches them self-regulation and respect for themselves and others.

78. B: Although sharing control over the classroom may sometimes be a positive, many teachers may struggle to work together to make co-teaching successful. Unless the roles and responsibilities of each teacher are clearly defined, it may be difficult for each teacher to share control of the classroom. It may also be difficult to find time to plan lessons together, which could potentially make it a struggle to have a shared vision. Answer a is incorrect because co-teaching can increase the amount of attention that students receive because there are multiple teachers in the class. Answer c is incorrect because differentiation should be increased in the co-teaching model because one of the teachers in the class is focused on the struggling learners. Answer d is incorrect because typically in the co-teaching model one of the teachers is an expert in the subject area and the other is a special education teacher.

79. D: Under IDEA, students with disabilities must be educated in the least restrictive environment, meaning they should be placed with nondisabled peers to the maximum extent appropriate. Removing this student from the general education setting for all classes when he only struggles in English violates LRE, because he could remain with his peers for subjects in which he is performing adequately while receiving targeted support for reading and writing.

80. B: One of the main purposes of IDEA in 2004 was to protect the rights of individuals with disabilities and their families. These laws allowed for parents to be more involved in the special education process and understand and be involved each step of the way. This was important in ensuring that the decisions made were by members of the team rather than just the school. Answer a is incorrect because students with disabilities already had opportunities to learn under previous legislation. Answer c is incorrect because students with disabilities do not have protection from expulsion in most circumstances. Answer d is incorrect because although IDEA may have caused many school districts to implement new programming, it did not specifically call for it.

81. A: An IQ score one or more standard deviations below the mean, or a score of 85 or lower, is a criterion used in the definition by Heber of the American Association on Mental Deficiency (American Association on Intellectual disabilities) in 1961. Definitions widely used prior to 1961 did not include this criterion. Therefore option A is correct.

Social incompetence was included as one of six criteria for the definition of intellectual disabilities by Edgar A. Doll in 1941. (Doll developed the Vineland Social Maturity Scale, now the Vineland Adaptive Behavior Scales.) Therefore option B is incorrect.

Impaired adaptive behavior was cited in 1937 by Tredgold of Great Britain: "...the individual is incapable of adapting himself to the normal environment..." Therefore option C is incorrect.

Being essentially incurable is another one of Doll's 1941 six criteria for the definition of intellectual disabilities. Therefore option D is incorrect.

82. C: Adaptive behavior scales are used to determine which independent living skills a student has and what the student may need to work on. These assessments are typically used for students with intellectual disabilities or other severe disabilities to understand what instruction needs to be implemented. These tests typically consist of an evaluation of a student's social skills, daily living skills, communication skills, and other skills that the student will need after high school. Answer A is incorrect because the primary purpose of these scales is to identify skill deficits, not to diagnose behavior problems. Answer B is incorrect because the adaptive behavior scale is not used to determine whether or not a student needs a behavior plan. Answer D is incorrect because while adaptive behavior scales can inform curriculum, answer C is more specific about what needs to be taught (independent living skills).

83. D: All students can benefit from movement activities as a method of stimulating their brain, so incorporating this strategy for all students would be the most beneficial. Although it may not always be possible each class period, finding creative ways to get Zachary up and moving with the rest of the class will make him feel less singled out. It is important to develop a plan for when these movement breaks are needed for students like Zachary and how they can be implemented for the entire class. Answer A is incorrect because Zachary may take advantage of the pass system and use it more than he really needs to. Answer B is incorrect because giving him a timer also might become a distraction to Zachary and other students around him. Answer C is incorrect because giving a student his own area might end up making him feel singled out.

84. B: It helps students to stick to a task if the task is made more fun by adding novelty to it through games or personal interest materials. For students who have difficulty staying with and completing routine tasks, the teacher can employ certain strategies that will encourage the child to stick with the work. One way is to explain to the students about the importance of remaining on-task and monitoring oneself. Another way is to eliminate any part of the routine that really isn't necessary, such as copying sentences. Still another way is to break up the task into smaller time commitments. In this way, the student doesn't get too bored before being allowed to go to something else, but he or she is nonetheless required to come back in a timely manner to finish.

85. D: For a student who is new to a classroom, it is important that the general education teacher and special education teacher come up with a plan together. This collaboration is crucial to the success of the student because preparation can limit potential issues that may arise. Although some students may not require as much preparation, students like Justin with deaf-blindness will likely require a plan in order to meet their needs. Answer A is incorrect because simply giving the teacher the IEP will likely not prepare them as much as a collaborative conversation. Answer B is incorrect because allowing the general education teacher to teach on their own without collaboration may leave them unprepared. Answer C is incorrect because although asking the district for assistance can be beneficial, working with the general education teacher will likely have a greater impact.

86. B: Telling the parents what she suspects would be inappropriate. This SPL is very observant and has a talent for diagnosis as well as being well-educated about and experienced with autism. And SPLs do work with some autistic individuals. Regardless of these things, she is not qualified to make such a diagnosis. This should be done by a licensed psychologist, behavior specialist, or psychiatrist. Telling the parents what she suspects could alarm them unnecessarily – especially if she turns out to be wrong or if a psychological practitioner disagrees and/or makes a different diagnosis. Therefore option A is incorrect.

Referring the parents to a clinic for more thorough evaluation by qualified psychological personnel is the right thing to do. If her suspicions are confirmed, the diagnosis will be made by someone with credentials to back it up and who can recommend appropriate interventions. Referring to a free clinic is also helpful since the parents cannot afford to pay a private practitioner. Therefore option B is correct.

Asking the referring kindergarten teacher to tell the parents is as inappropriate as telling them herself, since the teacher is also not qualified to make such a diagnosis. The SPL would also be evading personal responsibility by diagnosing outside of her role but using the teacher to deliver the information, which is not confirmed. Both actions would be unethical. Therefore option C is incorrect.

Ruling out other physical or medical conditions is a good idea, and an astute physician may recognize early signs of autism just as the SPL did. But this step in itself is insufficient. To recommend a physical checkup and also refer the parents to a clinic for behavioral evaluation would be an acceptable action plan. Therefore option D is incorrect.

87. B: Supplementary curriculum is typically designed to provide opportunities for students to explore experiences that they might be interested in after high school. This may look different for each student, but it can be beneficial in providing students opportunities that they may not otherwise have. A supplementary curriculum can be used for all students but is typically designed for students who may need additional support in accessing a job after high school. Answer A is incorrect because supplementary curriculum typically does not simply mean that the students can access their accommodations. Answer C is incorrect because although assistive technology can be involved in supplementary curriculum, it may not always be. Answer D is incorrect because a supplementary curriculum is not meant to create more work for the students.

88. C: Factors that can often prevent diverse parents and families from communicating and participating in the education of their children include language barriers, which frequently stop them from communicating (A); unsuccessful parent school histories, which can make them feel ineffectual to participate (B); feeling alienated from school processes because of their differing cultures (C) and/or languages; and poor past experiences with schools, which can make them reluctant to participate (D).

89. D: To advise against the placement goes against the policy of inclusion. A student in a wheelchair has the right to be integrated into the general education classroom if he has the ability to participate in the educational activities of that class. Therefore option A is incorrect.

Transferring Stewart from his wheelchair to a regular student desk and back again is unrealistic and impractical. It would require help, which might not be available. It would also be more restrictive. Staying in his wheelchair, Stewart has mobility in and out of the classroom, but if he cannot transfer between the wheelchair and another chair on his own, he will be dependent on somebody else to help him. Therefore option B is incorrect.

Limiting Stewart's placement to only classes with other students in wheelchairs is not the least restrictive environment. Additionally, such a class may not be available. Or, even if there are other classes with students in wheelchairs, those classes may not be the most appropriate to Stewart's educational needs. Therefore option C is incorrect.

To integrate Stewart into a classroom with no other wheelchairs, personnel should make sure that the room is wheelchair-accessible and that Stewart can navigate in the room. They should also instruct the other students how to avoid such things as tripping over footrests, accidentally kicking Stewart, bumping into his chair, getting their feet run over, blocking Stewart's path, and so forth. As long as accommodations are made in terms of the room's physical arrangement and everybody learns how to behave around a wheelchair, Stewart can be integrated into the classroom. Therefore option D is correct.

90. B: There are a variety of types of emotional disturbances that can impact the way they learn and process both stressful and typical environments. The most generally appropriate strategy for helping Christina complete her work is to modify the environment by allowing her to work in a separate setting if she is unable to focus in the typical setting. Stress management techniques should also be taught, but they are a less-direct method of helping Christina achieve in her classwork. Rewards for completing work may be additionally helpful in strengthening Christina's ability to stay calm and focused under stress, but they are generally not helpful in reducing stress after it has already initiated. Rewards are a method of cognitive-behavioral therapy, which can be an effective method of teaching a student how to handle stressful situations or re-direct their own thinking patterns. Implemented incorrectly, behavior reinforcement can backfire and cause the negative behavior to be reinforced, rather than the intended behavior management skill. Providing Christina with choices about what work she does is not likely to be the best overall situation as she needs to complete the work that is required by the curriculum. If she is able to perform the work that is assigned with more minimal modification, that is the better option.

91. C: The primary purpose of universal newborn hearing screenings is early identification of hearing loss, which affords early intervention. Professional organizations such as ASHA advocate universal screening because not all infants are screened even though hearing loss is the most common congenital disability. Educational planning (A) is a purpose of later educational testing of a child, not of newborn hearing screening. Disability diagnosis (B) requires a complete audiological evaluation defining type, degree, and configuration of hearing loss instead of just a screening, because that only identifies presence or absence of hearing loss. Eligibility for special education services under the IDEA (D) is a purpose of later, comprehensive assessments of preschool- and school-aged students, not infants.

92. D: Students with learning disabilities often avoid asking questions in large classes/groups. Teachers can encourage them to take risks by giving cues that support their asking "wh-" questions. Pairing students to discuss teacher questions (A) is a good strategy to engage all LD students in a large class. Asking LD students to summarize main lesson points (B) is a good strategy to discern whether they understand these, and reviewing benefits all students. Having LD students complete reminder worksheets at the end of the lesson (C) is a good strategy to see what they have learned, what they enjoyed, and what else they know about the subject.

93. B: All students have different capabilities and capacities for learning, but teachers should not lower expectations for individuals based on perceived limitations or initial difficulties; doing so would unnecessarily limit or put pressure on individual students. If a majority of students are having difficulty with an assignment, they may need more scaffolding or teaching. Lowering expectations assumes students are incapable of success when they might have succeeded with more help. Making no changes will only result in students failing to finish the assignment or producing low quality work. Removing all expectations eliminates intentional instruction that is often required for students to progress.

94. D: Ms. Ross is presenting new words in multiple exposures to enhance vocabulary acquisition. Appropriate word choice (A) entails selecting words that are best suited to the particular instruction. Teaching word analysis (B) entails identifying word roots, prefixes, and suffixes, which greatly facilitates figuring out the meanings of new words. Contextual analysis (C) involves figuring out the meanings of new words by the context in which they occur.

95. B: Although schools will do everything they can to provide students with disabilities the best possible education, this is not stated in the law. Schools must provide an appropriate education to students with disabilities, but this is not defined and may be different for each student. It is important to ensure that students are receiving FAPE and have access to general education and special education services. Answer a is incorrect because one of the requirements is to have parents be a part of the IEP team discussion. Answer c is incorrect because parents have the right to be informed whenever there are changes made to the IEP. Answer d is incorrect because parents may have an outside evaluation conducted if they disagree with the results of the special education evaluation.

96. D: The purpose of the prereferral process is to put supports in place before obtaining consent for a special education evaluation. Obtaining consent would typically occur after the referral for special education services rather than during the prereferral process. The prereferral process is important in determining whether or not the student needs to be evaluated for special education services. Answer a is incorrect because evaluating a student's strengths and weaknesses is important to determine which supports need to be put into place. Answer b is incorrect because putting accommodations and interventions into place is helpful in evaluating what works for a student and what doesn't. Answer c is incorrect because evaluating the accommodations and interventions is important in deciding if they need to be continued or if another action should take place.

97. A: Textbooks incorporate informational structure, such as presenting items in chronological order, comparisons and contrasts, and pointing out causal relationships. They also use informational features such as boldface type, sub-headings, bullet points, review questions, glossaries, an index, etc., to assist students in organizing, remembering, and applying information, even though many students may not use them. The simplest, most direct and efficient way that Mr. Stewart can help his students is to point these out and explain how to use them. Creating separate handouts (B) takes more time and work and may duplicate what the text already does. Graphic organizers (C) are excellent aids, especially for students who learn more visually than verbally, but they also involve more work than using the text. Mr. Stewart's students have good reading comprehension but cannot organize whole chapters. A slide show is an excellent supplement to the text, but it should not replace explaining the text's informational aids.

98. C: Medicating Bart due to his anxiety is not a good idea. Nothing was stated about his having an anxiety disorder. Anxiety about such a big change would be natural in many students. Despite his accomplishments Bart may lack confidence or he may simply feel threatened by change. This is situational anxiety, not organic anxiety, and drugs are not the answer in this case. Therefore option A is incorrect.

Putting off the move is counterproductive since Bart is ready now in terms of his skills. His anxiety over a big change is unlikely to go away simply by delaying the move. Therefore option B is incorrect.

Bart's teacher can teach him various coping skills specifically aimed at managing transitions such as this. Once he learns these strategies, he is likely to feel more equipped to deal with changes and with the feelings of anxiety they provoke. Therefore option C is correct.

Forcing the move and ignoring Bart's anxiety is like throwing an unwilling child who cannot swim into a swimming pool to force the child to adapt or drown. It is likely to be traumatic. Such a decision is also unnecessary since Bart's teacher can help him feel more prepared before the move by teaching him coping skills. Therefore option D is incorrect.

99. D: Although all of these strategies may be useful for Bobby in the long term, having a job is something that he is likely going to need the most. Students who are at risk and infrequently see their parents need to develop some of these independent skills sooner than other students. Because of this, they are more likely to need a job in order to be able to provide for themselves. Answer a is incorrect because students like Bobby may or may not even be thinking about going to college. Answer b is incorrect because simply giving him extra support may not help him very much in the long-term. Answer c is incorrect because although teaching him executive functioning skills may be helpful, he is more likely to need assistance in finding a job.

100. B: A class may not be available. If one were available, it might teach useful skills but it would not be the same as gaining real-life experience. Also, William will be attending college classes and working part-time, so enrolling in another class on top of these commitments could overload his schedule. Therefore option A is incorrect.

Since William is proficient with computers, referring him to a website is a natural choice. The TASH website, for example, has a link to its Bridge Network, a free resource network that provides access to a database of contact information incorporating many needs of persons with disabilities. It includes resources for transitions from school to adult life, self-determination, and community living, among many others. Telling William about a website like this would enable him to locate resources on his own and avail himself of the support he needs to make this transition. Therefore option B is correct.

Advising William to try living on his own with a roommate with no previous such experience would provide him with no transition. Being autistic and spending a lot of time with computers, William may not have the best social skills for living with a roommate. Since he is interested in doing this but feels unsure how to go about it, he should not just attempt it without any preparation. He is less likely to experience success that way. Therefore option C is incorrect.

William could feasibly choose to stay at home while he attends classes and works. In many ways it would be easier than making a change. However, since he is interested in independent living, continuing to live at home would be a lack of progress. It would be better to encourage him to pursue his interest in progress and offer him sources of support and information to accomplish his objective. Therefore option D is incorrect.

ILTS Practice Tests #2 and #3

To take these additional ILTS practice tests, visit our online resources page:
mometrix.com/resources719/iltslbsi290

How to Overcome Test Anxiety

Just the thought of taking a test is enough to make most people a little nervous. A test is an important event that can have a long-term impact on your future, so it's important to take it seriously and it's natural to feel anxious about performing well. But just because anxiety is normal, that doesn't mean that it's helpful in test taking, or that you should simply accept it as part of your life. Anxiety can have a variety of effects. These effects can be mild, like making you feel slightly nervous, or severe, like blocking your ability to focus or remember even a simple detail.

If you experience test anxiety—whether severe or mild—it's important to know how to beat it. To discover this, first you need to understand what causes test anxiety.

Causes of Test Anxiety

While we often think of anxiety as an uncontrollable emotional state, it can actually be caused by simple, practical things. One of the most common causes of test anxiety is that a person does not feel adequately prepared for their test. This feeling can be the result of many different issues such as poor study habits or lack of organization, but the most common culprit is time management. Starting to study too late, failing to organize your study time to cover all of the material, or being distracted while you study will mean that you're not well prepared for the test. This may lead to cramming the night before, which will cause you to be physically and mentally exhausted for the test. Poor time management also contributes to feelings of stress, fear, and hopelessness as you realize you are not well prepared but don't know what to do about it.

Other times, test anxiety is not related to your preparation for the test but comes from unresolved fear. This may be a past failure on a test, or poor performance on tests in general. It may come from comparing yourself to others who seem to be performing better or from the stress of living up to expectations. Anxiety may be driven by fears of the future—how failure on this test would affect your educational and career goals. These fears are often completely irrational, but they can still negatively impact your test performance.

Elements of Test Anxiety

As mentioned earlier, test anxiety is considered to be an emotional state, but it has physical and mental components as well. Sometimes you may not even realize that you are suffering from test anxiety until you notice the physical symptoms. These can include trembling hands, rapid heartbeat, sweating, nausea, and tense muscles. Extreme anxiety may lead to fainting or vomiting. Obviously, any of these symptoms can have a negative impact on testing. It is important to recognize them as soon as they begin to occur so that you can address the problem before it damages your performance.

The mental components of test anxiety include trouble focusing and inability to remember learned information. During a test, your mind is on high alert, which can help you recall information and stay focused for an extended period of time. However, anxiety interferes with your mind's natural processes, causing you to blank out, even on the questions you know well. The strain of testing during anxiety makes it difficult to stay focused, especially on a test that may take several hours. Extreme anxiety can take a huge mental toll, making it difficult not only to recall test information but even to understand the test questions or pull your thoughts together.

Effects of Test Anxiety

Test anxiety is like a disease—if left untreated, it will get progressively worse. Anxiety leads to poor performance, and this reinforces the feelings of fear and failure, which in turn lead to poor performances on subsequent tests. It can grow from a mild nervousness to a crippling condition. If allowed to progress, test anxiety can have a big impact on your schooling, and consequently on your future.

Test anxiety can spread to other parts of your life. Anxiety on tests can become anxiety in any stressful situation, and blanking on a test can turn into panicking in a job situation. But fortunately, you don't have to let anxiety rule your testing and determine your grades. There are a number of relatively simple steps you can take to move past anxiety and function normally on a test and in the rest of life.

Physical Steps for Beating Test Anxiety

While test anxiety is a serious problem, the good news is that it can be overcome. It doesn't have to control your ability to think and remember information. While it may take time, you can begin taking steps today to beat anxiety.

Just as your first hint that you may be struggling with anxiety comes from the physical symptoms, the first step to treating it is also physical. Rest is crucial for having a clear, strong mind. If you are tired, it is much easier to give in to anxiety. But if you establish good sleep habits, your body and mind will be ready to perform optimally, without the strain of exhaustion. Additionally, sleeping well helps you to retain information better, so you're more likely to recall the answers when you see the test questions.

Getting good sleep means more than going to bed on time. It's important to allow your brain time to relax. Take study breaks from time to time so it doesn't get overworked, and don't study right before bed. Take time to rest your mind before trying to rest your body, or you may find it difficult to fall asleep.

Along with sleep, other aspects of physical health are important in preparing for a test. Good nutrition is vital for good brain function. Sugary foods and drinks may give a burst of energy but this burst is followed by a crash, both physically and emotionally. Instead, fuel your body with protein and vitamin-rich foods.

Also, drink plenty of water. Dehydration can lead to headaches and exhaustion, especially if your brain is already under stress from the rigors of the test. Particularly if your test is a long one, drink water during the breaks. And if possible, take an energy-boosting snack to eat between sections.

Along with sleep and diet, a third important part of physical health is exercise. Maintaining a steady workout schedule is helpful, but even taking 5-minute study breaks to walk can help get your blood pumping faster and clear your head. Exercise also releases endorphins, which contribute to a positive feeling and can help combat test anxiety.

When you nurture your physical health, you are also contributing to your mental health. If your body is healthy, your mind is much more likely to be healthy as well. So take time to rest, nourish your body with healthy food and water, and get moving as much as possible. Taking these physical steps will make you stronger and more able to take the mental steps necessary to overcome test anxiety.

Mental Steps for Beating Test Anxiety

Working on the mental side of test anxiety can be more challenging, but as with the physical side, there are clear steps you can take to overcome it. As mentioned earlier, test anxiety often stems from lack of preparation, so the obvious solution is to prepare for the test. Effective studying may be the most important weapon you have for beating test anxiety, but you can and should employ several other mental tools to combat fear.

First, boost your confidence by reminding yourself of past success—tests or projects that you aced. If you're putting as much effort into preparing for this test as you did for those, there's no reason you should expect to fail here. Work hard to prepare; then trust your preparation.

Second, surround yourself with encouraging people. It can be helpful to find a study group, but be sure that the people you're around will encourage a positive attitude. If you spend time with others who are anxious or cynical, this will only contribute to your own anxiety. Look for others who are motivated to study hard from a desire to succeed, not from a fear of failure.

Third, reward yourself. A test is physically and mentally tiring, even without anxiety, and it can be helpful to have something to look forward to. Plan an activity following the test, regardless of the outcome, such as going to a movie or getting ice cream.

When you are taking the test, if you find yourself beginning to feel anxious, remind yourself that you know the material. Visualize successfully completing the test. Then take a few deep, relaxing breaths and return to it. Work through the questions carefully but with confidence, knowing that you are capable of succeeding.

Developing a healthy mental approach to test taking will also aid in other areas of life. Test anxiety affects more than just the actual test—it can be damaging to your mental health and even contribute to depression. It's important to beat test anxiety before it becomes a problem for more than testing.

Study Strategy

Being prepared for the test is necessary to combat anxiety, but what does being prepared look like? You may study for hours on end and still not feel prepared. What you need is a strategy for test prep. The next few pages outline our recommended steps to help you plan out and conquer the challenge of preparation.

Step 1: Scope Out the Test

Learn everything you can about the format (multiple choice, essay, etc.) and what will be on the test. Gather any study materials, course outlines, or sample exams that may be available. Not only will this help you to prepare, but knowing what to expect can help to alleviate test anxiety.

Step 2: Map Out the Material

Look through the textbook or study guide and make note of how many chapters or sections it has. Then divide these over the time you have. For example, if a book has 15 chapters and you have five days to study, you need to cover three chapters each day. Even better, if you have the time, leave an extra day at the end for overall review after you have gone through the material in depth.

If time is limited, you may need to prioritize the material. Look through it and make note of which sections you think you already have a good grasp on, and which need review. While you are studying, skim quickly through the familiar sections and take more time on the challenging parts.

Write out your plan so you don't get lost as you go. Having a written plan also helps you feel more in control of the study, so anxiety is less likely to arise from feeling overwhelmed at the amount to cover.

Step 3: Gather Your Tools

Decide what study method works best for you. Do you prefer to highlight in the book as you study and then go back over the highlighted portions? Or do you type out notes of the important information? Or is it helpful to make flashcards that you can carry with you? Assemble the pens, index cards, highlighters, post-it notes, and any other materials you may need so you won't be distracted by getting up to find things while you study.

If you're having a hard time retaining the information or organizing your notes, experiment with different methods. For example, try color-coding by subject with colored pens, highlighters, or post-it notes. If you learn better by hearing, try recording yourself reading your notes so you can listen while in the car, working out, or simply sitting at your desk. Ask a friend to quiz you from your flashcards, or try teaching someone the material to solidify it in your mind.

Step 4: Create Your Environment

It's important to avoid distractions while you study. This includes both the obvious distractions like visitors and the subtle distractions like an uncomfortable chair (or a too-comfortable couch that makes you want to fall asleep). Set up the best study environment possible: good lighting and a comfortable work area. If background music helps you focus, you may want to turn it on, but otherwise keep the room quiet. If you are using a computer to take notes, be sure you don't have any other windows open, especially applications like social media, games, or anything else that could distract you. Silence your phone and turn off notifications. Be sure to keep water close by so you stay hydrated while you study (but avoid unhealthy drinks and snacks).

Also, take into account the best time of day to study. Are you freshest first thing in the morning? Try to set aside some time then to work through the material. Is your mind clearer in the afternoon or evening? Schedule your study session then. Another method is to study at the same time of day that you will take the test, so that your brain gets used to working on the material at that time and will be ready to focus at test time.

Step 5: Study!

Once you have done all the study preparation, it's time to settle into the actual studying. Sit down, take a few moments to settle your mind so you can focus, and begin to follow your study plan. Don't give in to distractions or let yourself procrastinate. This is your time to prepare so you'll be ready to fearlessly approach the test. Make the most of the time and stay focused.

Of course, you don't want to burn out. If you study too long you may find that you're not retaining the information very well. Take regular study breaks. For example, taking five minutes out of every hour to walk briskly, breathing deeply and swinging your arms, can help your mind stay fresh.

As you get to the end of each chapter or section, it's a good idea to do a quick review. Remind yourself of what you learned and work on any difficult parts. When you feel that you've mastered the material, move on to the next part. At the end of your study session, briefly skim through your notes again.

But while review is helpful, cramming last minute is NOT. If at all possible, work ahead so that you won't need to fit all your study into the last day. Cramming overloads your brain with more information than it can process and retain, and your tired mind may struggle to recall even previously learned information when it is overwhelmed with last-minute study. Also, the urgent nature of cramming and the stress placed on your brain contribute to anxiety. You'll be more likely to go to the test feeling unprepared and having trouble thinking clearly.

So don't cram, and don't stay up late before the test, even just to review your notes at a leisurely pace. Your brain needs rest more than it needs to go over the information again. In fact, plan to finish your studies by noon or early afternoon the day before the test. Give your brain the rest of the day to relax or focus on other things, and get a good night's sleep. Then you will be fresh for the test and better able to recall what you've studied.

Step 6: Take a Practice Test

Many courses offer sample tests, either online or in the study materials. This is an excellent resource to check whether you have mastered the material, as well as to prepare for the test format and environment.

Check the test format ahead of time: the number of questions, the type (multiple choice, free response, etc.), and the time limit. Then create a plan for working through them. For example, if you have 30 minutes to take a 60-question test, your limit is 30 seconds per question. Spend less time on the questions you know well so that you can take more time on the difficult ones.

If you have time to take several practice tests, take the first one open book, with no time limit. Work through the questions at your own pace and make sure you fully understand them. Gradually work up to taking a test under test conditions: sit at a desk with all study materials put away and set a timer. Pace yourself to make sure you finish the test with time to spare and go back to check your answers if you have time.

After each test, check your answers. On the questions you missed, be sure you understand why you missed them. Did you misread the question (tests can use tricky wording)? Did you forget the information? Or was it something you hadn't learned? Go back and study any shaky areas that the practice tests reveal.

Taking these tests not only helps with your grade, but also aids in combating test anxiety. If you're already used to the test conditions, you're less likely to worry about it, and working through tests until you're scoring well gives you a confidence boost. Go through the practice tests until you feel comfortable, and then you can go into the test knowing that you're ready for it.

Test Tips

On test day, you should be confident, knowing that you've prepared well and are ready to answer the questions. But aside from preparation, there are several test day strategies you can employ to maximize your performance.

First, as stated before, get a good night's sleep the night before the test (and for several nights before that, if possible). Go into the test with a fresh, alert mind rather than staying up late to study.

Try not to change too much about your normal routine on the day of the test. It's important to eat a nutritious breakfast, but if you normally don't eat breakfast at all, consider eating just a protein bar. If you're a coffee drinker, go ahead and have your normal coffee. Just make sure you time it so that the caffeine doesn't wear off right in the middle of your test. Avoid sugary beverages, and drink enough water to stay hydrated but not so much that you need a restroom break 10 minutes into the test. If your test isn't first thing in the morning, consider going for a walk or doing a light workout before the test to get your blood flowing.

Allow yourself enough time to get ready, and leave for the test with plenty of time to spare so you won't have the anxiety of scrambling to arrive in time. Another reason to be early is to select a good seat. It's helpful to sit away from doors and windows, which can be distracting. Find a good seat, get out your supplies, and settle your mind before the test begins.

When the test begins, start by going over the instructions carefully, even if you already know what to expect. Make sure you avoid any careless mistakes by following the directions.

Then begin working through the questions, pacing yourself as you've practiced. If you're not sure on an answer, don't spend too much time on it, and don't let it shake your confidence. Either skip it and come back later, or eliminate as many wrong answers as possible and guess among the remaining ones. Don't dwell on these questions as you continue—put them out of your mind and focus on what lies ahead.

Be sure to read all of the answer choices, even if you're sure the first one is the right answer. Sometimes you'll find a better one if you keep reading. But don't second-guess yourself if you do immediately know the answer. Your gut instinct is usually right. Don't let test anxiety rob you of the information you know.

If you have time at the end of the test (and if the test format allows), go back and review your answers. Be cautious about changing any, since your first instinct tends to be correct, but make sure you didn't misread any of the questions or accidentally mark the wrong answer choice. Look over any you skipped and make an educated guess.

At the end, leave the test feeling confident. You've done your best, so don't waste time worrying about your performance or wishing you could change anything. Instead, celebrate the successful completion of this test. And finally, use this test to learn how to deal with anxiety even better next time.

Review Video: Test Anxiety
Visit mometrix.com/academy and enter code: 100340

Important Qualification

Not all anxiety is created equal. If your test anxiety is causing major issues in your life beyond the classroom or testing center, or if you are experiencing troubling physical symptoms related to your anxiety, it may be a sign of a serious physiological or psychological condition. If this sounds like your situation, we strongly encourage you to seek professional help.

Online Resources

Due to our efforts to try to keep this book to a manageable length, we've created a link that will give you access to all of your online resources:

mometrix.com/resources719/iltslbsi290

It's Your Moment, Let's Celebrate It!

Share your story @mometrixtestpreparation